TOURISM PLANNING AND MANAGEMENT

TOURISM PLANNING AND MANAGEMENT

Atul Shrivastava

CENTRUM PRESS
NEW DELHI-110002 (INDIA)

CENTRUM PRESS

H.O.: 4360/4, Ansari Road, Daryaganj,
New Delhi-110002 (India)
Tel: 23278000, 23261597, 23255577, 23286875

B.O.: No. 1015, Ist Main Road, BSK IIIrd Stage,
IIIrd Phase, IIIrd Block, Bangalore-560085 (INDIA)
Tel: 080-41723429

Email: centrumpress@gmail.com
Visit us at: www.centrumpress.com

Tourism Planning and Management

First Edition, 2010

ISBN 978-93-80540-74-0

PRINTED IN INDIA

Printed at Balaji Offset, Delhi.

Contents

Preface

As the largest industry in the world, tourism has the potential to help deal with the key issues facing many parts of the globe and therefore can be seen as a positive and negative force. If the costs and benefits of tourism are understood from the outset, strengths and opportunities can be maximized while weaknesses and threats can be minimized. Each tourism planning situation will be different in terms of its tourism characteristics.

The costs and benefits of tourism will vary in each destination, and these can change over time, depending on tourism and other activities in the local and regional context.

Residents of a community must maintain control of tourism development by being involved in setting a community tourism vision, identifying the resources to be maintained and enhanced, and developing goals and strategies for tourism development and management. Equally important, community residents must participate in the implementation of strategies as well as the operation of the tourism infrastructure, services, and facilities. A long-tenD planning horizon needs to be adopted by businesses and destination tourism organizations to ensure that destinations are not used for short-tenD gain and then abandoned as visitor tastes and business interests move elsewhere. A longer-tenD horizon encourages the use of proactive strategies to ensure destination sustainability and the establishment of local linkages over time.

Many destinations are now pursuing strategies that aim to ensure a sensitive approach when dealing with tourism.

Many of these strategies are based on a formal expression of principles for sustainable tourism. Planners and others can use these principles as basic guidelines when attempting to incorporate the broad vision of sustainability into local policies and practices.

This book provides an insight and exhaustive tour of the exciting world of tourism with special reference to planning and management.

—*Atul Shrivastava*

1

Introduction

Over time, an increasing number of destinations have opened up and invested in tourism development, turning modern tourism into a key driver for socioeconomic progress, through the creation of jobs and enterprises, infrastructure development, and the export income earned.

Tourism has become one of the major international trade categories. The overall export income generated by international tourism including passengers transport reached US$ 1.1 trillion in 2008, or US$ 3 billion a day.

Tourism exports account for as much as 30% of the world's exports of commercial services and 6% of overall exports of goods and services. Globally, as an export category, tourism ranks fourth after fuels, chemicals and automotive products. For many developing countries it is one of the main income sources and the number one export category, creating much needed employment and opportunities for development.

The most comprehensive way to measure the economic importance of both international und domestic tourism in national economies is through the Tourism Satellite Account (TSA) Recommended Methodological Framework, *approved by the UN Statistics Commission.*

Though many countries are in the process of implementing the *Framework,* relatively few have full, comparable results available. As data is currently still fragmented, it is not feasible to provide precise and detailed worldwide results. However, the knowledge and experience gained through the TSA exercise has certainly contributed to a much better understanding of the role of tourism in economies worldwide and allows for a tentative approximation of key indicators. Based on the information from countries with data available, the worldwide contribution of tourism to gross domestic product (GDP) is estimated at some 5%. Tourism's contribution to employment tends to be slightly higher and is estimated in the order of 6-7% of the overall number of jobs (direct and indirect). For advanced, diversified economies, the contribution of tourism to the GDP ranges from approximately 2% for countries where tourism is a comparatively small sector, to over 10% for countries where tourism is an important pillar of the economy.

For small islands and developing countries, or specific regional and local destinations where tourism is a key economic sector, the importance of tourism tends to be even higher.

In 2008, international tourist arrivals reached 922 million, up from 904 million in 2007, representing a growth of 2%. This overall growth builds on the strong results of the first part of the year, before the collapse of the financial markets and the subsequent recession. The second half of the year showed an abrupt shift in trend, with international arrivals flat or showing negative growth in each of the last six months of 2008. Overall, the 5% growth between January and June gave way to a 1% decline in the second half of the year. Though not immune to the economic woes, tourism has so far resisted the economic downturn better than other sectors, such as construction, real estate and car manufacturing.

All regions had positive growth except Europe, which suffered stagnation in arrivals (+0.3%). The best performance was seen in the Middle East, where international arrivals reached 55 million, a rise of 18% over the previous year. Africa grew at half the rate of the previous year, but still registered an above-average growth of 4%. The Americas grew 3%, boosted by the strong performance of Central and South American destinations and the strength of traffic to the USA in the first half of the year. Asia and the Pacific saw a significant slowdown in arrivals as compared to its previous bumper years, growing just over 1% in 2008.

International tourism receipts rose by 1.7% in real terms in 2008 to US$ 944 billion (642 billion euros). Receipts from international passenger transport are estimated at US$ 183 billion, bringing the total international tourism receipts including international passenger transport (i.e. visitor exports) to over US$ 1.1 trillion, corresponding to US$ 3 billion a day. This represents around 30% of the worldwide volume of service exports and 6% of overall exports of goods and services.

Purpose of Visit and Means of Transport

In 2008, travel for leisure, recreation and holidays accounted for half of all international tourist arrivals (51% or a total of 467 million arrivals). Some 15% of international tourists reported travelling for business and professional purposes and another 27% travelled for other reasons, such as visiting friends and relatives (VFR), religious reasons/pilgrimages, health treatment, etc. The purpose of visit for the remaining 7% of arrivals was not specified. Slightly over half of travellers arrived at their destination by air transport (52%) in 2008, while the remainder travelled over the surface (48%) – whether by road (38%), rail (3%) or over water (6%). Over time, the trend has been for air transport to grow at a faster pace than surface transport, so the share of air transport is gradually increasing.

Growth in Receipts Mirrors that of Arrivals

Visitor expenditure on accommodation, food and drink, local transport, entertainment, shopping, is an important pillar of the economies of many destinations, creating much needed employment and opportunities for development. More than 80 countries earned over US$ 1 billion from international tourism in 2008.

UNWTO estimates that worldwide receipts from international tourism reached US$ 944 billion (642 billion euros) in 2008. In absolute terms, international tourism receipts increased by US$ 87 billion, but only by 16 billion euros due to the depreciation of the US dollar against several world currencies and, in particular, the euro (in 2008 the US dollar lost 7% against the euro).

In real terms, i.e. adjusted for exchange rate fluctuations and inflation, growth in international tourism receipts corresponded to 1.7%, only slightly lower than the growth in international tourist arrivals. After the substantial growth in 2006 and 2007 – of over 5% in both years – this represents a considerable slowdown.

All regions shared in the increase in tourism receipts in absolute values. In real terms growth was in all regions much weaker in 2008 than the year before with the exception of the Middle East, which registered a doubledigit growth of 17%. Asia and the Pacific grew by 2.7% (compared to +9.8% in 2007) and the Americas increased by 5.0%, slightly less than 2007's 6.3%. Both Europe and Africa (-1% each), however, suffered negative growth in receipts in real terms. By subregion, the strongest increases came from North America (+7%) and South Asia (+6%). In Northern, Western and Southem/Mediterranean Europe, North Africa, the Caribbean and Central America, receipts declined in real terms in 2008. In the case of North Africa and Central America, the decline followed two years of very strong growth.

For destination countries, receipts from international tourism count as exports and cover transactions generated by same-day as well as overnight visitors. However, these do not include receipts from international passenger transport contracted from companies outside the travellers' countries of residence, which are reported in a separate category, 'International Passenger Transport'. Although the availability of comparable international data is somewhat limited, the export value of international passenger transport has in recent years been estimated at around 16% of the combined receipts from international tourism and passenger transport, corresponding in 2008 to some US$ 183 billion against US$ 164 billion in 2007.

This takes total receipts from international tourism, including international passenger transport, to US$ 1.1 trillion in 2008. In other words, international tourism contributes over US$ 3 billion a day to the world economy.

No Major Changes in the Top Ten

When ranked according to the two key tourism indicators – international arrivals and international receipts –it is interesting to note that eight of the ten top destinations appear in both lists, even though they show marked differences in terms of the types of tourists they attract, as well as their average length of stay and their spending per trip and per night.

There were only slight changes in the ranking of the 'World's Top Tourism Destinations' in 2008. The top three places – both by international tourist arrivals and international tourism receipts – were still occupied by the USA, Spain and France, albeit in a different order. France continued to lead the ranking of the world's major tourism destinations in terms of arrivals, but ranked third in receipts. The USA ranked first in receipts, earning US$ 110 billion and regained its second position in arrivals, which it lost to Spain after 11 September 2001. Spain dropped to third place in terms of arrivals but maintained its position as the second biggest earner worldwide, and the first in Europe.

China and Italy both held on to their 2007 positions in terms of arrivals and receipts, with China ranking fourth in arrivals and fifth in receipts, while the reverse was true for Italy. The UK ranked sixth in arrivals and dropped to seventh place in receipts, after being overtaken by Germany (which ranked ninth in arrivals). Turkey moved up one rank in both categories, occupying the eighth position in arrivals and ninth in receipts. Completing the top ten ranking in arrivals were Ukraine and Mexico and in receipts, Australia and Austria.

The top ten tourism earners last year accounted for 49% of the total estimated US$ 944 billion in international tourism receipts. Their respective share of international tourist arrivals was slightly lower at 45%.

Europe – Noting the Effects of the Global Economic Crisis

Out of all regions in the world, Europe's tourism sector, the world's largest and most mature, was the most severely affected by the global economic crisis that emerged in mid-2008. The region, which accounted for over 53% of the world's international tourist arrivals and 50% of international tourism receipts in 2008, achieved the weakest growth in international tourist arrivals (+0.3% to 489 million arrivals). The impact was even more severe in terms of tourism earnings – while international tourism receipts increased by 5 billion euros (US$ 39 billion), to 322 billion euros (US$ 474 billion), this represented a negative growth of 1% in real terms.

Both Northern and Western Europe posted weaker arrivals figures for 2008. The world economic crisis and associated fluctuations in exchange rates heavily affected arrivals in both subregions, with many of their main tourism destinations recording negative results: the Netherlands (-8%), France (-3%), and the United Kingdom (-2%). A few countries, such as Germany, Switzerland and Austria, the latter two co-hosting the UEFA Football Championship, were able to maintain positive growth, with the first two increasing by 2%, while Austria experienced a 6% boost in arrivals.

Central and Eastern Europe bucked the trend with an increase of 3% in arrivals in 2008. Still, there was wide variation from one destination to another, with various destinations, including Bulgaria, Ukraine, Kyrgyzstan, Georgia and Armenia, recording double-digit increases. Southern and Mediterranean Europe recorded only slight increases in arrivals (+0.8%) with destinations such as Italy and Spain registering declines in arrivals. One bright spot in the region was Turkey which, with its attractive exchange rate and relaxed visa regime, achieved an increase of 12% in arrivals over 2007.

Asia and the Pacific – Rising Cost of Travel Dampens Growth

Asia and the Pacific experienced a significant slowdown in the growth pace of international tourist arrivals in 2008. The deceleration from +9.6% in 2007 to +1.2% in 2008 can be attributed principally to a rise in the price of tourism caused by increases in aviation fuel prices during the first half of the year. Growth in receipts in Asia outpaced that of arrivals. Year-on-year growth in receipts for the region was 2.7%, to US$ 206 billion, with South Asia (+6%) reporting the highest growth rate in real terms.

North-East Asia experienced a significant drop in arrivals growth, from 10% in 2007 to-0.1% in 2008. The dynamo for tourism in the region, China, experienced a 3% decrease in arrivals, which may be attributed to visitors' fear of congestion, higher prices and security concerns brought on by the 2008 Summer Olympics.

Playing host to the Olympics did, however, have a positive effect on China's tourism receipts, which grew by almost 10% (in US dollar terms). Arrivals in Japan stagnated in 2008, which can be explained in part by the Japanese yen's appreciation over the course of 2008. Destinations such as the Republic of Korea (+7%) and Taiwan (pr. of China) (+3%) bucked the trend and recorded above-average growth.

South-East Asia and South Asia were the strongest performing subregions of Asia and the Pacific, growing at 3% and 2% in 2008. In South-East Asia, countries like Indonesia (+13%), Cambodia (+7%) and Malaysia (+5%) grew at above-average rates. Arrivals in India, the dominant destination in South Asia, grew 6%.

Oceania reported the weakest arrivals figures in the region (-1%). The high costs of air travel – especially significant for distant destinations – coupled with the global economic environment and high exchange rates have negatively impacted international travel to Australia (-1%) and New Zealand (-0.3%). However, some of the Pacific Islands, such as Fiji (+8%), reported encouraging results in 2008.

Americas – Still Considerable Growth in Central and South America

International tourist arrivals in the Americas grew by 3% in 2008, to 147 million, where Central and South America led the way with above-average increases of 7% and 4% respectively. Growth in receipts in the region (+5%) tripled that of the world (+1.7%), with the strongest performance coming from North America (+7%). International tourism receipts for the Americas totalled US$ 188 billion in 2008, representing 20% of the world total. Arrivals in South America were up 4%, following 2007's increase of 7%. Strongest performers in the subregion were Uruguay (+10%), Chile (+8%), Peru (+7%) and Ecuador (+7%). International arrivals in Argentina and Brazil, on the other hand, grew at more modest rates of 2% and 0.5%, respectively. In Central America, Panama had an excellent year, showing double-digit growth of 17%, and other countries, like

Honduras (+8%), Nicaragua (+7%), Costa Rica (+6%) and Guatemala (+5%), also enjoyed above average growth in 2008. The results for North America were mixed. Mexico was up 6%, as against a flat 2007. The USA's performance was very strong in the first eight months but the looming recession in major source markets brought growth to a halt, ending the year at 4%. By contrast, arrivals in Canada continued to slide (-4%), due to factors which include a poor exchange rate, stricter travel restrictions to/from the USA, and reduced airline capacity from important source markets in Europe and Japan. The Caribbean saw arrivals grow by 2%. Cuba (+9%) and Aruba (+7%) posted excellent results and destinations such as Jamaica (+4%) and Puerto Rico (+6%) also did better than the subregion overall. Weaker results in the rest of the subregion can be attributed in large part on high airfares and decreased airline capacity, as well as economic difficulties in the USA and Europe.

Africa – above Average Growth in Arrivals

Africa's growth of 4% to 47 million international tourist arrivals, though at half the level achieved in 2007, was still very positive when compared to the world's performance overall. International tourism receipts amounted to US$ 31 billion, signifying a decrease of 1% in real terms. It is important to note that this decline followed a series of previous strong growth years.

North African countries Morocco (+6%) and Tunisia (+4%) posted good results, which can be attributed to strong government support coupled with easy access and attractive prices compared to 'euro' destinations on the northern shores of the Mediterranean. A number of Subsaharan African destinations reported positive growth, with Angola, Ghana, Mali and Uganda turning in double-digit results. Boosted by increased funding for tourism and targeted marketing promotions, South Africa, the leading destination in the region, increased international arrivals by 6%, boosted by the build-up to the hosting of the FIFA 2010 Football World Cup.

Middle East – Sustained Growth Amid Turbulent Times

The Middle East has succeeded in sustaining the high growth rate of the past few years. International arrivals in the region as a whole grew an estimated 18% to 55 million, and receipts increased 17% in real terms, reaching US$ 46 billion. Lebanon, Syria (both +31%) and Saudi Arabia (+28%) led the way in arrivals growth, followed by Egypt (+16%), Oman (+13%) and Jordan (+9%).

Middle East Outbound Market Continues Dynamic Growth Trend

Majority of international travel takes place within the traveller's own region, with about four out of five worldwide arrivals originating from the same region. However, travel between different regions tends to grow at a somewhat faster rate than intraregional travel. In 2008, interregional travel increased by 3.1% as against a growth of 1.7% for intraregional traffic.

Source markets for international tourism are still largely concentrated in the industrialized countries of Europe, the Americas and Asia and the Pacific. However, with rising levels of disposable income, many emerging economies have shown fast growth over recent years, especially markets in North-East and South-East Asia, Central and Eastern Europe, the Middle East, Southern Africa and South America. Europe is currently the most important source market, generating 55% of international arrivals worldwide in 2008, followed by Asia and the Pacific (20%) and the Americas (16%). All three regions grew at below average rates as the global economic crisis dampened growth in most source markets in the second part of the year. The Middle East, however, continued its dynamic growth, recording an annual increase of 16%. Outbound tourism from Africa also maintained growth at a rate of 5%.

International Tourism's Top Spenders – Virtually Equal to Last Year's Line-up

The ranking of international tourism spenders shows no major changes in 2008 apart from the fact that the Netherlands re-entered after a few years of absence, taking the number ten spot. Among the world's top ten spenders, apart from China (+21% in US$ terms), the Russian Federation (+12% in US$ terms) did particularly well in 2008, as did France (+10%) and Canada (+8%). Just one market, Japan, recorded negative growth (-8%), while world's top spender Germany increased spending only by a modest 2% for the year. In spite of an overall cooling of tourism growth in the second half of 2008, emerging source markets again turned in some of the best performances, with many registering growth rates of over 15% – Brazil, Hungary, South Africa, India, Bulgaria, Ukraine, China, Saudi Arabia, United Arab Emirates, Egypt, Malaysia and Argentina.

Hospitality and Travel

The hospitality and travel industry is comprised of companies enabling you to get from points A to B comfortably, as well as have a meal and some fun along the way. These companies may offer lodging, foodservice, gaming, travel services, attractions, recreation, or passenger travel. The Hospitality and Travel industry is fragmented. The production in this industry is divided among a few different companies, however, no single firm has large enough share of the market to be able to influence the industry's direction or price levels.

Primary Demand Drivers

- Business and tourist travel, which is closely linked to the health of the economy
- Competitive market conditions.

Profitability Drivers

- Efficient operations since many costs are fixed
- Effective marketing
- Increase the development of services offering additional conveniences.

Industry Composition: The hospitality and travel industry is a collection of companies catering to the needs of people with leisure time and money. These companies provide a range of services or products. The bulk of the industry is composed of lodging, from campgrounds to five star hotels; airlines and charters; and foodservice establishments, including restaurants, cafes, and catering. The industry also includes travel agencies and services, such as car rental or tours; gambling; and recreation and attractions, including sporting events, amusement parks, and roadside attractions. These different services also merge to offer options such as resorts or cruise lines-a mix of lodging, attractions, and even transportation. In the United States alone, there are over four million guest accommodations available, and many billions of dollars are spent on travel; with global travel becoming more affordable and in greater demand, the hospitality and travel industry will become increasingly important.

Leaders: American Airlines (AMR Corporation), United Airlines, and Continental proved best able to weather the rough U.S. market and have emerged as leaders in the industry, along with Air France. Providing travel services, resorts, restaurants, and cruises, Carlson Companies is another big name in the travel industry. Other big travel services providers include American Express, Expedia, and Travelocity. In term of lodging; Cendent, Hilton, Marriott, and Accor have succeeded at dominating the world market. Lastly, the big names in the global foodservice market are McDonalds, Yum! Brands, Starbucks Corporation, and Darden Restaurants. In the entertainment industry, Time Warner, Vivendi Universal, and Walt Disney are the major players.

Trends: The Internet has changed the shape of the travel industry; it is no longer necessary to call a travel agent, hotel, and airline to arrange a trip. Increased competition among establishments in this industry has spurred many independently owned and operated hotels and other lodging places to join national or international online reservation systems. Computer reservation systems have enabled the consumer to have direct control over the price and quality of a trip.

The foodservice industry is also being affected by technology as point-of-service (POS) systems enhance efficiency by combining functions such as keying in customer orders, sending them to the kitchen, totaling and printing checks, authorizing credit cards, and tracking sales. In the lodging sector, customer demand has shifted, with budget chains and extended-stay accommodations, such as time-shares, rising in importance.

The lodging industry is moving towards a more limited-service properties mostly in suburban, residential, or commercial neighborhoods, often putting hotels near popular restaurants. Full service properties are limiting the food service business and choosing to contract out their food service operations to third party restaurants, including some long-term arrangements with chain restaurant operators.

Recently, security has become a major issue for travellers. Across the globe, restrictions on what may be brought onto passenger airplanes are mounting, as well as preflight security measures. In addition, passports are now required for U.S. citizens travelling to Canada and Mexico. These measures have somewhat decreased airline demand, as much of the population does not possess a passport or is simply choosing not to fly due to the increased hassles of this mode of transportation. Increases in government-imposed taxes, such as fuel duties, are also shaving away at airline profit margins.

Future Outlook: The airline industry faces several challenges. After the September 11 events, network carriers faced reduced domestic capacity and several still remained in bankruptcy. Airlines must focus on cost control, cash preservation, and cautious growth. In the long run, inexpensive tickets and increasing demand for seats will bode well for the industry. Demand for air travel is expected to continue in the future. Growth in the more mature domestic markets is expected to be moderate, while travel between the U.S. and foreign points is expected to be moderate to strong. International travel will be spurred by the emerging economies in and around Asia, and by liberal regulations that allow U.S. carriers to fly to more foreign destination.

In the food services industry, competition remains steep and profit margins low, but studies in the U.S. have shown people are eating out more often. Demand is expected at the least to remain stable.

These companies must remain focused on cost control, but with a rise in consumer confidence, growth may be expected to continue. Lastly, the lodging industry has done well the last five years. National chains have seen the most growth, as they offer predictable prices with a consistent level of quality. The general expectation is that with the effect of globalization, travel and hospitality services will continue to increase in demand.

Air Transport

Airlines will achieve less turnover growth in 2008 and should post a loss of USD 2.9 billion (using a consensus oil price of USD 106.5 per barrel in 2008). The world economic slowdown and high fuel prices (34 percent of their operating costs) will prevent many sector companies from recovering. This turbulence will affect American airlines in particular.

The year will be all the more critical with the companies still subject to strict controls on the safety of their aging fleets and a the acceleration of new plane deliveries that will undermine their profitability. These elements confirm the return to red ink for American airlines, which have already reported initial losses for the first quarter this year. In this context the transatlantic open skies agreement in effect since April could prove less lucrative than expected with the airlines reluctant to continue to make the capacity reductions needed to restore financial health out of fear of losing their allotted take-off and landing slots the following season. The number of flights out of Heathrow is even supposed to increase by 25° percent with the pressure on prices intensifying in consequence particularly in business class. That will particularly affect British Airways and Virgin Atlantic, both very dependent on transatlantic routes, but less so Air France-KLM and Lufthansa thanks to their more balanced networks. European companies overall will take advantage of a durably weak dollar to compensate for higher fuel costs. That will also be the case for Asian carriers, which will moreover benefit from the regional dynamic. The profits of Middle Eastern companies will remain low during the current period of frenetic investment.

Low-cost carriers, meanwhile, will continue to diversify to more profitable medium and long-haul routes. Although the leaders will fare better thanks their lower debt burdens and more reasonable labour costs, weaker companies focusing on domestic markets will encounter difficulties. In such conditions the development of alliances and mergers not only between major companies but also involving low-cost operators should continue in industrialised and emerging countries alike to the detriment of smaller companies.

North America: airlines suffering from rising fuel costs and the world economic slowdown.

Passenger traffic in North America will grow 4.2 percent a year on average through 2011. American carriers are still the weakest in the industry according to Standard & Poor's. After returning to profitability just last year (USD 2.8 billion) they will likely slip back into the red in 2008 amid the ongoing rise of fuel costs and the marked slowdown of household consumption and corporate spending on travel. And American Airlines, United Airlines, Continental Airlines, and Delta Airlines duly reported first quarter losses.

Very Gloomy Economic Conditions for Domestic Airlines

Already contending with competition from low cost carriers (JetBlue, Southwest, AirTran), they will suffer from the slower growth of domestic passenger traffic.

Capacity Reduction

To limit the negative effects on profitability of the poor economic conditions, major airlines have already begun to reduce capacity. Even as many carriers decide to ground a portion of their existing fleets, the acceleration of new airplane deliveries will only increase the pressure on margins. With the transatlantic open skies agreement in effect since April moreover expected to trigger a price war, the airlines will likely maintain their capacity in that segment to protect their allotted landing and take-off slots for the next season.

A Fuel Bill Exacerbated by Structural Factors

Persistent shortcomings of air traffic control in the United States and antiquated infrastructure at some airports — affecting all airlines but especially those operating in the domestic market — will continue to add about 12 percent to airline fuel costs.

Volatile Ownership and High Debt

Although the major American companies carry high debt, their positive operating cash flow will, according to Calyon Securities, cover their operating costs this year based on average barrel prices around USD 100. That is not, however, the case for smaller airlines like Frontier Airlines that went bankrupt recently due to a lack of credit.

Ongoing Fleet Renewal

In the current context airlines may partially postpone the heavy investments required in the very near term and through 2020 to modernise their aging fleets — about USD 750 billion by

FAA (Federal Aviation Administration) estimates. They will not be able to delay them for long, however, with FAA inspections increasingly exposing fleet maintenance deficiencies, attributable to the cost cutting undertaken in past years.

This year began with the announcement of a far-reaching merger between Delta and Northwest that transformed Delta into the world leader. The two companies — partners to Air France-KLM — are thus expected to dominate the transatlantic sky with antitrust immunity granted to the Skyteam alliance by the Department of Transport. Continental Airlines may react by joining forces with British Airways and American Airlines.

Europe: Transatlantic open skies will give rise to consolidation moves and a price war.

Like in North America, passenger traffic in Europe is expected to grow five percent a year on average through 2011

Airline Profits in General will Slow in 2008

The transatlantic open skies agreement between the European Union and the United States in effect since April this year could weaken British Airways and Virgin Atlantic with both very dependent on flights between Heathrow and Washington: BA notably derives 60 percent of its operating income from that route. The open skies agreement means that European carriers can henceforth fly to any American city from any airport whatsoever in the European Union while American carriers can operate intra-European connecting flights to and from any EU airport. The agreement also increased from 25 to 50 percent the maximum stake a European carrier can hold in an American carrier. In the economic conditions prevailing so far this year, the agreement may prove less lucrative than expected. With companies reluctant to reduce their capacity on the routes involved out of fear of losing their allotted take-off and landing slots, prices could be subject to intense pressure particularly on the business travel segment.

To improve the profitability of those routes, the airlines have been forming alliances: Air France entered into a joint-venture with Delta Air Lines expected to generate USD°1.5°billion in additional turnover without requiring any major investments by either airline. In a countermove, British Airways may tighten its partnership with American Airlines or take a closer look at its British competitor BMI (British Midland Airways), also coveted by Lufthansa. The German airline has also shown interest in the 49 percent stake in Virgin Atlantic Airways put on the market by Singapore Airlines. And other moves are in the offing: With a view to a possible buyout of Iberia Lineas Aereas, BA has teamed up with the American equity fund TPG Capital while Lufthansa has joined forces with Apax Partners Worldwide. Spain's Spanair is also up for sale while Italy's AIitalia has yet to find a buyer.

The airlines will thus have to contend with profound changes while their margins remain under pressure from the rise of fuel prices and the need to continue renewing a portion of their fleets. In this context BA has announced having raised USD 1.7 billion in debt refinancing to cover payments for air plane deliveries over the next five years. And the turbulence has not spared European low-cost operators

Some fifty carriers, including subsidiaries of major airlines, have been waging a fierce price war with their margins squeezed as a result. With the leaders Ryanair and Easyjet likely to experience slower growth, weaker airlines like Spain's Vueling are expected to suffer significant declines in profits. The low-cost segment is also ripe for consolidations moves this year. The Lufthansa subsidiary Air Berlin, after having absorbed its fellow German operators DBA (Deutsche BA) and LTU (well positioned on long-haul routes), has its eyes on Condor, a Thomas Cook subsidiary, whose acquisition would give rise to a new low-cost heavyweight alongside Ryanair and Easyjet.

Asia: more intense competition likely in Japan; airlines often still weak in India and China.

Driven by regional economic dynamism, passenger traffic in Asia-Pacific will grow 5.9 percent a year on average through 2011. As a result of their investment efforts, however, airline profits will remain the lowest of the three regions with 0.9 percent expected by IATA estimates.

Japan's

National company Japan Airlines ended the 2007-2008 financial year with a EUR 100 million loss and will continue its restructuring programme this year with a view to restoring equilibrium. Conversely, its rival All Nippon Airlines will continue to capitalise on the regional expansion, especially in China. The Asia Gateway project up for discussion in 2008 for the purpose of opening

Japanese airports up more to international carriers is expected to spur trade with strong-growth countries. But that could also complicate matters for Japan Airlines and its efforts to return to profitability.

China

Three large, majority state-owned companies share the sky: China Eastern Airlines, Air China and China Southern. And the major international airlines have been working to establish positions in the country: Singapore Airlines — momentarily outmanoeuvred by Air China — has regained the upper-hand in negotiations over acquisition of a stake in China Eastern Airlines. And Cathay Pacific already has a reciprocal agreement with Air China concluded through the Hong Kong airline's Dragonair subsidiary and has announced the creation of a jointly-owned cargo carrier. Discussions are underway, meanwhile between Air France-KLM and China Southern. The opening of new routes between China and the United States will likely spur consolidation moves in this highly competitive segment especially with low-cost Chinese carriers like East Star Airlines now successfully penetrating international routes. Bankruptcies could increase among smaller companies like Oasis Hong-Kong Airline, which went into liquidation in April. All these developments, underpinned by large investments in airports and fleets, nonetheless remain dependent on airspace management still largely under military control.

India's

Two national companies, Air India specialised in international flights and Indian Airlines in domestic flights, merged in July 2007. Concentration moves have also developed among private companies with Kingfisher Airlines notably just taking a 26 percent stake in the low-cost carrier Air Deccan to rival the two leaders Air Sahara and Jet Airways. Although the government has implemented financial incentives to foster development of regional routes, the regulatory framework continues to impede the expansion of private companies with Jet Airways alone authorised to operate internationally.

Middle East: Booming Economic Conditions have Prompted Companies to make Heavy Investments

Passenger traffic in the Middle East : is expected to grow 6.8 percent a year on average through 2011, buoyed by a booming regional economy and the opening of new routes. And regional airlines have become fierce competitors via massive investments in new planes epitomised by Qatar Airways order for twentyfour A350 and ten A380 airbuses. Airline profits should nonetheless remain low at USD 0.2 billion this year.

Latin America: Antiquated Airports Pose a threat to Brazilian Airlines

Latin America : are expected to barely break even after suffering slight losses in recent years. The Brazilian sky has also been in the throes of consolidation. For the first time, a low-cost airline — Gol, Brazil's second largest carrier and the world's second largest low-cost operator behind Ryanair — has taken over a traditional airline, Varig, which filed for bankruptcy in 2005. With the revival of Varig's international routes and USD four billion in turnover Gol is now a worthy adversary for the leader TAM. Brazil's airport infrastructure has failed, meanwhile, to keep pace with the soaring growth of air transport in recent years, which could undermine the development of carriers operating in the country. In Mexico, after the sale of Mexicana in 2005, the transfer of Aeromexico to a group of investors led by the Banamex bank completed the privatisation of an air traffic sector characterised by competition between a large number of low-cost carriers.

The Product

With beauty and diversity, New South Wales has a wide range of experiences for international and domestic visitors. Tourists enjoy the big city buzz of Sydney, its great restaurants and shopping, the beauty of its world famous harbour. They can then step away to soak up the local flavours of regional of New South Wales. Visitors can laze on a beach, hike in fresh mountain air, journey to the red outback, soothe their soul in one of the World Heritage national parks, take a leisurely drive through the State's lush farm regions or stop in the quirky towns and cosmopolitan centres. Along the way visitors will be amazed at what they find – fine food and wine trails, lively festivals, Aboriginal heritage tours, amazing landscapes and friendly locals.

As a result, tourism products come in all shapes and sizes – from five-star hotels to boutique bed and breakfasts or trendy backpacker resorts. They also include iconic attractions such as the Sydney Opera House and Harbour Bridge, activities such as horse-riding, sea kayaking and rainforest tours, not forgetting ski, surf or circus schools, museums and galleries, aquariums, wineries, zoos and lots, lots more.

One of the challenges facing the tourism industry (and in particular tourism operators) is to develop and package tourism products in a way that people want, maintaining New South Wales' position as a premier tourist destination, as well as ensuring a viable business for the operator.

Tourism is Everyone's Business

Everyone gains from properly managed tourism. These benefits can be especially significant in regional areas by diversifying the area's economic base and expanding the employment market. In its broadest sense, the tourism industry is the total of all businesses that directly provide goods or services to facilitate business, pleasure and leisure activities away from the home environment. The chart below demonstrates the impact within our economy and community when someone goes on holiday. As you can see it is significant.

The Tourism System

Before developing a tourism product it is useful to understand how the tourism system operates. The following diagram shows the basic components involved:

The Consumer

In the tourism system the consumer is the most important element as the consumer is the reason tourism products and services exist. Everyone working in tourism must ensure that the consumer is fundamental to all business and planning decisions.

Consumers have many choices about how to spend their money and leisure time. If they choose to spend their money on a holiday, they will then determine their budget, decide how much time they have available and what types of activities they would like to do while away. Then they will begin to select a destination, decide how they will travel there and make reservations accordingly through a travel agent, wholesaler, over the Internet or directly from the tourism operator.

The Travel Experience

The travel experience relates to how the consumer travels to the destination and the experience they have along the way. The choices can include air, car, boat, coach, train, motorbike, hiking or a combination of the above. The mode of travel affects the type of experience, for example flying to a destination is a very different experience to driving.

A destination can suffer if transport options, links and support services are limited or below standard. Issues such as the variety of attractions, facilities and accommodation available en route, the road quality, signage and frequency of transport services, can all affect the quality of the travel experience.

The Holiday Experience

When consumers decide to take a particular type of holiday they have expectations of the experience they will have. This could relate to the quality of accommodation, service and food, the range and cost of activities available, the length of time they have, the weather, etc. Their satisfaction will be based on how well the holiday met their initial expectations or exceeded them.

Marketing Your Business

Marketing refers to a multifaceted, on-going process that any successful business is continually working through. It includes activities such as: researching the market, your consumers and products; evaluating research data; developing your business and products; developing your own skills; and promoting, advertising or working with the media to raise awareness of your product and generate sales. Marketing is often described as 'the four Ps': product, place, price and promotion. The product includes the physical attributes of the product, branding and packaging. Place is about distribution: the agencies, channels and institutions used to give consumers easy access to purchasing your product. Price must meet both the consumer's and your needs. Promotion is explaining destinations, products and services to consumers to help them choose their holiday. Promotion can use a range of media such as print (magazines, newspapers, brochures, posters displayed on billboards, bus stops, the sides of buses, trains etc), television, radio, direct mail, Internet, etc. Providing a holiday package as a prize for a competition or even staying in touch with customers provides promotion of your product.

Consumer Decision-Making

The above diagram assists in understanding the process consumers work through in deciding about taking a holiday. It is important to understand this process because it influences all stages of the previously discussed model, especially the marketing/ promotion element.

Needs – Going on a holiday allows people to take a break from their normal life, whether it's restful idleness in scenic spots or extreme sports in challenging terrain, on their own, with a partner or friends, or in a large group.

Awareness – Consumers may have a recognised or unrecognised need for a holiday. Promoting a holiday destination, product or service can help consumers recognise they need a holiday, then raise their awareness of the choices available.

Motivation – If the consumer is positively aware of a destination, product or service they are more likely to be motivated to visit.

Planning/Decision – Promotional information helps the consumer decide how to get there, and what they want to do.

Satisfaction – If a product delivers what has been promoted, the consumer is likely to be satisfied and have a quality holiday experience, and vice versa.

Word of Mouth – Consumers share their holiday experiences with friends, family and colleagues. Their word of mouth raises awareness of the destination, product(s) and service(s) with potential future consumers.

Tourism Growth

The 'Grand Tour' and the First Package Tours

In the early 19th century the aristocracy, and the 'new money' from trade were caught up in a fashion to show their refinement by educating themselves in the artistic treasures of Europe. Young ladies, especially, were taken on a 'Grand Tour' of Europe to complete their education.. and perhaps meet an eligible young man! Such journeys were complicated and expensive in the days before railways, and were restricted to the very rich. Later, English 'gentlemen' took skis to the Alps and strared the winter sports holiday!

Railways to the Seaside

It was the coming of the railways that gave Thomas Cook the opportunity to develop inclusive travel, where he started by inventing the return ticket. Day excursions gave way to travel with accommodation, and finally foreign travel. the link above tells the story.

The Middle Class go on Holiday

In the 20th century the better-off middle classes joined the rich in foreign travel. They had the time and the money for modest holidays, but most of their trips would have been organised by themselves, which involved skills not shared by the mass of the population.

The Rapid Growth of Tourism Since the 1960's

The great social upheavals of the Second World War saw most of the class barriers breaking down, saw service people travel the world and gain wider visions and appetites, and, in the 1950's onwards, exposure to television.. and travel programmes. With the additions of technical advances, such as the jet airliner, that could deliver holidaymakers to the Mediterranean in a couple of hours, and the computer, which would revolutionise bookings and accounting, the modern travel business has come of age.

Tourism is one of three growth sectors a recent study on Vanuatu's private sector has identified. Construction and agriculture are the other two.

"The number of tourists arriving by air rose by nearly 14% in 2007 and by over 16% in 2008," said a report called 'Sustaining Growth: A Private Sector Assessment for Vanuatu'. The study was commissioned by the Asian Development Bank (ADB).

"Remarkably, despite the global economic slowdown, tourist arrivals by air in January 2009 were 28% higher than in January 2008.

"Over the past few years, there has been a very large growth in the number of cruise ships visiting Vanuatu: the number of arrivals has tripled over the past five years.

"Anecdotal evidence suggests that these rose by nearly 40% in 2008 after increasing by 60% in 2007.

"A growing number of tour ship visitors later return as tourists, which bodes well for future tourism growth."

Vanuatu appears to have been successful too in attracting high-spending tourists, the report observed. In addition, improved policies towards the private sector contributed to growth in tourism, especially with the removal of the monopolistic hold of Air Vanuatu on international air services.

"Vanuatu recently opened its air transport market to international airlines, creating competition that has resulted in significantly lower airfares and higher tourism arrivals," said the ADB report.

"Recent figures illustrate the extent of this increase: international tourist arrivals were nearly 30% higher in January 2009 than in January 2008.

"These results reinforce the wisdom of opening the country to additional foreign airlines and demonstrate the benefits of greater competition.

"In another positive step—and as a result of pressures placed on the airline by greater competition—the government is considering options for restructuring Air Vanuatu."

Removing monopolies, the report said has also worked in Vanuatu's telecommunications sector. An overseas mobile phone operator—Digicel—was granted a licence to operate which immediately resulted – as it did with international airfares – in the slashing of phone tariffs.

Internet charges in Vanuatu, however, are said to be among the highest in the world, the ADB study found.

"However, government recently announced the issuance of three new licenses for the provision of internet and other telecommunication services which should lead to better service and lower prices."

The bank urged the Vanuatu Government to continue its policy of liberalising the country's telecommunications sector, as well as push on with the restructure of Air Vanuatu and "franchise out the domestic air routes that require operating subsidies (as was done successfully in Fiji)."

Further, management, air traffic control services, fire-fighting and aviation security at the country's three international airports (Port Vila, Santos and Tanna) should be out-sourced.

Tourism in developing markets has grown at an average rate of 6-8% over the past decade, twice the rate of traditional markets such as Europe, according to new figures released by the UNWTO.

It added that with international travellers projected to almost double by 2020, the most significant increases are expected to take place in markets like China (recent host of the World Travel Awards, with reigning Miss World one of the hosts, pictured above), India and destinations in South-East Asia. The Gulf States and emerging Eastern Europe complete this picture, followed by the Latin American and finally African markets.

Many of these are becoming important outbound markets, backed by growing middle classes on the one hand, and liberalising policies promoting mobility on the other. Chinese tourists already spent about US$30 billion abroad in 2007, according to UNWTO figures.

The domestic travel potential of emerging markets – in 2006 China registered 1.6 billion trips and India 461 million-is a further proof of their long term importance for international tourism.

Between 1996 and 2006, international tourism in developing countries expanded by 6% as a whole, by 9% for Least Developed Countries, and 8% for other low and lower-middle income economies. Against this backdrop, the sector will be more and more recognized as a key agent in national poverty reduction strategies and in development financing. Investment in infrastructure and human resource training, as key issues to make this trend sustainable. He also discussed the importance of credible long term climate response strategies – which allow these countries to realize their tourism growth potential.

World Travel & Tourism is expected to generate close to US$8 trillion in 2008, rising to approximately US$15 trillion over the next ten years, according to the latest Tourism Satellite Accounting (TSA) research launched today by the World Travel & Tourism Council (WTTC) and its strategic partner Accenture.

Overall, the new TSA results reveal a moderate impact on the Travel & Tourism industry as a result of the global economic downturn, with its annual growth rate experiencing a slowdown in 2008, to 3%, in comparison to 3.9% in 2007.

Looking past this present cyclical downturn, the long-term forecasts point to a mature but steady phase of growth for world Travel & Tourism between 2009 and 2018, averaging a growth rate of 4.4% per annum, supporting 297 million jobs and 10.5% of global GDP by 2018.

WTTC President Jean-Claude Baumgarten explained "Challenges come from the US slowdown and the weak dollar, higher fuel costs and concerns about climate change. However, the continued strong expansion in emerging countries-both as tourism destinations and as an increasing source of international visitors-means that the industry's prospects remain bright into the medium term."

Regionally Africa, Asia Pacific and the Middle East are experiencing higher growth rates than the world average, at 5.9%, 5.7% and 5.2% respectively, while the mature markets, most notably the Americas and Europe, are falling below the world average with a growth at 2.1% and 2.3 % respectively.

The overall impact of this slowdown for mature markets is expected to be offset by the strength of the emerging markets explains John Walker, Chairman of Oxford Economics "In particular, China, India and other emerging markets are still growing rapidly, which will increase both business and leisure travel, while many countries in the Middle East are undertaking massive tourism-related investment programmes."

Moreover, even in countries where economic growth slows, there is likely to be a switch from international to domestic travel rather than a contraction in demand for Travel & Tourism.

Among the 176 countries covered in the TSA research, the United States continues to maintain pole position as the largest Travel & Tourism economy, with its total demand accounting for more than US$1,747 billion this year. With a growth rate at 1.1% in 2008 the credit crunch is leading to a marked slowdown in US economic growth and is likely to restrict the business travel of those working in financial markets.

Considerable ground has been made by the emerging markets which are experiencing rapid economic growth. In 2008, China will jump from fourth to second position above Japan and Germany and is forecasted to increase its Travel & Tourism Demand four-fold by 2018, accounting for US$2,465 billion, with an annual growth rate of 8.9%. Among the fastest growers in 2008, Macau leads with a growth rate at 22%.

2

Product Development in Tourism

Knowing the Tourist Product

Many do not know what a tourist product is. Sadly, some in the tourist industry hardly know what tourist product is all about. Tourist product is intangible. When a tourist, guided by his motivations and the image of the tourist destination, decides on a trip somewhere outside his usual place of residence or work, he is buying a tourist product-a promise that will soon become a memory once he returns home.

Let's take the case of Aklan, Antique, Capiz, Guimaras, Iloilo or Negros Occidental as individual destinations or a multiple-destination, as the case may be. When one buys a trip to destinations like these, one does so in anticipation of a memorable experience. The experience at the airport, pier or bus station upon arrival in the destination is part of the tourist product. The quality of transportation and the behavior of the driver and other aspects of transport services all form part of the experience in the destination. They are important components of the tourist product. The residents' attitude towards visitors and tourists forms part of the tourist product, of the tourist experience.

The facilities and services of the accommodation establishment, shopping places and their wares, restaurants, food, local tours and security are all part of the tourist product. The fiesta and festival, tourist spot, accessibility experiences are all parts of the total tourist experience. All these elements should be attended to by tourism stakeholders in the destination if they want to fill their air, sea and land transport seats, hotel rooms and function rooms, restaurants, souvenir and delicacies stores all year round.

Does Aklan, Antique, Capiz, Guimaras, Iloilo or Negros Occidental have what it takes as a memorable tourist product? Is the Aklan Experience, Antique Experience, Capiz Experience, Guimaras Experience, Iloilo Experience or Negros Occidental Experience worth experiencing or re-experiencing, as the case may be? We only have to evaluate the destination against the above-cited criteria to know the answer.

There are tourist markets for every tourist product or combination of tourist products. Tourist markets level off with tourist products. Tourist destinations, therefore, should improve their tourist product if they want to attract high spending, discriminating tourists. They should know their markets and supply what they want. After all, the quantity and quality of tourists that a destination gets depend on the quantity and quality of the tourist products it offers.

New product development is one of the most important components of product policy and product management. Product lines and products are appraise and are positioned effectively. Brand decisions are taken wisely. For a higher level of growth, a firm has to look beyond its existing products. A progressive firm has to consider new product development as a cardinal element of its product policy.

Innovation is the essence of all growth. This is especially true in marketing. In an age of technological advancements, change is a natural outcome – change in food habits, change in expectations and requirements. Any business has to be vigilant to these changes taking place in its environment. People always seek better products, greater convenience, newer fashion and more value for money.

A business firm has to respond to these dynamic requirements of its clientele and these responses take the shape of new products and new services. Through such a response, the firm reaps a good deal of benefits. New products become necessary from the profit angle too. Products that are already established often have their limitations in enhancing the profit level of the firm. Profits from products decline as they reach the maturity stage of their life cycle. Thus, it is necessary for business firms to bring in new products to replace old, declining and losing products.

New products become part and parcel of the growth requirements of the firm and in many cases, new profits come to the firm only through new products. New products can be broadly classified into two groups: new products arising out of technological innovations and new products arising out of marketing oriented modifications. The first group involves innovations leading to intrinsically new products with a new functional utility behind them. The second group involves mere marketing oriented innovations in existing products; it gives rise to new versions of the existing products.

Tourism product development is mainly undertaken to facilitate product diversification, development or improvement of tourism products with the help of knowledgeable and qualified staff. It aims at enhancing visitor experience by building consensus and strategic alliances with business stakeholders in order to bring about socioeconomic growth. Tourism product development seeks to support in the maintenance, development and enhancement of the tourism product.

A large number of companies offer training programs and advice on tourism product development. The services include sustainable tourism product planning and development, presentations, seminars, campaigns and strategies for destination marketing organizations, individual operators and agencies. These companies make use of a community and stakeholder-based approach to assist businesses and destinations to plan for successful tourism in the long-term from cost-effective, environmental and communally sustainable perspectives. These companies provide an extensive range of specialized services designed to help individual tourism operators, associations and product clubs, educational institutions and government agencies effectively attain their short and long-term goals. Some of these companies are designed to assist government and quasi-government agencies in the development of the tourism industry, principally by coordinating and aiding timely action between public and private sector interests.

Tourism product development aims at long-term sustainable development by the execution of a number of strategies. These strategies bring into focus a generic idea to increase competitiveness, build an inclusive industry by promoting closer integration of people and develop and maintain the environment. Tourism product development is designed to increase the income in the sector. Tourism product development involves implementation of a comprehensive plan of action that will guide towards dealing with estimated increase in business over the short, medium and long-terms.

Tourism product development helps in improving product quality by complying with the standards set by international benchmarks. It helps in product improvement by tourism training. It helps in product diversification by acting as a channel, facilitator and controller for development through sports and community based development with stress on culture, heritage and ecotourism.

Pricing Tourism Products & Services

In general, tourism businesses appear to be in a highly competitive industry with limited flexibility to set prices. Either they sell at or below the established market price or see a rapid drop in sales. Establishing a firm's price under such circumstances is straightforward, although not always simple. All one needs to do is to identify what the competition is charging and price one's own product comparably.

Despite this apparent lack of flexibility, however, the uniqueness of tourism/recreation goods and services actually enables producers to establish prices. This uniqueness stems from a number of product attributes, including: business location, its natural environment, the types of facilities offered, the personal relationships that management and staff develop with customers, and real and perceived differences in the quality of the firm's products.

Because most tourism/recreation businesses have at least some flexibility to establish prices, this bulletin will address the key factors that should be considered in making pricing decisions. Keep in mind, however, that the same uniqueness which provides pricing flexibility also precludes development of a universally applicable formula for guiding pricing decisions. Furthermore, the goals of businesses in this industry vary widely and, because price is a major toot for achieving a business's goals, identical businesses under identical circumstances may logically establish different prices.

While it is not possible to prescribe a single formula for all price-setting decisions, it is possible to identify the primary components of a sound pricing strategy. These "ingredients" can be found in textbooks and by observing business pricing practices.

Both sources are drawn upon here to provide you with the ingredients to make sound pricing decisions. Ultimately, you must fit them to your business goals and circumstances to arrive at the best prices for your products.

The Basics of Pricing

Price theory is a keystone of economics. Because of this central role, no economics text would be complete without one or more chapters devoted to pricing. Many books have been written on this single topic. Successful business people, whether from books or practical experience, have learned to use basic pricing concepts for their products and services. These elements are introduced briefly below.

Economists begin their introduction to pricing by explaining the concept of demand. In simple terms, demand means that consumers will purchase more of a good or service at a low price than at a high price. Therefore, demand is the economists' term to describe the relationship between the varying quantities of a product which can be sold over a range of prices. Demand can be expressed in at least three ways:

a) in tabular form;

b) as a mathematical relationship; or

c) as a graph.

We will discuss demand as expressed in a graph, since that format is the easiest to visualize.

Note that as the price charged decreases from $3 to $2, the quantity which can be sold increases from five to ten units. Based only on this information, the operator of this particular business would maximize sales revenue by establishing a price of $2 for the product. At that price, gross revenue would equal $2 x 10 units = $20. At a price of $3 or $1 gross revenue would equal only $15.

If the unit cost of producing these 5, 10 or 15 units was identical—for example, $0.50 per unit, net revenue would also be maximized by setting the price at $2. Net revenue (gross revenue-production cost = net revenue) at a $2 price would equal $15. Note, however, that while gross revenue is $15 at both the $1 and $3 unit price, net revenue is not equal. At a$3 price, net revenue is $12.50 while at a $1 price net revenue is only $7.50. This illustrates the need to account for both demand and cost when setting prices.

In addition, unit costs contain both fixed and variable elements. Fixed costs include such items as rent, insurance and managerial costs which must be paid to be in a particular business. The per unit fixed cost burden declines as output increases. Doubling output, for example, would reduce fixed costs per unit by half.

Variable costs, on the other hand, vary directly with output. Examples of variable cost items include employee wages, laundry costs and supplies. Total variable costs increase as output increases but often will not be the same across all levels of output. Per unit variable costs typically are high at low levels of output and decline as output level expands because of economies of scale (e.g. volume discounts on large orders from suppliers). With reasonably good projections of a business's fixed and variable costs, it is possible to establish the minimum price required in order for the business to earn a profit. This is often referred to as a break-even price. This is the price per unit for a given volume of output at which total revenue is exactly equal to total costs. This relationship can be expressed algebraically as follows:

$$P \times Q = F + (V \times Q)$$

where

P = price per unit sold

Q = quantity produced and sold

F = total fixed costs

V = variable cost per unit.

Isolating price in the above expression yields the following:

$$P = F + (V \times Q)\ Q$$

Even though fixed and variable costs and quantity may not be known precisely, calculation of an appropriate range of break-even prices can often be very revealing. Indeed, use of this simple business technique could keep you from inadvertently investing in products unlikely to be purchased at the price required for you to break-even on the quantity you could produce. Occasionally, however, there are circumstances in which a rational business person may deliberately establish a selling price below the break-even point.

Pricing in Practice

The real world which the commercial recreation/tourism business faces is far more complex than the highly simplified theoretical economic models which we have been

Discussing

However, these models can help you to deal better with your real-world pricing problems and are a firm foundation upon which to build a more comprehensive tourism/recreation pricing strategy. When economists establish the price-quantity relationship which they refer to as demand, they mean it to apply to a single product which consumers perceive as being identical.

Billions of dollars are spent each year on advertising with the single purpose of convincing consumers that apparently identical products in fact possess important differences. These advertising dollars aren't wasted.

The boom in sales of certain designer jeans, headache remedies, soft drinks, and fast foods reflect consumer perceptions of differences among the products available to them, whether or not these differences actually exist.

Even without the influence of advertising, consumers' perceptions of products and services in the tourism and recreation industry do differ greatly. These differences in perceptions are extremely important to a business's pricing strategy. In essence, these perceptions define the competition. From a prospective consumer's perception, for example, the competition for a modern campground along a major highway, may be nearby budget motels, rather than less-developed campgrounds on the same route.

In such a setting, the modern campground owner might be able to price a night of camping considerably higher—near the level of nearby budget motels-than would be feasible if the competition was exclusively other campgrounds.

Thus, a first step in developing a pricing strategy is to establish from the consumer's perspective what other products in your market compete most directly with your offering. Be sure to include all significant attributes of your product such as: location, facilities and services you offer, and significant attractions in the vicinity of your business.

Many tourism/recreation businesses offer multiple products and/or services to the consumer. A marina, for example, may rent boat slips, sell boats, fuel, and equipment, offer maintenance and storage services, and even operate a grocery/beverage outlet. In establishing a pricing strategy, the marina must not only focus on demand, production costs, and its competitors' prices, but also must consider the impact of slip rental prices on the attractiveness of its other products and services.

The objective is to maximize profit across its entire product line. This might be achieved by charging slip rental fees below the competition and even below the break-even price.

Grocery stores commonly employ such a pricing strategy for turkeys at holiday seasons, since all but the most conscientious shoppers are likely to purchase the rest of the ingredients for the holiday meal wherever the best price on turkeys is offered. Restaurants with bars will often discount food prices in order to attract customers who will purchase drinks, which are a high profit product. Impact across a firm's product line is an important consideration in establishing pieces for an individual product offering.

Demand for tourism/recreation varies with the season and the day of the week. In some cases, demand may also vary across product offerings. For example, rooms with a scenic view or campsites near the water are in greater demand than others which a business may have to offer.

These differences can be exploited, since greater demand provides an opportunity to charge higher prices. Variations in demand also suggest that lowering prices during non-peak periods can yield added revenue.

As long as the price discounts offered aren't excessive (i.e. the established price covers all variable costs), offering reduced rates can actually enhance a firm's profit. To the extent that differences in demand can be identified, differential pricing should be an ingredient in a firm's overall pricing strategy.

Pricing is often employed to attract new customers, to maintain good customer relations, to help a new business to become known, and to "wage war" on competition. The latter seldom makes sense for small businesses, especially those with limited capital or lines of credit. Offering price discounts, however, can be effective in the other instances noted and is often feasible even for small businesses. For example, offering a price discount on occasion may yield more business than allocating an equivalent sum for advertising. On the other hand, a business in the hospitality industry must avoid the appearance of price gouging or risk loss of customers over the long haul.

Summary

This approach to making pricing decisions draws upon the concepts of demand and production costs. Break-even analysis reveals the minimum price to be charged in order for a firm to remain in business in the long run. In the "pricing in practice" section, we highlighted the importance of viewing your product from the consumer's perspective. Knowing the consumer's perspective helps identify your competitors. Assessing the impact of pricing decisions across your entire product line and using the concept of differential pricing were also noted as considerations in developing pricing strategies.

Finally, the idea of discount pricing as a promotional strategy to attract new customers or to maintain good relations with old customers was noted as a possible use of pricing strategy.

One point remains to be made. Regardless of how much you read about pricing, both in theory and in practice, and how much research you undertake to support your decisions, it is necessary to monitor the results of your pricing decisions.

Only through monitoring can you determine whether your pricing decisions are yielding the anticipated results. It is far better to adjust your strategy than it is to stick with a bad decision. Even good business people occasionally make bad decisions because of faulty information or incorrect analysis. The only way to determine what price to charge is to experiment. The ideas presented here should help you to narrow the focus of your experiments so that you can more quickly identify prices which are best for your business.

Distribution of Tourism Product

No matter how impressive your product, its success relies on customers knowing you exist in the marketplace. Choosing the most effective distribution system to reach and then sell to your target audiences will help you succeed.

Distribution Systems

A distribution system uses a variety of channels/intermediaries to not only raise product profile but also extend the points of sale, so that purchases can be made in locations other than the actual point of operation.

An efficient product distribution strategy should facilitate product sales in advance of their actual use.

This is significant if your target audiences include international visitors travelling on a structured prepaid itinerary; or domestic travellers who prefer to confirm their itineraries prior to travel.

Compiling a Distribution Strategy

Analysing which distribution channels will be the most profitable is crucial to an effective distribution strategy.

Major considerations include:

- How do your target markets currently purchase your type of product and how do you go about establishing a relationship with them?
- What distribution methods have you in mind that appeal to and reach your identified audiences?
- What sort of costs will be incurred by using these particular distributors?
- Are these proposed distributors enthusiastic about your product, and potentially good sales ambassadors?
- Do they handle products provided by your direct competitors?
- Are these proposed distributors familiar with your product? If not, what are the costs involved in developing product familiarity?
- What sort of incentive can you offer a distributor to encourage sales of your product? (An 'over-ride' commission, e.g. an additional 2-3% on top of existing commission rates.)

Ensure the response you receive from using your distribution channels meets your expectations and achieves anticipated sales.

Common Distribution Methods

Distribution channels are dependent on target markets.

Your options may include working with intermediaries like wholesalers; or more simply, using promotional material to not only spread the word about your product but to serve as a sales tool. Bear in mind that as you grow, the use of intermediaries as opposed to direct sales between you and your customers is often the most cost-effective means of increasing sales.

Your own Brochure

Before you produce a brochure you firstly need to determine how your prospective client will obtain it.

Effective distribution methods are important to brochure success. Secondly, consider the content of the brochure and how it may facilitate a sale. For example, a toll-free booking or enquiries phone number (or an Internet address) listed on your brochure provides a convenient means for customers to make direct bookings or purchases prior to travel. It enables you to quickly and easily convert a motivation to buy, to an actual sale. If you are targeting international markets, this phone service should operate 24 hours a day.

Also, as an added incentive, consider offering special discounts to customers making advance purchases.

Affiliations with Booking Agents

Establishing a relationship with an existing tourism-based booking agency selling a range of local tourism products can be a cost-efficient distribution channel. These agents are used by

travel planners (wholesalers, inbound tour operators etc.) and directly by individuals. Remember, commission rates should be allowed for in your price.

Tour Operator Brochures and Packages

Depending on your business, it may be possible to expand distribution by incorporating your product into tour operator packages. You may also consider participating in cooperative marketing programs with government tourism authorities, transport carriers, and major accommodation chains who often compile their own itineraries (e.g. weekend packages geared to domestic markets). To achieve such an arrangement it is expected that your product is established and well-regarded in the marketplace and has a price structure that incorporates commissions.

Travel Wholesalers and their Affiliated Travel Agents

Distributing your product through wholesalers and their affiliated travel agents can boost sales. Usually a wholesaler liaises directly with suppliers (or on an international level, with inbound tour operators) to collate a number of value holiday packages/ itineraries. These options are sold to the customer through a retail travel agent. Again, to be included in such packages, your product must be established, well regarded and, for international sales, 'export ready'. Visitor Information Centres and retail travel agents Many experienced, independent travellers with limited travel arrangements prefer to leave their itinerary open until they arrive. Therefore, do not overlook distributing your product through domestic outlets serving not only as booking centres but also information sources.

Direct Sales through the Internet

The Internet offers tourism operators an additional way to promote their product, provide information to potential travellers and sell their product. Increasingly, consumers are researching and planning their holidays online and similarly the rate of purchase online is increasing. In fact, online travel is the fastest growing consumer product sector. According to Roy Morgan Research, by December 2004, 26% of travel bookings by Australians were via the Internet, up from 15% in 2002.

While use of the Internet for research, planning and booking or purchase is widespread, it has particular appeal to independent travellers who conduct extensive destination research prior to travel. Furthermore, there has been a tendency for both younger and upmarket travellers to purchase online.

Direct sales on the Internet can take two forms:

(a) enabling transactions on your own websites

(b) providing allocations to other online sellers.

In both cases, consider the costs, resources and security measures involved. To reach your target market and maximize the appeal, you may consider as part of your marketing plan links with major tourism authorities' websites.

An 'Export Ready' Product

Presenting a product that is considered 'export ready' is crucial if you plan to sell to international markets. To see if you are 'export ready', answer the following questions.

- Is your business established in the domestic market? (i.e. do you have a good level of domestic distribution and do you have a successful domestic marketing strategy?)
- Do you have a phone/fax booking service with confirmations available within 24 hours?
- Are you experienced with the concept of wholesale commissions and nett rates?
- Do you understand the concept of pricing and yield management?*
- Do you clearly understand the differing needs of international markets compared to domestic markets?
- Do you have an active quality assurance program to maintain your product to a high standard?

International Product Distribution

International markets are very competitive. To succeed you require an 'export ready' product; suitable cashflow; and the ability to forge positive relationships with intermediaries

specialising in international markets. You must also be patient as financial returns can be slow. As a rule of thumb, the experience in the industry is that it takes 2-4 years to become established in the international market.

Inbound Tour Operators

These operators coordinate itineraries specifically for international travellers, providing a complete, costed travel schedule that is marketed to international tour wholesalers and travel agents. They usually coordinate tours around 12 months in advance so you will need to plan ahead.

Distributors and their Commission Rates

Commission rates paid to tourism intermediaries vary depending on the channel of distribution, and are only paid after a sale of your product is made. Industry standards for commissions paid from the usual retail price are generally:

- 10-15% of the retail price for retail agents
- 20-25% of the retail price for wholesalers
- 25-30% of the retail price for inbound tour operators – ITOs.

Inbound tour operators receive this level of commission to pay international intermediaries on your behalf, and to allow for their own profit margin.

The Link between Distribution and Promotion

The extent of your sales relies not only on the most effective distribution of sales intermediaries but also associated product promotions and where these are distributed. Promotions must be placed in locations that guarantee extensive exposure to your target markets. If compiled and distributed effectively, advertising brochures, and publicity featured in targeted publications (including travel guide books and maps) can successfully project your product and stimulate sales.

To maintain good relations with your sales intermediaries, keep them informed of any product developments through regular newsletters and industry familiarisations ('famils').

3

Sustainable Integrated Tourism Planning

The Costs and Benefits of Tourism

As the largest industry in the world, tourism has the potential to help deal with the key issues facing many parts of the globe and therefore can be seen as a positive and negative force. If the costs and benefits of tourism are understood from the outset, strengths and opportunities can be maximized while weaknesses and threats can be minimized.

Each tourism planning situation will be different in terms of its tourism characteristics. The costs and benefits of tourism will vary in each destination, and these can change over time, depending on tourism and other activities in the local and regional context.

Tourism can be Seen as having the following Benefits and Costs

Economic Benefits:

- Tourism generates local employment, both directly in the tourism sector and in various support and resourcesm anagemenst ectors.
- Tourism stimulates profitable domestic industries-hotels and other lodging facilities, restaurants and other food services, transportation systems, handicrafts, and guide services.
- Tourism generates foreign exchange for the country and injects capital and new money into the local economy.

- Tourism diversifies the local economy, particularly in rural areas where agricultural employment may be sporadic or insufficient.
- Increased tax revenues from tourists can be reaped if a local sales tax is added to the provincial and federal taxes already in place.
- Employment opportunities will be created in the business communities due to the influx of tourists who will need goods and services.
- Increased entrepreneurial opportunities will provide goods and services not already available in the community and create new tourist products.
- Improved road systems and infrastructure can be financed through tourism attractions.

Economic Costs

- The jobs created through tourism may be low paying and require few skills.
- Inflated prices may result from local businesses attempting to raise profits or cover the cost of extra employees.
- Inflated property values may occur if the community becomes a tourist 'hot spot'. This will result in higher property taxes that may be unfavourable for local residents.
- If tourism is seasonal at a destination, so too will be the injection of income into the community.
- Health service provision and police services can increase during the tourist season at the expense of the local tax base.
- Affordability and availability of staff housing can be problematic.

Social Benefits:

- The quality of life of a community can be enhanced by economic diversification through tourism, following the principles of sustainable development.
- Tourism creates recreational and cultural facilities that can be used by local communities as well as domestic and international visitors.
- Public spaces may be developed and enhanced through tourism activity.

- Tourism enhances local community esteem and provides the opportunity for greater understanding and communication among peoples of diverse backgrounds.

Social Costs

- Rapid tourism growth can result in the inability to meet the capacities of local amenities and institutions; quality of amenity services can be diminished by over-use.
- Litter, vandalism, and crime are concerns associated with tourism development that will be the responsibility of the community.
- Tourism can bring overcrowding and traffic congestion. Congestion can result in the perception of inconvenience by the residents, which is interpreted as a negative impact on their quality of life.
- Foreigners bring with them material wealth and apparent freedom.

Young members of the host community are particularly susceptible to these economic expectations that tourists bring. The result can be a complete disruption of the traditional way of life in the community.

An increase in crime may result from tourism. The community structure may change (including community bonds, demographics, and institutions). The authenticity of the social and cultural environment can be changed. Organized events for tourists based on local social behaviour and culture can become distorted in their authenticity, which may not be a valid representation of the local environment. Lifestyles may be disrupted beyond levels acceptable to the host community.

Cultural Benefits

- Tourism can enhancel ocal cultural awarenessb, ut eventually might distort it.
- Tourism can generate income to help pay for preservation of archaeological sites, historic buildings, and districts.
- Despite many criticisms about alteration of cultures to unacceptable levels, the sharing of cultural knowledge and experience can be beneficial for both the hosts and the guests at tourist destinations, and could result in the revival of local traditions and crafts.

Cultural Costs

- Youth in the community could begin to emulate the speech and attire of tourists..Loss and damage to historic sites may occur through tourism development and pressures.
- Long-term damage to cultural traditions, and erosion of cultural values, resulting in cultural contamination beyond the level acceptable to the host destination.

Environmental Benefits

Nature tourism encourages productive use of lands that are marginal for agriculture, enabling large tracts to remain covered in natural vegetation.. Parks and nature preserves may be created, and ecological preservation supported as a necessity for nature-based tourism. Improved waste management can be achieved. Increased awareness and concern for the environment may develop.

Environmental Costs

- Negative changes in the physical integrity of the area may occur.
- Rapid development, over development, and overcrowding can forever change the physical environment and ecosystem of an area.
- Litter, erosion, overtaxed sewage, a and waste management systems may occur.
- Sensitive areas and habitat may be lost.
- Degradation of parks and preserves through over-use and poor management ay result.
- Excessive waste may be generated.
- Water and air pollution may occur.
- Wear and tear on infrastructure is accelerated.

The Basis of Sustainable Tourism

Over the past two decadest, he inter-relatedness fall earth systems and human systems has become abundantly clear. We have clearly understood that no human action ever occurs in total isolation from other natural systems, and we have appreciated the reality that humans are dependent on the earth's limited resources. We have realized the fundamental importance of somehow finding ways to live within the carrying capacity of the earth. Over the last twenty years, the global community has been primed for some fundamental changes, including a search for "sustainable development" that is based on new modes of resource allocation and accounting, new attitudes toward the preservation of environmental integrity, and new ways of making decisions in all sectors.

Among the imperatives that promote and enhance the vision of sustainable futures, including that of a sustainable future for tourism, are the following:

- prudent use of the earth's resources within the limits of the planet's carrying capacity; devolution of top-down decision-making responsibilities and capabilities to a broader range of the destination's stakeholders; the abatement of poverty and gender inequalities, and respect for fundamental human rights;
- enhancement of the quality of life through improved health care, shelter, nutrition, and access to education and income-generating skills;
- preservation of biodiversity and life support systems for all natural habitats; and
- preservation of indigenous knowledge and ways of living, and respect for the spiritual and cultural traditions of different people. In fulfilling these imperatives, governments and other societal agents must struggle to find an appropriate balance between different, sometimes apparently conflicting needs and value systems. Sustainable development must meet three fundamental and equal objectives, namely:
- economic: production of goods and services (the overriding criterion in fulfilling this objective is efficiency);
- environmental: conservation and prudent management of natural resources (the overriding criterion is the preservation of biodiversity and maintenance of ecological integrity); and
- social: the maintenance and enhancement of the quality of life (equity is the main consideration in meeting this objective) and inter-generational, as well as intra-generational equity in the distribution of wealth.

Achieving sustainable tourism development requires that the private sector and the public sector cooperate as partners in working toward a sustainable society. Making decisions about sustainable tourism development also requires that governments work within a broader framework than may have been used traditionally, working toward decisions that are:

- longer-term: to better anticipate and prevent problems;
- multi-sectoral: to include the full range of functions of the tourism environment;
- ecosystem based: to recognize the cumulative and synergistic effects of actions;
- wider: to recognize the impacts of their actions on other sectors, regions, and communities;
- deeper: to recognize that the causes and consequences of the problems they seek to solve may involve others and other institutions; and
- full-cycle: to consider the full context of resource use from initial extraction to end use.

Individual tourist resource management decisions will have to be taken with increased understanding of all these dimensions if the goal of sustainable futures is to be attained. Achieving sustainable futures requires the development of appropriate tourism on a continuum where growth decisions, development viewpoints and sustainability issues are balanced with environment and economy. In order to achieve profitability and environmental sustainability in the tourism industry, the tourism industry as a whole must take a different approach to planning and development.

Relationships

We can examine the interdependent relationships between tourism and the environment in terms of the interaction of the visitor, the place, and the host community, using the framework of the tourism system described in Section I. These three elements interact with each other and are affected by external influences. The relationships are essentially two way and can be either positive or negative.

In ten Ds of visitors, we are aware of the range of impacts that growing numbers of visitors and their growing demands have on the places and host communities where tourism opportunities exist, and we know that an increasing number of visitors are searching for higher quality and more satisfying experiences. These trends can bring positive results if there is appropriate and sustainable tourism development in order that the health and well-being of visitors and local residents is ensured, so that communication, education, awareness, and understanding grow from tourism opportunities provided by a community and its location. If tourism is poorly managed, negative results-such as scarred landscapes from overuse, crowding, and traffic problems-will reduce the quality of the tourism experience and quite possibly lead to a hostile and/or exploitative host community.

The concept of sustainability can be interpreted in a number of ways, for example, as a philosophy, as a set of principles and/or values to guide development, or as criteria or tests for determining sustainability. Sustainability is possible only if tourism resources (natural, human-made or cultural) can be maintained over time. The idea of stewardship/trusteeship-to hold the resources of a country in trust for future generations and the responsibility to pass them on in good condition-is applicable here. This means that we want to achieve a situation that can be maintained without depleting the resource, cheating the visitor or exploiting the local population. Achieving sustainability (economic, political, social, cultural, and environmental) requires an ability to accept and accommodate change. It implies, also, that mechanisms are in place to mediate between different interests, which mayor may not be true in any particular setting or situation.

In general, the terminology associated with sustainable tourism is inconsistent and frequently confusing. In spite of this variability in terminology, various actors, and interests have attempted to define their perspectives on goals, practices, effects, and expectations of tourism.

Principles for Sustainable Tourism

Many destinations are now pursuing strategies that aim to ensure a sensitive approach when dealing with tourism. Many of these strategies are based on a formal expression of principles for sustainable tourism. Planners and others can use these principles as basic guidelines when attempting to incorporate the broad vision of sustainability into local policies and practices.

The list of principles provided below are important for destinations and organizations that wish to be guided by the ethic of sustainable and responsible tourism.

Residents of a community must maintain control of tourism development by being involved in setting a community tourism vision, identifying the resources to be maintained and enhanced, and developing goals and strategies for tourism development and management. Equally important, community residents must participate in the implementation of strategies as well as the operation of the tourism infrastructure, services, and facilities.

A tourism initiative should be developed with the help of broad-based stakeholder input. Tourism development must provide quality employment. The provision of fulfilling jobs has to be seen as an integral part of any tourism development. Part of the process of achieving quality employment is to ensure that, as much as possible, the tourism infrastructure (hotels, restaurants, shops, etc.) is developed and managed by local people. Experience has demonstrated that the provision of education and training for local residents and access to financing for local businesses and entrepreneurs are central to this type of policy. Broad-based distribution of the benefits of tourism must occur at the tourism destination. Local linkages and resident participation in the planning, development, and operation of tourism resources and services will help to ensure that a more equitable distribution of benefits will occur among residents, visitors, and other service providers.

Sustainable tourism development has to provide for intergenerational equity. Equitable distribution of the costs and benefits of tourism development must take place among present and future generations. To be fair to future generations of tourists and the travel industry, society should strive to leave a resource base no less than the one we have inherited. Sustainable tourism development must, therefore, avoid resource allocation actions that are irreversible.

A long-ten D planning horizon needs to be adopted by businesses and destination tourism organizations to ensure that destinations are not used for short-ten D gain and then abandoned as visitor tastes and business interests move elsewhere. A longer-ten D horizon encourages the use of proactive strategies to ensure destination sustainability and the establishment of local linkages over time.

Hannony is required between the needs of a visitor, the place, and the community. This is facilitated by broad stakeholder support with a proper balance between economic, social, cultural, and human objectives, and a recognition of the importance of cooperation among government, the host communities, and the tourism industry, and the non-profit organizations involved in community development and environmental protection.

Tourism strategies and plans must be linked with a broader set of initiatives and economic development plans. A need exists for more coordination at both policy and action levels among the various agencies involved and among different levels of government. This is particularly relevant to tourism and environmental policies. Service provisions such as transportation, parking, and water and sewer capacities must also be considered in conjunction with tourism plans and developments. Cooperation among attractions, businesses, and tourism operators is essential given that one business or operation can be directly affected by the performance or quality of another.

There is a definite need for impact assessment of tourism development proposals. The capacity of sites must be considered, including physical, natural, social, and cultural limits and development should be compatible with local and environmental limits. Plans and operations should be evaluated regularly with adjustments as required. Guidelines have to be established for tourism operations, including requirements for impact assessment. There should be codes of practice established for tourism at all levels-national, regional and local. There is also a need to develop indicators and threshold limits for measuring the impacts and success of local tourism ventures. Protection and monitoring strategies are essential if communities are to protect the resources that form the basis of their tourism product.

Tourism planning must move away from a traditional growth-oriented model to one that focuses on opportunities for employment, income and improved local well-being while ensuring that development decisions reflect the full value of the natural and cultural environments. The management and use of public goods such as water, air, and common lands should include accountability on behalf of the users to ensure that these resources are not abused.

Sustainable tourism development requires the establishment of education and training programmes to improve public understanding and enhance business, vocational and professional skills.

Sustainable tourism development involves promoting appropriate uses and activities that draw from and reinforce landscape character, sense of place, community identity and site opportunity. These activities and uses should aim to provide a quality tourism experience that satisfies visitors while adhering to the other principles of sustainable tourism.

The scale and type of tourism facilities must reflect the limits of acceptable use that resources can tolerate. Small-scale, low impact facilities and services should be encouraged, for example, through financing and other incentives.

The tourism process must also ensure that heritage and natural resources are maintained and enhanced using internationally acceptable criteria and standards.

Sustainable tourism marketing should include the provision of a high quality tourist experience which adheres to the other principles outlined above, and whose promotion should be a responsible and an ethical reflection of the destination's tourism attractions and services.

These principles are ambitious, and it is fair to say very difficult to achieve so that tourism developments that will always adhere to all of these principles. However, these principles must be seen as targets for all tourism planning.

Strategic Integrated Sustainable Tourism Planning

The nature of sustainable tourism development requires a process of planning and management that brings together a series of interests and concerns in a sustainable and strategic form of planning and development. Tourism planning continues to be contentious and somewhat nebulous, because most government officials and tourism industry practitioners harbour their own definitions and parameters of the task. By its very nature, planning is multi-dimensional and is purposely integrative. Even in the less complex circumstances of some Asian and Pacific countries at early phases of tourism development, it is necessary for those with the responsibility to oversee-or administer tourism planning in the public interest to be cognizant of two special dimensions: strategic planning and integrated planning.

Need for Integrated Tourism Planning

Although there is evidence that some tourism destinations have been developed without conscious, strategic and integrated planning, many of them have experienced unforeseen consequences that have led to their deterioration.

(a) *The need for planning:* Some managers and decision-makers argue that we are overwhelmed with plans and planning processes. Others argue that we require more regulation and planning in order to ensure that the goals of sustainable tourism can be met. There are others who maintain that we require less planning and possibly less regulation. There is no right answer to the level of planning that a particular situation calls for and clearly every societal context will determine what is appropriate. Similarly, though sustainable tourism calls for a high level of local involvement in planning and developing tourism, the amount and quality of resident participation will vary depending on the cultural and political factors in the destination. It is obviously useless to develop a sophisticated planning system if there is no political or community support for it. In these cases, one might first have to create an appropriate setting or structure for a planning process that avoids the failures of past planning practices.

(b) *The failures of traditional planning:* Many people are sceptical about the effectiveness of planning. They see it as a waste of time since most plans never see the light of day and end up on a shelf. In many cases, planning in the past has tended to be very much based on developing regulatory procedures as opposed to creating suitable mechanisms for achieving the goals and objectives developed within the planning process. The failure of traditional and rational approaches to planning can be attributed to a number of factors as discussed below.

(i) Lack of flexibility: The logical, rational approach to planning, it has been argued, has made plans far too rigorous and unable to adapt to changing conditions. Unless the external environment is perceived to be quite static, a detailed stepwise approach that is rigorously adhered to could make it very difficult for the organization or destination to create an optimal fit between its resources and the forces influencing tourism in its setting. A dynamic approach as provided through strategic planning principles enables a dynamic planning process, better able to adapt to changes.

(ii) Lack of strategic thinking and vision : A major criticism has been launched against traditional, rational planning approaches by some researchers who argue that such plans lack leadership vision in the process of formulating strategies. The inclusion of "strategic vision" by leaders and decision-makers (not technical planning experts) ensures that the plan is not merely an operational plan, but provides direction and concepts for achieving the organizations broad goals and interests.

(iii) Ineffective top-down planning : Planning by the destination's planning officials or by retaining planning experts from outside the destination results in a plan which is unable to effectively represent the diverse opinions, needs and attitudes of a range of tourism stakeholders. The chances of successful implementation of such a top-down plan is further inhibited by the lack of community support and involvement in the process, particularly in political systems where residents seek greater participation in the decision making of their community direction.

(iv) Poor linking of formulation and implementation : Another major impediment to planning has been the inability to link formulation of the plan to the outcomes of implementation so as to ensure accountability and to measure the success of the planning exercise. The lack of clear, easy to implement actions and responsibilities to ensure accountability for carrying out the actions, has been a deterrent to effective implementation. A clearly deemed relationship between the planning and implementation of action steps must be present to ensure effective delivery of both the tourism experience and the sustainability of the destination's assets and resources.

(c) *Strategic tourism planning-an action planning approach:* A strategic planning approach is essential for sustainable tourism, whereby the disparate planning and development activities related to tourism are linked to an overall, broad strategic tourism plan to provide an integrated framework for directing tourism.

Strategic planning seeks an optimal fit between the system and its environment. Hence, it:

- Residents is long-term;
- contains vision;
- specifies goals (ends);
- specifies major actions (means) to achieve goals;
- specifies the major resource allocations to arrive at (ways);
- is dynamic, flexible and adaptable;
- ensures that formulation and implementation of the strategic plan are not discrete, but linked closely through constant monitoring, environmental scanning, evaluation and adjustment; and
- is not a linear process (e.g., constant environmental scanning occurs throughout the process to enable proactive response and adjustment; monitoring can start as soon as target indicators and levels are established to provide base line information).

A strategic approach to a sustainable community tourism plan also requires:

- close coordination with local and regional legislative and political
- structures; community participation and support;
- a new role for planners as educators and providers of technical expertise, but not solely plan designers; the plan is designed
- primarily by those who have a stake in the outcome;
- an innovative and inclusive organizational structure for joint planning; a learning community that is informed, educated and aware;
- applying the principles of sustainable tourism development to ensure the long-term sustainability of the ecology, the local economy and the sociocultural values of the host community, while distributing the benefits equitably among the stakeholders.

The nature of strategic tourism plans: Sustainable tourism planning requires a strategic planning approach, which seeks an optimal fit between the system and its environment through the creation of a long-term direction (vision), goals and strategies for the allocation of resources and monitoring impacts, and detailed action plans. This is achieved through dynamic, flexible and adaptable planning, where:

- The fomulation and implementation are closely linked through constant environmental scanning, monitoring, evaluation and adjustment of the strategic plan.
- The plan is created by a broad and diverse group of actors (stakeholders) whose needs, attitudes and values are closely reflected in the plan's philosophy, vision and contents.
- There is a clear recognition of the interdependence among the various components of the plan, which is considered in the creation and implementation of goals and strategies.
- Planning approaches span a broad spectrum, ranging from a rational, lockstep approach all the way to strategic, broad-based plans.

Despite this proliferation, a good plan generally contains the following elements and action steps:

- Vision and/or mission statement
- Situation (issues) analysis
- Strategic goals
- Strategies.

Implementation of strategies (measurable objectives and detailed action plans) Monitoring and evaluation of implementation strategies and action plans Adjusting the strategic and operational plans based on information feedback from evaluation and constant scanning of the external environment.

Strategic planning principles: Strategic tourism planning requires careful consideration of the goals and principles of sustainable tourism. Some of the goals and principles that should be considered in tourism planning are:

Economic

- Development which takes into account the full costs and benefits of the alternatives and decision embarked upon, from an overall economic and social perspective.

- Broad-based distribution of benefits among all stakeholders..Provision of a quality visitor experience that is compatible with the destination's goals and values.
- Ensure that fiscal costs of infrastructure provision and marketing do not outweigh the benefits (for example, residents may end up paying higher taxes to subsidize tourism development but may not benefit from improved income, social services, use of or access to the publicly constructed infrastructure, education and training opportunities, etc.

Social

- Steady employment avoids the underemployment and unemployment associated with seasonal hiring for peak tourism periods.
- Better employment opportunities than the low pay positions typically associated with tourism services.
- Quality jobs that encourage the use of local knowledge, skills and traditions, and offer a sense of fulfilment and satisfaction to the residents.
- Improved standard of living and equitable distribution of benefits within (and between) generations in the present and future.

Ecological

- Maintenance of essential ecological processes, biological diversity and non-renewable resources for future generations (through preservation or conservation strategies).
- Planning at a scale and pace that enables effective and ongoing monitoring and mitigation of long-term impacts.
- Full-cost accounting of environmental resources in cost-benefit analyses.
- An environmental and cumulative impact that analyses important prerequisites to development, and environmental management systems needs to be implemented by businesses and organizations.

Cultural

- Tourist activities and behaviours should be respectful of cultural activities, sites and values.

- Designs should be compatible with national and local heritage and character and should foster the community's identity or sense of place.

Tourist types and activities should match the needs and expectations of the local people, with protection of sensitive and indigenous cultures against any adverse impact.

Political

- Compatibility between overall economic development goals of regional and community interests and tourism goals.
- Integration of plans and planning with other relevant community and regional plans and processes.
- Balance top-down planning with resident input and participation in planning and development.

(d) Strategic tourism planning-an action process

The major steps in a strategic planning process for tourism for a community-based destination is outlined in the figure that follows. Note that while the steps appear sequential, the process is an iterative one, with feedback loops connecting the various stages. It is also important to note that this is a recommended process-each nation/destination may need to tailor this process to suit its own requirements, norms and values.

Means of Achieving Strategic Action Oriented Integrated Tourism Policy

Tourism planning can operate at many levels:

- The individual site. (Examples include a beach, heritage site, park or theme park.)
- The destination. (In some cases the site and the destination may be the same, but usually it refers to the larger geographical setting where the site is situated.)
- A region within a country. (This can be a geographic or political boundary or it can be based on tourism attraction factors.)
- The nation. (Especially true in the case of smaller island countries.)
- Several countries. (A good example is the area around the Mekong River that is being presented as a theme-related destination involving several countries.)

There can be little argument that there should be integration within each of the levels and across all levels, so as to achieve balance, aesthetic harmony, cooperation, confidence (for investment), efficiency, identity, sensitivity and most importantly sustainability.

These aspirations of integration can be achieved through preparation of a tourism policy, which is a policy for tourism following a systematic process.

Developing a Tourism Policy

Policies can help guide a government and other stakeholders' programmes of action and provide a frame of reference for the tourism industry's actions. If we are to achieve sustainable tourism, it is always preferable that a set of tourism policies be developed either as a set of distinct tourism objectives or better still that all levels and areas of policy formation integrate tourism directives in their decision-making process.

Such a Policy should

- provide a set of guidelines for the actions of all stakeholders;
- specify the broad objectives to be achieved;
- specify action plans; and
- identify areas of responsibility and power for policy implementation.

Tourism objectives should be the product of stakeholder participation and recognize the complexity of tourism development and management. It is rare where there will be a classic policy development process. Political priorities, power realities, economic development requirements and industry pressures will very much influence what occurs in the policy development process. Ideally at least, the role that tourism should play in the overall national as well as regional development should be clearly articulated and understood. Only then can other areas of public and private development reflect tourism objectives and priorities. The officials responsible for economic development, environmental protection and tourism are just examples where the policy and decision-making areas of activity meet or should meet.

Each objective should be tested for its general applicability and contribution to broad objectives related to overall sustainable development with specific attention to:

- energy and water conservation;
- employment;
- economic growth;
- infrastructure plans;
- environmental and resource conservation;
- urban and rural revitalization;
- heritage conservation;
- consumer protection;
- community welfare; business creation.

A commitment to the achievement of a satisfactory tourism policy requires a set of objectives that focus on the following issues:

Economic

It is necessary to optimize the contribution of tourism and recreation to economic prosperity, full employment, regional economic development, and improved international balance of payments.

Sociocultural

It is essential to contribute to the personal growth and education of the population and encourage their 'appreciation of the local geography, history, and ethnic diversity. Social policy should also seek to avoid activities that have the potential to undennine or denigrate the social and cultural values and resources of the area and its traditions and lifestyles.

Market Development Oriented

Policies must encourage the free entry of foreign visitors, while balancing this goal with the need to monitor persons and goods entering the country with laws protecting public health.

Resource Protection and Conservation

Policies must protect and preserve the historical and cultural foundations as a living part of community life and development and to ensure future generations an opportunity to enjoy the rich heritage of the area. These policies will also ensure the compatibility of tourism, recreational, and activity policies with other broader interests in energy development and conservation, environmental protection, and judicious use of natural resources.

Human Resource Development

It is important to ensure that tourism has an adequate supply of professionally-trained skilled and managerial staff to meet future needs. Human resource policies should also ensure that the education and training programmes and materials are available to meet the needs of tourism.

Government Operations Concerns

Policies must help to coordinate government activities related to tourism while allowing the public sector to take a leadership role by supporting the needs of tourists, residents and tourism businesses with appropriate legislation and administration. Most countries will have developed their own style of policy-making. It is important that the policy for tourism be consistent in its general aim and orientation and be readily integrated with other policy areas. Lateral (with other policy areas) and vertical (internal) linkages must be integrated. A policy process progresses to strategies plans, programmes, legislation and regulations. It is important that each stage at any level (national/regional/local) be carefully integrated laterally and vertically.

Developing the Tourism Plan

There is no single model of tourism plan or one process. There are many variations in content, style, approach and emphasis, and some possibilities are identified here.

Alternative plan approaches: A master plan is the principal instrument of planning for tourism. Such a plan may be comprehensive and wide-ranging, or it may focus on one or a combination of:

- physical/environmental issues;
- economic issues;
- promotion and marketing;
- conservation (of environment or heritage resources);
- sociocultural issues;
- investment;
- human resources development.

On a temporal scale, the master plan may focus on a short-term time scale (five years, perhaps to coincide with the cycles of the national economic strategy), or it may focus on an indeterminate scale with indications of preferred end-states or achievements, not associated with particular time periods.

Other differences in approach may cover:

- attitudes to spontaneous development (strict or flexible planning);
- degree of incentives and technical assistance;
- apportionment of benefits;
- integration with tourism-related activities;
- certainty of site prescription;
- supervision;
- regulation and strategy support.

An important element in any tourism plan is the degree to which it is integrated with the nationwide or region-wide economic, welfare and physical development plan.

Tourism plans prepared in recent years, and those to be prepared, should include specific reference to:

- ecological sustainability;
- environmental conservation;
- heritage (built environment) and cultural heritage conservation;
- sustainable development of heritage resources.

Content: For any particular nation, the plan could adopt a particular focus, perhaps for only one of the review phases. However, a generalized prospectus of contents would include:

- the institutional or organizational framework, setting out:
- the principal organizations;
- the principal responsibilities;
- the legislative framework;
- the roles and functions of the private and public sectors.
- the principal plan elements, such as:
- infrastructure;
- facilities and services;
- visitor attractions.
- development implications-economic, environmental, and sociocultural;

- the principal means of securing implementation, including:
- financing and investment;
- incentives;
- marketing;
- promotion;
- tourism information systems;
- tourism awareness programmes;
- human resources development.

The plan of any nation may refer to regional cooperation in the various aspects of tourism planning and development, and the contribution which can be made to the regional circumstances.

In some cases, the emphasis of the plan may direct the considerations away from the physical dimensions of the tourism development.

This would be unfortunate, because no matter what form the development takes, the tourism experience of the visitor will take place in a region, in a destination, at a site. Therefore, it is important that these particular aspects of tourism planning are given due attention.

The form and structure of physical plan elements: Tourism planning may focus on the nation, the region, a destination, or a site. Integration of all these will achieve the most satisfactory outcome. In the context of physical development, tourism planning at any level can be conducted with attention to spatial form and structure.

Regional: There are various operational issues linked to the principal detenninants of regional form and structure. Experimentation is ongoing, but there are some constant principles. The basic options include:

- using existing developments as magnets and regional control factors;
- creating new developments;
- creating a hierarchical network of tourism destinations by devising a balanced strategy;
- developing a region-wide strategy, eliminating those areas that have little tourism potential, devising a destination-focused strategy, devising a tour or circuit strategy; and

- developing a strategy of complementary tourism destinations, with each destination specializing in focus or market segment.

The basic fond and Structural Patterns include:

- concentration of tourism development:
- major resorts;
- tourism destination areas; and
- base camps on the threshold of a tourism region.
- gateways or points of entry into the destination areas.

Variants on this basic spatial formula exist in tourism planning literature and in many case studies worldwide.

The dilemma for the Asian and Pacific region is to reinterpret the land-based concepts of regional form and structure into a region specific idiom.

Destination Area: The destination area contains the critical mass of resources, facilities and amenities that contribute to the satisfaction of tourists. The basic elements of a tourism destination area or zone are:

- one or more communities to supply the utilities, services and facilities;
- one or more attraction complexes;
- transportation linkages between the communities and the attractions; and
- an entrance or gateway at the destination.

An important principle in the planning and design of tourism destinations is that they be distinctive places with unique internal relationships between the various parts (other places and the various facilities and services). The destination is what attracts the tourist. To be successful, the tourism destination should be planned to maximize:

- the locational advantage;
- the product advantage (in comparison with competitor destinations);
- the advantage of proximate cultural resources and natural resources;
- transport linkages; and
- hospitable host attitudes.

There is no single formula for successful destination tourism, but there are planning and design principles appropriate to the destination scale.

These Include:

- the destination should be integrated into a region-wide strategy;
- the destination should attract (or create) a distinctive image;
- successful destination planning will involve:
- public-private partnership;
- integration; and progressive accumulation of the critical mass of attractions, services, facilities, amenities, and transport linkages-all within carrying capacity limits.

Site scale: The scale of this tourism planning is a particular challenge, because at this scale a single, functional or aesthetic problem can seriously disrupt the image of a tourism destination. If the tourism business on any site fails, it becomes a monument to bad decision-making that may affect an entire destination by association.

At this level, "place" takes on a particular important meaning. It is not only the contribution each place makes to the entire destination, but also a geographical reference point and landmark. It is at the site scale that regional and destination tourism planning yield concrete outcomes, and at this level the projections and predictions of demand for facilities, services and experiences materialize. Therefore, a special understanding of the site characteristics, their potential and constraints, and the contribution of the site to the wider destination area become crucial. It is also critical that the planning, management and monitoring processes be efficient at this scale. In order to avoid the repetition of inappropriate design and development, post-development evaluation should become an integral part of the planning process, especially to determine the validity of the predevelopment design decisions.

Physical Development Strategy

In order to implement the tourism development proposals examined at the various levels (national, regional, destination and site), it is necessary to provide a suitable physical development planning strategy. An important element of any physical development strategy is land use planning. It is important to recognize that many countries may have land use strategies but they are unevenly enforced and lack support at local levels. In some cases, there may not yet be a policy.

There are Four Different Approaches to Land use Planning

Blueprint planning, which is based on the expectation that the full plan as prepared will be implemented exactly and in its entirety. Such an expectation is unrealistic, because no plan ever starts with complete information and functions within a completely controlled operational environment. Such a plan type is too inflexible. Regulatory planning, which relies upon the application of development provenance standards with the possibility of all development eventually conforming to previously set model codes and standards. While easy to implement, the built environment may become monotonous and repetitive. Even so, some fond of regulatory planning is inevitable.

Market-driven planning, which is best suited to individual projects, rather than to planning strategies for entire communities or regions. A systems-driven approach to planning which is becoming more common, especially as planning functions are needed to address increasingly complex situations involving threats to the environment and as development is increasingly scrutinized according to ecologically-sustainable principles. This approach provides for review, monitoring and adjustment as circumstances change in the plan.

The land use planning system most likely will combine the compatible elements of the systems-driven methodology and the regulatory approach to planning.

In many cases, the system of land use planning control is derived from standard European or North American codes of planning practice and then modified to meet the needs of national governments and administrative systems. Usually, a land use planning control system in force for the planning system is backed by appropriate legislation which provides for control over land use and development, specified administrative procedures, and necessary infrastructure development.

For tourism development, the most important issues in land use planning and development will include:

- location of tourism uses;

- accessibility to and travel within tourism districts/zones;
- development standards;
- design standards;
- traffic problems;
- quality of the built environment;
- landscaping of tourism developments;
- free-standing major developments;
- tourism attractions in rural environments;
- location of the major transport interchanges such as airports, and bus/coach terminals; and
- impact of tourism development on local architectural styles and
- important areas of heritage.

To achieve a good standard of land use development, the planning system should:

- coordinate development-relegating frastructurer equipements;
- implement appropriate concepts and ideas in order to achieve acceptable, conventionals tandards of aesthetics, health, convenience and diversity (of interest, experience, and culture);
- promote development where and when appropriate;
- provide the developer with prior knowledge of the development requirements (in the form of performance standards);
- prevent prejudicial development (by type, location, timing, or quality);
- reflect acceptable changes in standards and fashions; and facilitate innovation.

It may be claimed that the best plans and developments have been the outcome of deliberate planning using a systematic planning and decision-making process, but there are examples of successful plans and developments which have not emerged from the application of a systematic process. Such development may be considered to have been fortuitous, fragile, or both. In any case, the pursuit of a systematic process should offer the best chance of successful and harmonious tourism development.

Implementation of a Tourism Plan

It is preferable to consider the planning process as a continuum that integrates the steps of plan creation with its implementation.

Stages of implementation can include the following:

- preparing and putting into practice guidelines, regulations and
- policies necessary to bring the plan to fruition;
- undertaking development in accordance with the plan;
- supervising that development
- preparing the community for the impact of tourism development;
- preparing and providing training facilities for those intending to work in the tourism/travel/hospitality industry;
- collecting information to monitor the progress of the plan as it is put into practice;
- undertaking marketing and promotion to ensure that the tourism destination is known and appreciated for what it has to offer.

A tourism plan is a tool to guide development. Little, if anything, will happen without:

- a suitable legislative and administrative structure;
- suitable sources of finance;
- suitable entrepreneurial interest;
- evidence of demand for the tourism product at the destination; and
- certainty of access by visitors.

In addition, a tourism plan At any level, especially at national and regional levels, will need desegregation so that the various resource needs-land/water, labour and capital-are seen in their spatial, temporal, financial, infrastructure, and social inter-relationships.

An additional consideration is the likely impact of forces external to the destination area, especially the impact of decisions, international airlines that service the region, and the international tour operators who facilitate the arrival of tourists.

Institutional Framework

There is considerable evidence of the need for an effective institutional framework if tourism developments to be coordinated, efficiently supervised, monitored and integrated into the overall scope of national economic, environmental and social planning. It is important that the institutional framework encompasses organizations from both the public and the private sector. A coordinated framework is necessary because of the fragmented nature of the tourism industry.

The tourism palling process provides the catalyst for inputs from the various stakeholders with the outcome of decisions affecting tourism development. Even after the preparation of a tourism development plan, the final outcome is dependent upon the integrated realization of a series of independent development decisions based upon the pursuit of individual opportunities.

The public sector, the private sector, non-profit organizations, the community, and tourists play important roles in tourism planning and development.

In each case, there will be particular perspectives on tourism development, the need for tourism planning, and the shape of that planning. The principal perspective of the public sector is to manage development to achieve community goals in the public interest. For the private sector, the principal function is to provide facilities and services to tourists while maximizing returns on investment. The private sector has also come to accept that it has social and environmental responsibilities. It is recognized that entrepreneurial flair may create tourism development opportunities beyond those identified in the prepared tourism plan.

The formal plan should be composed with sufficient flexibility to accommodate such initiatives, especially if it is responding to shifts in tourist preferences. Some changes in preferences may be identified through the constant monitoring and evaluation of tourism activity by consultants, market research investigators, design professionals and project managers. Financial institutions and corporate lending agencies will have a particular interest in the changes of fashion and the dicates of the tourism market.

The World Tourism Organization (WTO) has described the distinct roles of the public and private sector by the principle that governments should not seek to do what the private sector is able and willing to do. However, in many cases of large-scale development, the private sector and government may work in a partnership. Other partnerships may develop where governments assist indigenous landowners to start an enterprise that will be managed eventually by indigenous communities. The perspective of the tourist on tourism planning is different from the other stakeholders.

The interests of every tourist cut across the various independent decisions made by governments and the private sector, and the tourist is concerned with the experience that can be gained. One of the main purposes of tourism planning is to create a harmonious balance between the different interests of the various stakeholders. This balance may be achieved through the establishment of an appropriate multifaceted institutional framework. In some tourism development lands, an effective institutional framework is considered to be one of the principal determinants of successful tourism development.

Sustainable Tourism

Sustainable tourism is an industry committed to making a low impact on the environment and local culture, while helping to generate income and employment for local people. The aim of sustainable tourism is to ensure that development is a positive experience for local people; tourism companies; and tourists themselves. But sustainable tourism is not the same as ecotourism.

Overview

Global economists forecast continuing international tourism growth, ranging between three and six percent annually, depending on the location. As one of the world's largest and fastest growing industries, this continuous growth will place great stress on remaining biologically diverse habitats and indigenous cultures, which are often used to support mass tourism. Tourists who promote sustainable tourism are sensitive to these dangers and seek to protect tourist destinations, and to protect tourism as an industry. Sustainable tourists can reduce the impact of tourism in many ways, including:

- informing themselves of the culture, politics, and economy of the communities visited
- anticipating and respecting local cultures' expectations and assumptions

- contributing to intercultural understanding and tolerance
- supporting the integrity of local cultures by favouring businesses which conserve cultural heritage and traditional values
- supporting local economies by purchasing local goods and participating with small, local businesses
- conserving resources by seeking out businesses that are environmentally conscious, and by using the least possible amount of non-renewable resources.

Increasingly, destinations and tourism operations are endorsing and following "responsible tourism" as a pathway towards sustainable tourism. Responsible tourism and sustainable tourism have an identical goal, that of sustainable development. The pillars of responsible tourism are therefore the same as those of sustainable tourism – environmental integrity, social justice and economic development. The major difference between the two is that, in responsible tourism, individuals, organisations and businesses are asked to take responsibility for their actions and the impacts of their actions. This shift in emphasis has taken place because some stakeholders feel that insufficient progress towards realising sustainable tourism has been made since the Earth Summit in Rio. This is partly because everyone has been expecting others to behave in a sustainable manner. The emphasis on responsibility in responsible tourism means that everyone involved in tourism – government, product owners and operators, transport operators, community services, NGO's and CBO's, tourists, local communities, industry associations – are responsible for achieving the goals of responsible tourism.

Responsible Tourism

Responsible Tourism can be regarded as a behaviour. It is more than a form of tourism as it represents an approach to engaging with tourism, be that as a tourist, a business, locals at a destination or any other tourism stakeholder. It emphasises that all stakeholders are responsible for the kind of tourism they develop or engage in. Whilst different groups will see responsibility in different ways, the shared understanding is that responsible tourism should entail an improvement in tourism. Tourism should become 'better' as a result of the responsible tourism approach. Within the notion of betterment resides the acknowledgement that conflicting interests need to be balanced. However, the objective is to create better places for people to live in and to visit. Importantly, there is no blueprint for responsible tourism: what is deemed responsible may differ depending on places and cultures. Responsible Tourism is an aspiration that can be realised in different ways in different originating markets and in the diverse destinations of the world (Goodwin, 2002).

Focusing in particular on businesses, according to the Cape Town Declaration on Responsible Tourism, it will have the following characteristics:

- minimises negative economic, environmental, and social impacts
- generates greater economic benefits for local people and enhances the well-being of host communities, improves working conditions and access to the industry
- involves local people in decisions that affect their lives and life chances
- makes positive contributions to the conservation of natural and cultural heritage, to the maintenance of the world's diversity
- provides more enjoyable experiences for tourists through more meaningful connections with local people, and a greater understanding of local cultural, social and environmental issues
- provides access for physically challenged people and
- is culturally sensitive, engenders respect between tourists and hosts, and builds local pride and confidence.

Sustainable tourism is where tourists can enjoy their holiday and at the same time respect the culture of people and also respect the environment. It also means that local people (such as the Masaai) get a fair say about tourism and also receive some money from the profit which the game reserve make. The environment is being damaged quite a lot by tourists and part of Sustainable tourism is to make sure that the damaging does not carry on.

There are many private companies who are working into embracing the principles and aspects of Responsible Tourism, some for the purpose of Corporate Social Responsibility activities, and others such World Hotel-Link, which was originally a project of the International Finance Corporation, have built their entire business model around responsible tourism, local capacity building and increasing market access for small and medium tourism enterprises.

Responsible Hospitality

As with the view of Responsible Tourism, Responsible Hospitality is essentially about creating better places for people to live in, and better places for people to visit. This does not mean all forms of hospitality are also forms of tourism although hospitality is the largest sector of the tourism industry. As such we should not be surprised at overlaps between Responsible Hospitality and Responsible Tourism.

In the instance where place of permanent residence is also the place where the hospitality service is consumed, if for example a meal is consumed in a local restaurant, this does not obviate the requirement to improve the place of residence. As such, the essence of Responsible Hospitality is not contingent upon touristic forms of hospitality.

While Frideman (1962) famously argued that, admittedly within legal parameters, the sole responsibility of business was to generate profit for shareholders the idea that businesses' responsibility extends beyond this has existed for decades and is most frequently encountered in the concept of corporate social responsibility (Carroll, 1999).

There are numerous ways businesses can and do engage in activities that are not intended to benefit shareholders and management, at least not in the short term. However, often acts of corporate social responsibility are undertaken because of the perceived benefit to business. Usually in hospitality this relates to the cost reductions associated with improved energy efficiency (Pizam, 2009) but may also relate to, for example, the rise in ethical consumerism and the view that being seen to be a responsible business is beneficial to revenue growth.

As per the Cape Town Declaration on Responsible Tourism, Responsible Hospitality is culturally sensitive. Instead of then calling for the unachievable, Responsible Hospitality simply makes the case for more responsible forms of hospitality, hospitality that benefits locals first, and visitors second. Certainly, all forms of hospitality can be improved and managed so that negative impacts are minimised whilst striving for a maximisation of positive impacts.

Coastal Tourism

Many coastal areas are experiencing particular pressure from growth in lifestyles and growing numbers of tourists. Coastal environments are limited in extent consisting of only a narrow strip along the edge of the ocean. Coastal areas are often the first environments to experience the detrimental impacts of tourism. A detailed study of the impact on coastal areas, with reference to western India can be an example.

The inevitable change is on the horizon as holiday destinations put more effort into sustainable tourism. Planning and management controls can reduce the impact on coastal environments and ensure that investment into tourism products supports sustainable coastal tourism.

Some Conceptual Models in Coastal Tourism

Some of the recent studies have led to some interesting conceptual models applicable for coastal tourism. The 'inverted funnel model' and the 'embedded model' can be good metaphors for understanding the interplay of different stake-holders like government, local community, tourists and business community in developing tourist destinations.

Community-based Management

There has been the promotion of sustainable tourism practices surrounding the management of tourist locations by locals or more concisely, the community. This form of tourism is based on the premise that the people living next to a resource are the ones best suited to protecting it. This means that the tourism activities and businesses are developed and operated by local community members, and certainly with their consent and support. Sustainable tourism typically involves the conservation of resources that are capitalized upon for tourism purposes, such as coral reefs and pristine forests. Locals run the businesses and are responsible for promoting the conservation messages to protect their environment. Community-based sustainable tourism (CBST) associates the success of the sustainability of the ecotourism location to the management practices of the communities who are directly or indirectly dependent on the location for their livelihoods.

A salient feature of CBST is that local knowledge is usually utilised alongside wide general frameworks of ecotourism business models. This allows the participation of locals at the management level and typically allows a more intimate understanding of the environment. The use of local knowledge also means an easier entry level into a tourism industry for locals whose jobs or livelihoods are affected by the use of their environment as tourism locations. The involvement of locals restores the ownership of the environment to the local community and allows an alternative sustainable form of development for communities and their environments that are typically unable to support other forms of development.. However, recent research has found that economic linkages generated by CBST may only be sporadic, and that the linkages with agriculture are negatively affected by seasonality and by the small scale of the cultivated areas. This means that CBST may only have small-scale positive effects for these communities.

Stakeholders

Stakeholders of sustainable tourism play a role in continuing this form of tourism. This can include organizations as well as individuals.

Non-Governmental Organizations

Non-governmental organizations are one of the stakeholders in advocating sustainable tourism. Their roles can range from spearheading sustainable tourism practices to simply doing research. University research teams and scientists can be tapped to aid in the process of planning. Such solicitation of research can be observed in the planning of Cat Ba National Park in Vietnam. Dive resort operators in Bunaken National Park, Indonesia, play a crucial role but developing exclusive zones for diving and fishing respectively, such that both tourists and locals can benefit from the venture

Large conventions, meetings and other major organized events drive the travel, tourism and hospitality industry. Cities and convention centres compete to attract such commerce, commerce which has heavy impacts on resource use and the environment. Major sporting events, such as the Olympic Games, present special problems regarding environmental burdens and degradation. But burdens imposed by the regular convention industry can be vastly more significant.

Green conventions and events are a new but growing sector and marketing point within the convention and hospitality industry.

More environmentally aware organizations, corporations and government agencies are now seeking more sustainable event practices, greener hotels, restaurants and convention venues, and more energy efficient or climate neutral travel and ground transportation. Additionally, some convention centres have begun to take direct action in reducing the impact of the conventions they host. One example is the Moscone Centre in San Francisco, California, which has a very aggressive recycling program, a large solar power system, and other programs aimed at reducing impact and increasing efficiency.

Tourists

With the advent of the internet, some traditional conventions are being replaced with virtual conventions, where the attendees remain in their home physical location and "attend" the convention by use of a web-based interface programmed for the task. This sort of "virtual" meeting eliminates all of the impacts associated with travel, accommodation, food wastage, and other necessary impacts of traditional, physical conventions.

Travel over long distances requires a large amount of time and/or energy. Generally this involves burning fossil fuels, a largely unsustainable practice and one that contributes to climate change, via CO_2 emissions.

Air travel is perhaps the worst offender in this regard, contributing to between 2 and 3% of global carbon emissions. Given a business-as-usual approach, this could be expected to rise to 5% by 2015 and 10% by 2050. Car travel is the next worst offender.

Mass transport is the most climate friendly method of travel, and generally the rule is "the bigger the better"-compared to cars, buses are relatively more sustainable, and trains and ships are even more so. Human energy and renewable energy are the most efficient, and hence, sustainable. Travel by bicycle, solar powered car, or sailing boat produces no carbon emissions (although the embodied energy in these vehicles generally comes at the expense of carbon emission).

Sustainable Tourism CRC

Sustainable Tourism Cooperative Research Centre (STCRC), headquartered in Gold Coast, Queensland, Australia is an Australian Cooperative Research Centre established by the

Australian Government's Cooperative Research Centres Program to establish a competitive and dynamic sustainable tourism industry in Australia.

STCRC is a not-for-profit company owned by its industry, government and university partners. STCRC stands as the world's largest travel and tourism research centre.

Organisational Aims

STCRC's aims are the development and management of intellectual property (IP) to deliver innovation to business, community, and government enhancing environmental, economic and social sustainability of tourism – one of the world's largest, fastest growing industries.

In doing so, STCRC aims to develop Australia's long-term tourism research capactities through a vigorous postgraduate research education programme. Presently this programme has produced a number of PhD students and the program is supported by scholarships for students in industry-designed projects, and by developing and distributing education and training products.

Commercialisation Unit

The Commercialisation of STCRC research, sustainability oriented technologies and certification programs is done through EC3 Global which is wholly owned by the STCRC. EC3 Global provides an array of programs and services for companies, communities and other interest groups to set and achieve sustainability targets. With origins leading back to 1987, EC3's research encompasses 250 tourism and environmental sustainability leaders in 16 universities. EC3's influence has grown to encompass hundreds of projects, creating a strong market presence in over 50 countries. Presently EC3 Global commercialises four main products, Decipher, Earthcheck, IPAT and Green Globe.

History

STCRC was established under the Australian Government's Cooperative Research Centres Program to underpin the development of a dynamic, internationally competitive, and sustainable tourism industry. Since its inception the STCRC has supported over 170 PhD scholars through a suite of scholarships and the provision of a Career Development Program. STCRC currently supports over 90 postgraduate students. All are of exceptional academic standard. Most hold a first class honours degree and many have also received university awards for excellence. All supplementary scholarship holders also hold an APA or university-equivalent scholarship.

University Partners

There are currently 16 Australian universities who are partners with the STCRC, these are listed below.

Charles Darwin University

Charles Darwin University was formed in 2003, with over 50 years history delivering tertiary education to the Northern Territory. Charles Darwin's Main Campus is located in Darwin, Australia and is named after Charles Darwin, the English Naturalist Formed in 2003 through a merger between the Northern Territory University, Alice Springs-based Centralian College, NT Rural College in Katherine and the Menzies School of Health Research. Charles Darwin University is the largest university in the Northern Territory.

Curtin University of Technology

Curtin University of Technology formed in 1986 is Western Australia's Largest University with over 40,000 students presently. Curtin University has a strong emphasis on innovation and technology, which are the main themes of the university. Curtin University has an important Research & Development history, with an annual income from research of around $12 Million Australian Dollars annually.

Edith Cowan University

Edith Cowan University is the second largest university in Western Australia and has approximately 23,000 students of which over 3,000 originate from countries outside Australia. It was established in 1991, and is the only Australian university named after a woman, Edith Dircksey Cowan. The university specialises in the service professions, and the teaching of education remains a key focus. Joint research and study with other universities and international consultancies remains an important area for the university.

Griffith University

Griffith University is an Australian public university with five campuses in Queensland between Brisbane and the Gold Coast.

As of 2008, there were more than 37,000 enrolled students and 3,500 staff. As such, Griffith stands as one of Queensland's largest universities and holds Queensland's oldest academy.

Griffith has diverse multidisciplinary teaching and research fields, and comprises of students and academic staff from over 120 countries throughout the world.

James Cook University

James Cook University is a public university based in Townsville, Queensland, Australia and was proclaimed on 20 April 1970 in Townsville. James Cook University is the second oldest university in Queensland. James Cook University is listed as one of the best universities in Queensland and is one of only 17 in Australia that was listed in the ARWU top 500 academic world universities in 2007.

The main fields of research include marine sciences, biodiversity, sustainable management of tropical ecosystems, tropical health care and tourism. James Cook University receives over $23 Million dollars in research funding annually, highlighting the importance of its ongoing research projects.

La Trobe University

La Trobe University is a multi-campus university in Victoria, Australia. La Trobe is generally considered to be ranked amongst the top ten universities in Australia and in 2005 was ranked in the top 100 universities in the world. Presently La Trobe university has over 28,000 enrolled students and has become a well established centre for teaching, training, scholarship and research.

Monash University

Monash University is a public university with campuses located in Australia, Malaysia and South Africa. It is Australia's largest university with about 55,000 students. Monash consistently ranks amongst the top universities in Australia and the world.

The University has a total of eight campuses, and also a centre in Prato, Italy. This makes it by far Australia's most internationalised university. Indeed, it is arguable that Monash has the greatest international presence of any research-intensive university in the world. It was recently ranked by The Times Higher Education Supplement (THES) at number 43 in its annual ranking of the world's top 200 universities for 2007.

Murdoch University

Murdoch University is located in Perth, Western Australia and has three campuses at Murdoch, Rockingham and Peel. It currently has a student population of over 15,000 studends including 3,000 international students. Murdoch is a modern Australian university with a national reputation for excellence in teaching and research.

Southern Cross University

Southern Cross University (SCU) is a university based on the Mid North and North coast of New South Wales, Australia. It is a regional University with more than 14,000 students. The University is the country's seventh largest provider of distance education. It also has international students from more than 50 countries. More than 700 students are enrolled on-campus and with on-shore partners in Australia, with a further 1300 enrolled in overseas programs.

The University is renowned for its tourism studies, especially in the local Northern Rivers area.

University of New South Wales

University of New South Wales (UNSW) is one of Australia's largest and most prestigious research institutions, the UNSW has over 40,000 students including 8,800 international students from 90 different countries.

It is a member of Australia's "Group of Eight" lobby group, and is also a founding member of Universitas 21, an international network of leading research-intensive universities. UNSW ranks third for both total funds allocated and the number of grants from the Australian Research Council among Australian universities following University of Sydney and Australian National University, by securing more than $26 million in Discovery Project grants. The University also gains the highest number of Linkage Project grants of any university.

University of Canberra

The *University of Canberra* is an Australian university, located in Canberra, the capital of Australia. It is the second largest university in Canberra. The University was one of nine Australian universities recognised by the Australian government in 2006 for high achievement in learning and teaching. In a 2005 ranking of the international standing of Australian universities, University of

Canberra received 44% and ranked approximately two-thirds down the list of Australian universities. Presently it has over 10,000 students, from over 80 different countries and more than 1,000 staff.

University of Queensland

The *University of Queensland* is Queensland's first university, being founded in 1909. Presently it has over 37,000 enrolled students. The University of Queensland also prides itself on being one of Australia's foremest research institutions, the University is a founding member of the Group of Eight, an alliance of research-strong "sandstone" universities in Australia.

UQ remains the most successful Australian university in winning and being shortlisted for Australian Awards for University Teaching since they were established in 1997. On a variety of measures it is one of the top three or four research universities in the country.

University of South Australia

The *University of South Australia* is a public university in the Australian state of South Australia. It was formed in 1991 with the merger of the South Australian Institute of Technology and Colleges of Advanced Education. The university is a leading expert in technical education and applied research, as well being a founding member of the Australian Technology Network.

University of South Australia is ranked as the 291st university in the 2007 Times Higher Education Supplement Top 400 Universities list. The University has nearly 32,000 enrolled students as of 2008.

University of Tasmania

The *University of Tasmania* is an Australian university, with three campuses in Tasmania. A 'sandstone university', it is the fourth-oldest university in Australia, and was established over a century ago. It was founded on 1 January 1890, and is a member of the international Association of Commonwealth Universities.

The university works with overseas universities to offer students an international experience, with exchange arrangements in place with over 40 institutions throughout Europe, Asia and North America. The university has a particularly notable and long-standing reputation in examining the practical and theoretical challenges involved in addressing social and environmental concerns.

University of Technology, Sydney

The *University of Technology, Sydney (UTS)* is a university in Sydney, New South Wales, Australia. It is part of the Australian Technology Network of universities, and is the third largest university in Sydney in terms of enrollment numbers. Founded in its current form in 1988, it is also the only university with its main campuses within the Sydney CBD. UTS has been ranked in the World's Top 100 universities by the Times Higher Education Supplement and was given A1 ratings across all major disciplines in 2007 by the Federal Government Education department.

Victoria University

The *Victoria University* is a University in Melbourne, Victoria. The University offers both Higher Education and Technical and Further Education (TAFE) courses. Presently there are over 45,000 enrolled students, including over 8,500 international students. Founded in 1916, it is one of Australia's older universities, with a rich history and many successful students.

4

Tourism Planning and Sustainability

Steps to Sustainable Tourism

Sustainable tourism development meets the needs of present tourists and host regions while protecting and enhancing opportunities for the future. It is envisaged as leading to management of all resources in such a way that economic, social and aesthetic needs can be fulfilled while maintaining cultural integrity, essential ecological processes, biological diversity and life support systems.

World Tourism Organisation

Environment refers to ecosystems, and also to cultural qualities and characteristics of places. *Heritage* embraces our natural, Indigenous and historic inheritance — what we think our descendants should, and would want to, inherit.

Generally, these two terms are interchangeable. Environment and heritage are valued differently by different people. Those working in tourism recognise them as assets of mainstream and niche tourism products and are in a position to do much to educate visitors about the values of our natural and cultural heritage places.

Achieving sustainable tourism requires motivation, determination and a systematic approach. Its core is proper planning. The 10 steps form an entire planning process that can be applied from start to finish, or can be used in part if more appropriate. It can be followed in large planning exercises such as a 'big picture' regional planning process or by small interest groups or individuals wanting to promote a single attraction.

Following these steps thoroughly will assist you meet the needs of the visitor, the environment, business and the local community. There can be a sustainable future for them all. The 10 steps can be used in many different ways. They can help to:

- develop audits, scoping projects and preliminary assessments of tourism development potential in regions
- identify tourism and heritage issues which need to be considered in management, regional or business planning
- develop regional heritage and tourism strategic plans and action plans
- assist in developing business plans for new or existing heritage tourism products
- foster more effective planning for infrastructure development at heritage places
- evaluate options and establish a stronger business case for an idea or proposal.

Sustainable Development

Sustainable development needs to address economic, social and environmental issues. Many businesses now include social and environmental factors as part of their performance measurement. Sometimes referred to as 'triple bottom line' measurement and reporting, this approach focuses on accountability, transparency, commitment to stakeholder and community engagement and systematic measurement and reporting.

Tourism and Heritage Principles

An important complementary publication to this framework is *Successful Tourism at Heritage Places*. It sets out principles, guidelines and case studies that illustrate success factors in tourism at natural and cultural heritage places.

The principles from *Successful Tourism at Heritage Places* underpin this framework and should be a starting point for discussions and collaboration. They are:

1. recognise the importance of heritage places
2. look after heritage places
3. develop mutually beneficial partnerships
4. incorporate heritage issues into business planning

5. invest in people and place
6. market and promote products responsibly
7. provide high-quality visitor experiences
8. respect Indigenous rights and obligations.

Appropriate Tourism Development

Sustainable Tourism sets out an approach to help develop appropriate longterm solutions for tourism at places with natural and cultural heritage values. It also seeks ways to support growth in the tourism industry while ensuring that conservation needs are met.

Tourism will not be an option for some environments or heritage places where it is incompatible with the special values or management objectives of a place. Using the process in this guide will enable you to assess whether this is the case.

What do we want to do?

This step will help you to:

- define your aims
- understand the context.

Whether you're using this process in relation to a region, a particular place or a tourism product, your first step is to determine what you would like to achieve and to understand the context of your project.

The statement of aim that you produce will become an important reference for briefings, consultation, media communications and proposals, as it will help others to clearly understand what you're trying to achieve. If a number of people are involved, you must all agree on your aims before going any further.

What are Your Aims?

A clearly defined aim will guide the work ahead. It can be as simple as you like and can be worded many different ways such as in a vision statement, mission statement or statement of purpose. Invest a little time in making sure this statement is tight, clear and achievable.

In developing your aim, consider:

- what are we aiming to achieve
- in the short term?

- in the long term?
- why do we need to do this?
- what time frames are we working to?
- What is the context for your region, place or project?

To help you and others better understand the context of the region, place or project, you will need to set the scene in a brief overview statement. This statement should cover:

- social setting
- economic conditions
- current political climate
- natural environment setting *and*
- cultural considerations.

Some of the key questions you may need to answer succinctly are:

- what are the key natural and cultural assets for tourism?
- what are the current visitor numbers?
- what is the potential for future growth in visitor numbers?
- how well is the current situation working?
- is the place or region appropriate for tourism use and development?

If at all possible clearly identify common ground or potential areas/points of conflict between those interested in the place/ project. Defining common ground early in the process can be important in assisting progress. How to manage issues and conflicts will be explored in later steps.

Who is, could be or needs to be Involved?

This step will help you to:

- identify stakeholders
- consider when and how people should be consulted and involved
- work out how to develop effective working relationships.

It is important to find out who is concerned about and responsible for tourism, environment and heritage issues relating to your place or region. If you systematically and strategically identify and involve those with a stake in your place, region or tourism product, you will:

- ensure the right people are involved in planning and future activities
- help determine heritage significance of places involved
- help make sure all the important issues are considered
- help to decide what future actions are realistic and will best meet everyone's needs and
- help build support for regional plans, management plans and development proposals.

This step is important as it will underpin all future steps and will need to be revisited and updated continually.

Initially, everyone who is, could be or needs to be involved or considered in future decisions should be identified and the nature of their interest noted. From here, various forms of consultation, as appropriate, can be considered and this can then lead some form of involvement in the process, project or business.

Who are the Stakeholders?

Determine who is, should or could be involved by listing all potential stakeholders.

You can identify stakeholders by:

- talking to people
- reading existing reports *and*
- if necessary, publicly or formally seeking interested persons or organisations.

Start using existing networks and communication forums to identify the people who

might be involved. Ask your colleagues:

- who else should I talk to?
- who is not involved who should be?

Some or all of the following questions may help you to identify the people, groups and organisations who may need to be informed, consulted or involved in some way. Understanding the nature of the interest of each stakeholder helps, whether it is statutory, professional, economic, cultural or personal. Depending on their interest, stakeholders may just need to be kept in mind in future steps, others will need to be included in some form of consultation and a smaller set will need to be involved. The essential or key stakeholders should be identified as early as possible.

How to Consult and Involve People

Informing and involving people can be challenging and time consuming but can make a huge difference to successful projects, plans and tourism products. Consultation processes can be targeted at your key stakeholders for specific purposes, or might be designed to generally inform the community, build support and seek willing involvement. There are many different consultation techniques. Choosing the best one for you will depend on the context, type of people involved and the available human and financial resources. Some techniques are formal, others are targeted and specific. The range of techniques includes, but is not limited to:

- community meetings
- interviews
- public exhibitions, displays and information sheets
- advisory committees
- media placements seeking input
- written submissions
- telephone polls and surveys
- focus groups
- open days
- guided information tours
- conferences or workshops
- residents' feedback sessions
- visual mapping
- pictorial and photographic illustration.

If you would like help in developing your consultation approaches, you may like to engage someone who is trained or experienced in consultation techniques. Additional resources detailing consultation methods are listed in the references section. Working out the appropriate people to involve is often a matter of common sense, but it can be important to involve people other than the usual suspects. Sometimes these people can be a breath of fresh air, and bring with them new and interesting perspectives.

How to Develop Effective Working Relationships

Several other factors may make a big difference in establishing or developing effective working relationships, such as:

- identifying the 'drivers' or champions

- identifying the key people to be involved in regular communication *and*
- identifying important partnerships.

Drivers and Champions

Every project or process needs someone to coordinate activities, bring people together and be the central contact point. This individual may be the initial person to get the process rolling before handing it on to others, or they could be nominated as the coordinator by superiors or a project team. This person, along with other contact people, should be clearly identified, and all key stakeholders notified of their role, and provided with their contact details.

Project Teams, Working Groups or Steering Committees

Where possible, use and build on existing communication mechanisms to coordinate work. If a suitable consultative group does not already exist, it may be useful to set up a working group to address issues relevant to your region, place or tourism product. The aim of the working group should be to communicate across organisations, integrate the needs of tourism, heritage and the environment and foster support for the process.

Possible Participants for a Working Group

Appoint members and use them as conduits for information into the group and out to the broader community. Your group can be as formal or informal as you like. It can provide a focal point for reporting and communication between people, accessing information, exploring options, making decisions and communicating to the broader community. It should reflect all key interests, and should involve key people or organisations at the core of decision-making.

Developing Partnerships

Successful tourism often requires resources that no one organisation can offer so partnerships can be an effective tool when dealing across tourism and heritage issues. They can help to build support, and to coordinate rather than duplicate efforts. Taking a partnership approach early on, may help you when seeking approvals and may ensure that you have all the right information as a project progresses. The key steps to developing partnerships are:

1. identifying what key partnerships will help you to achieve your goals
2. identifying the people who are or should be involved
3. building the relationships (using this document is a good start)
4. developing mutual understandings of issues and the natural and cultural heritage involved
5. jointly developing goals and objectives
6. expressing commitment to the partnership, and to implementing agreed future actions.

What is Known?

This step will help you to:

- identify existing studies or sources of information relevant to your process or project
- locate and summarise available information on the current and potential market for tourism
- determine the heritage assets, their heritage values and themes Information is a powerful tool so drawing together relevant facts and figures will provide a solid grounding for future decisions. As you look for material on planning and managing tourism at heritage places, and the current and potential tourism market, you may find that much useful information already exists.

Where to look

You might have a look at books, newspaper articles, sound recordings, council records, tourism brochures, annual reports, tour operator records, park management plans and research reports. Information can also be found:

- by talking to knowledgeable individuals and through observations, interviews, questionnaires and focus groups
- in local and state libraries
- in private collections
- on websites
- through various local or regional organisations
- in universities
- at heritage site management authorities

- at state and Australian Government departments
- with tour operators.

Questions to Ask

Are there any:

- regional plans for economic development?
- relevant local government plans?
- expressions of community aims/aspirations?

If you can, also try to identify what areas of information seem to be missing as these might be important parts of the overall picture and may need to be obtained some other way if they are important for making future decisions.

Other Sources

Environment and Heritage Information

A useful starting place for environment and heritage information is through the internet at sites such as the Australian Heritage Directory. The websites of the Australian Government Department of the Environment and Heritage, and state environment, park and heritage agencies are also useful.

What makes this Region, Place or Product Special?

In this step you need to identify the important values of your place, region or product, and the ways in which they are understood and communicated. Places can be special for all kinds of reasons — they may be important to the local community or to the world as a whole.

Tourism, heritage and local community interests will benefit from developing a common understanding of what is significant so that they have a unified approach to presenting local and regional heritage to visitors.

Identifying Natural and Cultural Heritage Values

Natural and cultural heritage places are often the key assets for tourism. The unique qualities of a place, or its values, can be a large part of a tourism business and its key selling points.

Understanding the values of your heritage places is essential for effective product development, planning, marketing, management and interpretation. It is also important when considering the appropriateness of introducing or expanding tourism activities at your heritage place. This understanding helps to ensure that future development is as compatible as possible with the ongoing care of the values.

You may find that the values have already have been documented by natural and cultural heritage specialists or are known to locals. Heritage professionals have developed considerable expertise and have structured methods (including criteria) for assessing the significance of a place. Information they can offer on aesthetic, historical, scientific, social and spiritual significance will be valuable. Hunt out this information. A good place to start is to check local, state or national heritage registers.

Identifying other Values

Other values, aside from those formally recognised by heritage specialists, are also important. These may be the less tangible aspects that make a place, region or experience special to the local community or to visitors. They may relate to its cultural, community, recreational and economic uses.

The Tourism Perspective

Stories based on heritage values, particularly those provided by local people, are often what make a place attractive to visitors. These stories are also what visitors take away with them and share with others when they return home. The combination of values, stories and landscapes, can create a total 'experience' for the visitor.

What are the Issues?

This step is about identifying all the important issues or factors that might affect what happens in the future. This means talking to people and looking at the information you have collected to date. Tease out the important matters that are unresolved or that will impact on your place, region or tourism product. Before you start, remember:

- issues are not always problems — they can be worked on and with
- identify conflicts in perspectives or issues — flag these for further clarification and analysis so that you can find ways to address them later
- focus on the issues and not the people raising them
- if people have identified issues, make sure these are considered through the next steps. People's views need to

be reflected in the process and individuals should also be able to see their input

- in identifying issues, you may come across some which require expert advice or further investigation. This could include professional assessments of the condition of places, market potential, and visitor management and interpretation. Obtaining professional advice or digging out extra information may help to build a sturdier foundation for planning future work, forecasting budgets and preparing for any necessary approvals
- a thorough knowledge of issues will also help you to develop performance measures and monitoring indicators as you address the issues over time.

Ways to Identify Issues

Identify issues clearly and thoroughly. Where necessary, consider using professional skills and approaches, such as those offered by facilitators experienced or trained in techniques for working with stakeholders and identifying issues. If you are undertaking this step yourself, think of running separate meetings or separate parts of meetings, so that people have a chance to think and talk about issues concerning them. Record what people say. Ensure everyone has an opportunity to express their view.

Further checks that can help you to identify important issues are:

- *Revisit step 2* (who is involved?) and consider the issues that might come from different perspectives and stakeholders. If you don't have an understanding of issues from their point of view, how might you find this out?
- *Revisit step 3* (what do we know?) to consider issues raised previously. Are there any recommendations that have been made before?
- *Revisit step 4* (what is special?) and consider issues that arise when we understand what makes a place, region or tourism product special.

Identifying Issues

To help consider and cover the range of issues relevant to both tourism and heritage, it may be useful to consider:

- consumer/visitor experience

- community experience
- environment/heritage management and impacts
- infrastructure issues
- market/marketing issues
- tourism product availability
- economic cost/benefit issues
- training/capacity building
- strategic and resource context
- approvals and regulation.

Sometimes an issue is broadly identified, but not enough information exists on which to base a reasonable judgement. In this case, either you need to gather more information about the issue, or use some sort of analytical technique to develop a clearer picture. Various types of analysis appropriate for tourism, heritage and business planning are detailed in the next step.

Handling Conflicts

It is important to identify areas of conflict, as these can reappear later as barriers to progress or action. Looking beyond the conflict of different ideas and people and getting to the root cause can often help to resolve the issue. Conflict is often inevitable. It can make ideas or projects unworkable, but it may also present opportunities for innovative solutions.

Various methods of conflict resolution and mediation processes exist. Rather than focusing on the particular individuals and their views and creating an adversarial situation, there are ways of working with interests to acknowledge views, explore issues and develop solutions cooperatively.

In some cases informal cooperative and collaborative approaches will be successful, others may require more formal approaches such as negotiation, arbitration or mediation. Using the services of a professional and 'neutral' facilitator can produce a good result.

Keys to managing and resolving conflicts include:

- having an inclusive participatory process
- maintaining open and effective communication
- being responsive and adaptable *and*
- building consensus between a majority of stakeholders.

Analysing Issues

Now that the issues have emerged from the last step, you may need to delve further to clarify what is going on. Important issues need to be fully understood if the right decision is to be made about a particular course of action.

Concentrate your efforts on analysing priority issues. If resources are limited you may need to make a judgement based on available information and analysis. Analysis may simply be a matter of presenting a reasoned judgement about an issue with justification of how you came to that position and citing what data or information supports this. More sophisticated analysis may help you to make better business and management decisions, but this can also be time-consuming and costly, so compromises may have to be made. In any case you should clearly state how you have reached your current understanding of the situation.

Many of the methods of analysis described below are standard approaches used in strategic planning. Some of them, such as market analysis, are essential components for business plans. You will need to decide what types of analysis are relevant or appropriate to your situation. The aim of using any analytical technique is to better understand factors at play in what might be a very complex situation. Analysis will also help to further identify and prioritise fundamental issues.

Key analytical methods may include, but are not limited to the following:

- market analysis
- heritage conservation analysis
- SWOT analysis
- situational analysis
- cost–benefit analysis
- priority analysis.

Market Analysis

A number of market-related issues would have emerged in the previous step. A market analysis is an analytical summary of how your region, place or product fits into the marketplace. It takes into account the saleability or profitability of a product or service, based on information about the product and the potential market. Market analysis may include an assessment of how your region, place or tourism product compares with existing competition.

- Are there others around competing for a similar market?
- What are their strengths?
- What are yours?
- Is the market big enough for people to share?
- How can your region, place or product be presented in the marketplace to maximise the fit between what you can offer and what people want?

Basically a market analysis should assess the supply and demand for tourism product, accommodation, transport and associated services relating to your situation. This type of analysis helps in positioning your product intelligently in the marketplace. You can estimate the market potential for a product using information on sales volumes for similar products or in similar regions. Industry statistics collected regularly across Australia may also be available from you state or territory tourism organisation (refer to contacts information).

Market analysis often includes a forecast of where the market is going. Trends over time may indicate how your product or service may fare in the future. In the summary of your market analysis you should explain the potential for future development opportunities based on market and trend information.

Heritage Conservation Analysis

In Step 4 you identified the factors that make your place special — its heritage values. In some cases, when the implications of tourism on a heritage place become clearer, you may need to revisit this question with further specific studies on the heritage values, or on particular technical issues that may affect how the site is used. One important type of conservation analysis is a condition analysis. This method uses trained heritage conservation experts to look closely at buildings, Indigenous sites or natural features and assess their physical condition, and their capacity to withstand visitors or other possible indirect impacts.

Situational Analysis

This is a description of the context in which tourism is currently occurring. It includes the main determining factors such as the seasonal or geographic flow patterns and the functional relationships at play. Understanding the situation is the first step in designing the response. A situational analysis involves analysing needs and assets, understanding what works well and what doesn't and the capacity of those involved. Including others in situational analysis helps to build a better understanding of the context or situation.

SWOT Analysis (Strengths, Weaknesses, Opportunities and Threats)

This is a very standard way to help identify and consider the issues identified in Step 5. A SWOT analysis is a simple and useful part of many types of strategic plans, including business plans.

In this process you will need to consider the *present* strengths and weaknesses of your situation and *future* possibilities for opportunities and threats. Remember, that the weaknesses and threats can become strengths and opportunities if addressed. This analysis will help you to get an overview of key issues, and will help to articulate issues that may not have come out in other ways. It is useful to undertake SWOT analysis after you have collected and considered information from issues identified in the last step.

Cost–benefit Analysis

This is a relatively simple and widely used technique. As its name suggests, simply add up the value of the benefits of a particular approach or idea and then subtract its associated costs. Costs are either one-off or ongoing. Benefits generally accumulate over time.

Costs and benefits can be financial, environmental and social. Putting a financial value on intangible costs and benefits can be more challenging and highly subjective. Cost–benefit analysis is linked to the concept of the 'triple bottom line' which is used as a framework for measuring and reporting performance against three key areas — economic, social and environmental.

Cost–benefit analysis can be done formally, using quantified financial measurement, or informally. A simple way to do this is to list in a table all of the expected costs and benefits.

Some cost–benefit analysis questions that could be asked in relation to a region, place or project:

Priority Analysis

You can determine priorities in many different ways, but one simple way is to look at the importance and urgency of the issues.

Consider each issue and its place on the chart. Issues that are judged to be both very important and urgent will obviously need to be addressed as a top priority.

The priorities for issues which fall elsewhere on the chart will depend on the issue and context.

The following questions may help you consider priorities, and place issues on the chart:

- are there options or actions that address important needs or gaps?
- which options or actions advance and support set priorities or responsibilities?
- is there a particular action that, if not taken, would result in negative consequences?
- what opportunities present themselves that should be pursued?

Ideally, you should do this analysis with a group of your stakeholders so that you develop a common understanding of your key issues. It will help point towards particular options and future courses of action, and will also help to build agreements between stakeholders on possible future directions.

Principles or Objectives to Guide Action

Now that you have an understanding of tourism and heritage values and the key issues at play, you need to consider more specifically what you want to achieve. This should be a balance between looking after heritage and developing tourism if, and where, appropriate.

In Steps 2 to 6 you drew together all the relevant background material and knowledge. Using this as your foundation you now need to consider where you want to go in the future. In this step you will develop specific objectives, or if appropriate, a general set of principles, to guide future work.

These principles or objectives, need to deal with the realities of tourism while maintaining and protecting what is special about the area's natural and cultural heritage.

It is very important that principles or objectives are agreed by key stakeholders and that they have a high level of ownership. Implementation of the principles works best when people feel they have played an important part in their development.

Principles

In some cases a general set of principles is the most appropriate way to guide the direction and breadth of future work. Principles can be expressed in the form of guidelines, protocols or policy statements.

For example, a tourism business might develop a set of responsible tourism principles, or a set of protocols might be developed with Indigenous communities covering issues relating to Indigenous heritage and tourism.

In historic heritage conservation plans, you can often find a statement of 'conservation policies'. Where these policies exist, they should be included in the principles as they are likely to guide the development of heritage tourism.

Objectives

Setting objectives is one of the most common ways of planning for the future. Objectives are sets of short statements that are like goal posts. They are something to aim towards, and can give a clearer focus to your plan and efforts.

Objectives should be written in clear language, be specific, measurable, realistic, and have a time frame. They are an important part of many planning documents, including business plans.

Objectives are created by thinking how you want the future to look. Build into your objectives words which reflect economic and community aspirations as well as the intention to take care of heritage. Objectives should be developed and owned collectively by stakeholders or business partners.

They can be written in several different ways. One approach is to state your intent, for example, *"to improve directional signage at..."*. The other way is to state the desired end result, for example *"signs installed at all..."*. The form you use will depend on personal preference and the context in which they are to be used.

You can measure whether or not you have met your objectives by developing indicators or tangible evidence of attaining your goals. You may also want to think about what milestones would help to break down your work into achievable stages. As your work proceeds, any reporting should focus on your progress towards achieving your objectives. This is the means by which you and others can monitor performance.

Example of Objectives

- To develop a regional tourism strategy focusing on key areas which are linked by a particular theme
- To build relationships and communication between tourism operators, attractions and regional managers of natural and cultural heritage places through regular reporting meetings
- To improve the regional directional and interpretive signage relating to tourist and heritage attractions
- To maintain and enhance the region's international profile as an ecotourism destination
- To ensure that educational materials are available relating to the values of particular places
- To secure increased financial resources to promote the distinctive natural and cultural heritage assets of the region
- To build the capacity in the local community to support and participate in tourism through awareness raising and training activities
- To increase market share from 2% to 5% within two years.

What are your Ideas and Options?

You will have generated ideas and concepts as you have progressed through Step 3 (what information is there?), Step 4 (what makes this region, place or product special?), Step 5 (identifying issues) and Step 6 (analysing issues). The aims and objectives identified in Step 7 can help you to develop ideas and options in this step.

It's likely that you will have many different options and pathways to your final goal or goals. If you are working in a region or community, you may need to consider many possibilities before making a final decision. In planning for tourism the feasibility of one or more options may need to be tested and presented before funding or approvals are granted.

This step will help you to clarify your ideas and options, make decisions and prepare you for taking action.

Consider options by…

1. developing ideas
2. presenting ideas or options for testing
3. analysing issues further, if needed

4. developing recommended option/s
5. seeking agreement on preferred option/s.

Developing Ideas

As you have worked through this process, many ideas will have emerged or will have been put forward by the people with whom you have been working. Now you can bring those ideas forward and show how they might work. You may need to bundle together specific ideas into packages or groups of actions. You will need to take into account key issues and to ensure that you maximise opportunities and manage any threats. If clear ideas and options do not emerge at first, you may need to develop them through discussions, brainstorming sessions, focus groups or workshops.

In general, ideas and options should include:

- the visitor experience
- community engagement
- care of heritage assets
- infrastructure
- marketing
- product development
- stakeholder communication
- training and capacity building *and*
- necessary resources and support.

Consider Questions

Visitor Experience

- What will help improve the visitor experience?
- What specific interpretation activities could be undertaken to improve visitor experience?
- How are we meeting demand for the particular natural and/or cultural heritage experience being offered?
- How will interpretation be delivered/improved? (*Successful*
- *Tourism at Heritage Places* provides guidance on this)
- What heritage themes will be used?
- What activities will visitors undertake?

Community Engagement

- How can community engagement be maximised?

- Can community representatives be included in key decision making processes?
- How can the community be involved in tourism at a heritage place?
- What sort of regional cooperation will be pursued?
- Who will be involved in developing tourism?
- What partnerships could be further explored?

Care of Environment and Heritage

- How can heritage assets be best cared for?
- How will visitor impacts on values be managed?
- Will it be necessary to limit use of a place?

Assets

- What activities will directly contribute to maintaining a heritage place/asset?
- What steps will be taken to work cooperatively with park managers, site managers etc?
- What sort of actions will be taken to ensure the appropriate people are consulted in relation to Indigenous tourism, gender protocols, intellectual property etc?
- Are there significant plant or animal species requiring protection?
- Are there significant landscape values at the place —are they acknowledged or protected, how accessible are they and are they sensitive to visitor impacts?

Infrastructure

- How can you best plan for infrastructure?
- How can tourism planning integrate with current local/ regional planning?
- What will be pursued in terms of transport, waste, water and other services in order to meet visitor demand?
- What signage will be developed?
- Will the proposed infrastructure use sustainable energy sources, practices and technologies?

Marketing

- How can marketing be more effective?
- How will visitors find out about the product/place?

- Can marketing be done cooperatively at a regional level?
- What key information, such as minimal impacts on heritage values, can be communicated?
- How will marketing of Indigenous tourism be strategic and coordinated?
- A What is the marketing strategy?
- What are the place, regional and national themes?
- Will the product be promoted in visitor centres?

Product Development

- How can tourism products be developed?
- Is there good match between the product and the market?
- How will your product/experience complement regional tourism product/experiences?
- How can a better understanding of heritage values lead to new tourism products and marketing opportunities?

Communication

- What is the best way to maintain, maximise and improve communication between interests?
- Are new communication forums needed?
- How will you report progress on achieving aims to people who need to know or who might be interested?
- What representation should be sought in government and industry forums? and capacity building
- What capacity building is needed in the community and in individuals?
- What skill levels will be needed for staff to perform at the standard required?
- What business skills need to be developed?
- Can formal training, industry development or accreditation programs assist?

Resources and Support

- What resources and support are needed?
- What advice may be needed at different times and where can this be found?
- What best practice environment and heritage management

- will be adopted?
- What research is desirable or useful?

Baseline Data and Monitoring

- What data is needed about the physical condition of the environment or heritage places that will assist in monitoring potential positive and negative outcomes for conservation?
- What data is needed about and from visitors to ensure that in the future we can determine how effectively we are meeting customer demand and expectations?
- What data is needed about local community attitudes, issues, amenity and social conditions that will enable effective monitoring of the potential positive and negative effects of tourism?
- Who is responsible for collecting baseline data?
- What specific monitoring will be undertaken to ensure that significant impacts on environment and heritage assets, community health and business development are identified?
- What indicators might be necessary as a measure of performance for sustainable practice?

Presenting Ideas or Options for Testing

Once you have put together your ideas into a package or proposal that you think will work you can then present this to a group of informed people, a business or project team or a stakeholder group.

Use their knowledge and experience to test how your ideas might meet the needs of key interests while also addressing the issues and opportunities of the situation. When presenting the options you should give a realistic assessment of their feasibility and include information on proposed timing and required resources.

Analysing Issues Further, if Needed

When developing your ideas or options, you may discover that you don't have a clear picture of some important elements. If so, go back to Steps 5 and 6 to gather more information or further analyse your situation. If you have several possible scenarios, you can test how each scenario might fare in light of your market analysis. You might even want to conduct specific market testing of your ideas or product.

Developing Recommended Options

Once you have tested your ideas and gathered any extra information that you need, you can then develop your preferred options. These should be backed up by a clearly reasoned statement supported by the information you have collected in the steps so far. These options can then be presented in a proposal, feasibility study or strategic plan. Good communication and people skills can make a big difference when it comes to convincing others of the benefits of your recommended option/s.

Seeking Agreement on Preferred Options

Negotiating over the best course of action can be complicated by tensions between competing interests. Different stakeholders are likely to have different but equally legitimate priorities. At this point it is important to focus on the positive mutual interests that can link tourism, heritage conservation and communities and that can form the basis for cooperation.

Once a particular idea or option looks like meeting most people's needs, your next step will be to seek agreement through the necessary formal and informal processes. As you obtain agreements and support, make sure you document this for future reference.

How to do it?

The preferred options or ideas from the previous step now need to be turned into actions that you can implement! Making new projects or ideas happen may involve many stakeholders, organisations and groups. Even if implementation is the responsibility of one organisation or business, you will probably need to gain the support or approval of others. Whatever your situation, a clear implementation plan is essential. This not only makes sound business sense but is standard practice in project management. This plan can also be called an action plan or a work plan. In addition to developing this plan, each participating organisation may need to look at its own planning documents to ensure that the implementation plan links to existing planning documents. It may be worth having an overall implementation/ action plan for heritage tourism issues as a common agreed framework.

Additional Factors

Additional factors that are crucial to address include:

- strategies for political support
- communication
- capacity building
- making links
- staging
- influence.

Strategies for political support — consider and include actions that help build political support for what you want to achieve. Lobbying can be a legitimate and necessary activity.

Communication — good mechanisms for communicating are vital in bringing together diverse interests and helping them to work together. Consider and include any actions or activities that will make this happen. Too often these communication activities are not given the resourcing or attention that they deserve.

Capacity building — while training and staff or community development may be included as an objective of the plan, you may also want to think carefully about whether implementing the plan will need specific training or capacity building. What support or additional capacity do individuals or groups need to participate and play an effective role in implementation?

Making links — consider how different activities can link together to create a whole which is greater than the sum of its parts. Often the most efficient use of resources comes from piggy-backing on other initiatives and pursuing activities with multiple outcomes.

Staging — consider how actions can build up in stages over time to reach the desired result. At times you may need to reach one stepping stone before reassessing where to go next.

Influence — gain the support of other key players and influence other plans or activities to increase your ability to make a difference. Ways of gaining support need to be considered and included in your planning and activities.

Keeping on Track

Any strategic plan, development plan or action plan needs to be followed and referred to regularly to be kept relevant. The best way to use a plan is to constantly check and report on progress. You can do this through:

- performance measures or indicators
- monitoring and reporting *and*
- evaluating and reviewing.

Performance measures or indicators — these can be used to monitor progress and identify what is being achieved They help to demonstrate how well an organisation, program or strategy is meeting its objectives or when actions are not proceeding as planned. They can also show where performance can be improved.

Performance indicators can use qualitative and quantitative information. They should be relevant to the program's desired outcomes and objectives, be quantifiable, verifiable and free from bias. Indicators can be relatively simple, cheap and easy to measure. You can develop these yourself or use existing indicators. Monitoring and reporting — build into your implementation plan key points at which to check your progress. It is a good idea to give formal progress reports to the group with responsibilities across both tourism and heritage interests. This will help keep attention on what has been achieved and what still needs to be done.

Timeframes for monitoring and reporting are important and should be carefully thought through. You need to allow enough time to determine if the outcomes are successful or whether you have made a significant impact. If unforeseen obstacles arise you may want to report sooner rather than later to avert negative consequences. You also need to consider how much time it takes to collect and collate monitoring data.

Evaluating and reviewing — your plan should also include a timeframe (three to five years is typical). A major evaluation and review should be conducted at the end of this time. This may lead to the plan being refreshed or the process being repeated to produce a new plan. Keeping track of progress means that efforts can be redirected and management continually adapted to suit changing circumstances.

Statement of Directions

If you are writing up a plan, this step is simply like the conclusion or executive summary. It summarises in as succinct a form as possible:

- the key heritage and tourism assets of the region, place or product
- the key issues *and*
- the agreements and outcomes reached between parties.

If you are using this process to run a meeting or series of meetings, or a major project, this step comes at the end so that all the people involved can see what they have achieved and can be clear about the outcomes. There may also be other creative ways to present your outcomes through images or other forms of communication. Whatever case, you will find this summary very useful for briefing colleagues, superiors and for including in newsletters, electronic information or media materials.

Planning for Tourism Marketing

Many businesses nowadays are working towards incorporating sustainability into the core of their products. Quite often these products are the result of a well thought sustainability concept, and yet the entrepreneurs behind it fail to reach the marketplace, because they lack marketing expertise and knowledge of the tourism industry's distribution channels. These tourism companies, and particularly small firms from developing countries, suffer from poor targeting, market segmentation and positioning, low consumer product knowledge, and consumer risk perception.

Distribution channels are key to increase the exposure of sustainable suppliers, and to capitalise on the latent market demand for sustainability by changing behaviour in non-sustainable firms. Each channel has strengths and weaknesses which are reviewed with a range of examples showcasing good practice. These channels are analysed from the point of view of the supplier for equity, cost-benefit, market penetration and normalisation potential. The results show that few channels have high equity, but many of them offer a good cost-benefit ratio, hence efforts are needed to provide opportunities for businesses. The market penetration and normalisation potentials show the channels with the greatest overall scope.

Policies should encourage industry associations and individual distribution channels to introduce sustainability criteria for their suppliers. A stepped approach could first introduce criteria where eco-savings can be made, and where sustainability is part of the quality evident to the client, as well as customer education. This first step aims to allow companies with low access to training and know-how to repay their investment through the eco-savings, and develop a proactive culture. A second step would require industry associations to introduce more complex standards such as labour and other fair trade specific issues, as well as deepening into the many aspects of sustainability that the clients may not notice during their visit, but will have great importance to the long term wellbeing of the destination.

Destination management organisations and tourist boards are useful to create destination brands and can act as sales portals. They can strengthen their role by setting standards and providing training. Tour operators are key sales channels that allow tourism companies to sell large volumes, usually at a lower price than if selling direct. Large operators, but also increasingly smaller ones are setting sustainability standards for their suppliers as well as support mechanisms. Guidebooks are very successful marketing tools but they require products to be unique and a long lead time, and as such are mid-term investments.

Media can be a powerful tool for consumer education and the challenge here is to feed interesting unique stories to the press that change consumer behaviour, as suchfor example a public relations clearinghouse on sustainability would be an attractive tool. Certification schemes are increasingly setting standards for tourism firms and providing guidance, but their implementation is not widespread and with low equity and low consumer recognition they are a tool for business to business lobbying. As such the recommendation is to experiment with their implementation.

Travel fairs are useful venues to for learning about the market and renewing contacts but their negative costbenefit means they are not accessible to most, and they should, therefore, be seen more as events to educate suppliers on marketing, and be packaged by tourist boards as part of training for developing companies. Internet retailing has the potential to reach a broader market but for the inexperienced tourism firm much training is needed, with priorities such as managing risk perception of consumers if operating their own website, to possibly paying high commissions for discounted last minute travel sites. More regulation of internet retailing will increase consumer trust and particularly help small firms. Finally, consumer organisations are powerful brands to endorse products, but as in the case of guidebooks, are mid-term investments and require clearer sustainability criteria, as well as a stronger contribution to consumer education.

Marketing Sustainable Tourism Products

Many entrepreneurs fail to understand the nature of the tourist industry as a marketplace, and assume that because they have an authentic and exciting tourism product, clients will find them. Many donors and policy makers also make the same mistake, funding conservation projects expecting that tourism will generate sufficient revenues for the long term survival.

Underestimating the challenge, as well as the cost of distributing tourism products is a key reason why new tourism ventures fail, and why many donor projects do not survive beyond the initial subsidised period. The challenges mentioned here apply in the majority both to sustainable and non sustainable tourism products.

Reviewing the key stages of a marketing plan provides some background to this report. The first stage is a thorough analysis of the market, resources, competitors and the business environment. The second stage is to decide on the strategic choices of how to segment markets, to determine the markets to be targeted, and to plan an appropriate product positioning.

The latter part is to determine the marketing mix, which in its most basic sense means how the product will be offered to tourists, the price that will be charged, how the product will be communicated, and how it will be distributed. It is through examining the requirements of these promotion and distribution channels that projects and firms face the reality check of what the market wants.

Key Stages of the Marketing Plan

Three key issues are highlighted below that influence the success of marketing efforts by tourism companies. Many of these cannot be solved by individual tourist firms or even through collaboration at a destination level; it is however important to be aware of them to consider how they will affect the promotion and distribution of tourism products.

Analysis

- Market
- Resources

- Competitors
- Environment.

Strategy

- Segmenting
- Targeting
- Positioning.

Marketing Mix

- Product
- Price
- Promotion
- Distribution.

Three key issues are highlighted below that influence the success of marketing efforts by tourism companies. Many of these cannot be solved by individual tourist firms or even through collaboration at a destination level; it is however important to be aware of them to consider how they will affect the promotion and distribution of tourism products.

Targeting, Segmenting and Positioning

There are many examples of sustainable tourism products that are not viable because the supplier has failed to understand market needs, often through a failure to engage the industry in product development. This is sometimes the result of agencies working with host destinations that have suffered the negative impacts of unsustainable development, and then fail to involve operators, on whom marketing success often ultimately depends.

Resource based Instead of Market Led

Sustainability means authenticity, which in turn suggests that the tourism product should not be changed just to please tourists. But in doing so tourism products often do not take into account the expectations of tourists and the needs of tour operators.

Targeting International Markets

Too many businesses expect international markets to become the key source of income. This should be balanced with filling a good percentage of the capacity with domestic and short haul regional markets. This is partly to mitigate a destination's exposure to the vagaries of international tourism trends, but also because advertising in regional markets is almost always more cost effective.

Sustainability as Unique Selling Proposition

Marketing on the basis of sustainability is not going to suffice for most tourist segments and products, even when sustainability could be at the core of the product itself, and could be one of the determining attributes that the tourist looks for. For the vast majority of consumers, sustainability will only be a consideration when other criteria, such as price, choice of accommodation and availability of activities have all been satisfied.

Sustainability as Part of Quality

In the past, too many sustainable products in tourism and elsewhere, have performed worse in the basic quality attributes. Tourists are willing to purchase sustainable once the basic attributes of product quality are met. The win-win products in the sustainable, organic, fair trade sectors are those that provide added value.

Consumer Product Knowledge

If a tourist market knows the product well, the type of promotion can emphasise characteristics of the product or place that are meaningful to the tourist, whereas first time tourists will need more information about the product as prior knowledge cannot be assumed. Also repeat tourists are more likely to buy directly from suppliers that first time tourists.

Inexperienced Product Users

Tourists that buy a certain type of holiday for the first time are more open to education, but it is also less likely that their behaviour will be in-keeping with that of locals. First time tourists on a package such as trekking, diving or homestays have specific awareness raising and education needs before and during their experience, that will mark their behaviour for future trips. The product and the message to these first time users will need to be tailored to emphasise safety and customer care, whilst also communicating the need for cultural sensitivity and respect – insofar as tourism involves interactions that necessarily include an active and a passive experience.

Price Sensitive First Time Visitors

Many tourists experiment with destinations, visiting just once, making it hard for the service providers to communicate product quality, and relying on price alone to secure sales. Uniqueness and authenticity need to be reinforced for these first time visitors who lack the knowledge to demand them for themselves. Information sources that can be trusted such as travel guides and signs of quality for example are good vehicles to reinforce such messages.

Repeat clients encourage sustainability. Repeat clients are more likely to appreciate the unique characteristics of a place, usually related to sustainability. Lack of loyalty to destinations often means service providers do not see a short term benefit from providing the required services of quality, as those tourists leaving will not come again, and others just as gullible will follow.

Risk Perception

Tourists often do not want to book directly with service suppliers because they perceive risk. Small firms are perceived as more risky because they do not have strong brands to support them, and for this reason they will need to work in partnership to ensure purchases. Sustainable tourism products will have to work on reducing the perception of risk, by tackling the following:

Risk of the Unknown

A large volume of internet sales at present are repeat sales once the client knows the business, and they are mainly for airline tickets, car rental and hotel rooms in global companies with standardised products. This increases when travelling to countries for the first time, particularly when these countries are very different to the country of origin of the tourists.

Risk of Fraud

Secure purchasing systems that can give confidence to clients are necessary for small tourism firms to sell directly. At the moment a large percentage of direct sales are with large firms. The perception of potential fraud from giving credit card details to companies outside the tourists' home country is high, also raising concerns about data protection and the possibility of identity theft.

Risk of Virtual Companies

Tourists are less likely to want to book with small companies because of the perceived threat that these might not be real companies, the client has paid in advance for the service but once they arrive at the destination the company does not exist. Small tourism firms need the backing of stronger brands to provide reassurance to the client that they are sound companies. Retailing through a link at the national tourist board, or having the backing of consumer organisations can provide the kind of quality assurance that will increase bookings.

Risk of no Consumer Protection

Purchasing directly from tourism suppliers means that clients will not have the same legal protection as when they purchase a product from a tour operator in their own country. This is clearly the case in Europe, where the Travel Packages Act places responsibility for the quality of the product including health and safety on the tour operator. There is little regulation and only very limited consumer protection against false claims made on the internet by direct suppliers.

Distribution Channels: Current Practice and Prospects

The tourism marketplace is made up of a large number of tourism service suppliers trying to reach a multiplicity of tourist markets. They do so targeting the tourists directly, developing positive messages about their product through promotion channels, and working with intermediary distribution channels that will sell a range of services tailored to the market's needs.

Business to Consumer (B2C)

Tourism service suppliers can use a range of direct marketing channels such as database and internet marketing to attract tourists. The advantage is having a greater control over the message sent and the type of tourist attracted. The disadvantages are that this is done at a greater financial risk, with potentially high start up costs. Box 2 includes a summary of main channels for direct marketing.

Business to Business (B2B)

The main focus of this report is for suppliers to trade through intermediaries that take the role of either selling individual services, packaging them or doing the marketing and booking. Tourism suppliers benefit from outsourcing the cost and risk of marketing. The advantages are diversification of markets that reduce risk, a potentially secure level of business, and fixed commissions that facilitate financial planning. The challenges are less control over marketing messages, markets and income streams.

Most often, tourism suppliers combine the two: direct (B2C) and via distributors (B2B). In the latter case, intermediaries are used to provide a baseline level of business that ensures minimum occupancy rates or load factors, which provides a contribution towards fixed costs of capital repayment and salaries. Direct marketing is used to capture repeat visitors, particular market segments and for specific promotions. The balance between the two types of marketing is determined by how entrepreneurial the company is, the availability of knowledge and funds, and the interest of intermediaries to work with it. Promotion strategies are the consequence of the distribution strategy, with some of the promotion tools used to generate direct sales, or to increase the interest of distribution channels in working with these suppliers.

This section reviews the potential and challenges faced by different promotion and distribution channels to contribute to the marketing of service suppliers that are sustainable.

While eight distribution and communication channels are reviewed here, some of these (particularly tour operators) are much larger than the others, whereas some of them only have an impact on a niche market, or are highlighted here because of their potential for the future.

Direct Marketing Channels

Database marketing. This is more likely for national than for international clients, and few small companies hold databases of past clients. These can work with specialist outbound tour operators to be included in their client reminder newsletters, usually generated as part of database marketing tactics, by providing up to date copy on the product and destination.

Internet marketing. Service providers frequently try to promote individual products without any coordination. Too often, suppliers perceive all others as competitors, when in fact key consumer motivators are 'choice' and 'range', which means that products are only enhanced by demonstrating links to other local products and suppliers. Whereas some confident travellers would be happy to seek out extremely remote products, many would prefer to know that they form part of a more substantial product cluster in the chosen destination.

Affiliate marketing. One of the most effective forms of marketing is for suppliers to establish relationships with other organisations, often unrelated to tourism, who can market their products to their own customers. This might be through special interests, such as wildlife, heritage or sports, or through particular groups, such as clubs and associations or faith groups. Sometimes these can be arranged simply by identifying that a satisfied customer is involved in a particular group and that they would be enthusiastic about promoting the product to fellow members.

Joint marketing portals. National and regional tourist boards and incoming tour operators need to pull together different services through joint marketing portals. Selling individual products, however sustainable, will not get tourists to a destination.

To be meaningful, these products need to be grouped by their appropriateness to specific market segments and price ranges.

Repeat business and word of mouth. Established companies fulfil a large percentage of their capacity through repeat business, as it generally accepted that it costs five times as much to gain a new customer as to maintain an old one. At its most sophisticated, this can involve a powerful multi-media CRM (customer relationship management) system, but it can simply be the good practice of maintaining a record of all customers' (and enquirers') contact details-albeit subject to relevant data protection legislation, which should not be underestimated.

Destination Management Organisations (DMOs) and Tourist Boards

DMOs are agencies or marketing consortia (normally publicly funded, sometimes supplemented by membership subscriptions) that promote a 'destination' to outbound tour operators and both domestic and foreign consumers through a variety of media, and provide information on local products and suppliers. Sometimes, suppliers (e.g. subscribed members) receive preferential treatment.

The challenge for destinations is to identify the environmental constraints and impacts of tourism development, and to then engage local destination suppliers, buyers (foreign and domestic) and all visitors in embracing sustainability as a key element of the tourism proposition. The opportunity is to make excellent environmental management part of consumer motivation, in order to help ensure the sustainable development of tourism.

Some destinations have marketed themselves as being totally sustainable, although in reality this often reflects an emphasis on natural heritage, rather than indicating product sustainability. Tourism New Zealand's campaign "100% Pure New Zealand" is a good example of this approach, where this DMO concentrates on presenting a consistent message to position New Zealand as a sustainable destination.

There are examples of tourist boards giving additional promotion to firms that have met certain standards of sustainability. Places as far apart as Scotland and Costa Rica are promoting companies certified as sustainable, either by highlighting certified suppliers with an additional logo in their promotional material or by creating a separate dedicated brochure for sustainable products.

Oman's Ministry of Tourism, which is responsible for developing and promoting the country's tourism product, has designed a policy that places 'sustainable tourism' at its heart. But, whilst many foreign tour operators are enthusiastic about 'ecotourism', sustainability of the product is not really a consideration-their key requirements are the availability of airconditioned tourism facilities, 4x4 vehicles and 5* accommodation. Local expertise is generally focused on the physical environment, rather than an appreciation of the cultural and social dimensions of sustainability in tourism.

The challenge for DMOs is often less about marketing sustainable tourism products, but more about raising awareness of what the sustainable development of tourism means for suppliers, which in turn will help to ensure the more sustainable development of tourism products. Remarking that the term "'responsible tourism' is more meaningful to suppliers", Oman's Dr. Aziz stated that the development of "the responsible tourism sector is one of the guaranteed ways of achieving sustainable development for the Sultanate of Oman." Thus the motivation for sustainable tourism products is national self-interest, and the opportunity is to encourage and facilitate more sustainable supplier practices. Oman is working to achieve this outcome through a programme of training and awareness raising, and by offering preferential terms to suppliers that adopt more sustainable practices. The former will be achieved through a national training programme, primarily targeted at tourism

SMEs, whilst the latter will involve a schedule of discounts on marketing activities, including attendance at international tourism fairs. There can be other priorities that DMOs must tackle before they can even begin to focus on sustainability issues, but such circumstances can bring benefits, allowing DMOs to approach product development as a 'blank canvas'. Although it has a tremendous product, Yemen has been the subject of much negative publicity in recent years and has been considered by tour operators and consumers alike to be too outlandish a destination for mainstream tourism. This means that the focus has been to rebuild the country's image as a viable tourism destination. In fact, this challenging marketing environment also enables Yemen to highlight the sustainability of its products, adding real value to the destination. This involves all the *usual marketing activities, such as organisation of familiarisation visits for journalists and tour operators, production of promotional media in paper and electronic formats and attendance at major international tourism fairs.*

With a particular emphasis on cultural and nature-based tourism, the main themes being promoted are 'ecotourism' and activity tourism, especially diving, deserts, mountains and climbing, which are attractive to tour operators. With 70% of visitors coming from the MENA region (Middle East & North Africa), the Yemen Tourism Promotion Board (YTPB) is focusing on several key foreign markets and plans to develop a new multi-lingual website. This will be in Arabic, English, French,

German and Italian and in the future also in Japanese and Russian, in order to communicate directly with the consumer. According to the YTPB's Director, "sustainable tourism is fundamental, because it helps the economy of Yemen through the creation of jobs and investment; tourism is Yemen's future". With many diverse products and micro enterprises, YTPB's challenge is simply to "get Yemen into tour operators' brochures". Marketing sustainable tourism is not simply a marketing exercise, but requires integration across all social and economic sectors. Thus, echoing the approach of Oman's Ministry of Tourism, Yemen's General Authority for Tourism Development

(GATD) is focused on the sustainable development of tourism. Observing that Yemen's tourism product is essentially its "environment and culture", the GATD stated that the challenge is to keep this "intact", because "if changed, then Yemen loses". The aim of sustainable tourism is therefore to "encourage investors, reduce poverty and preserve cultural and natural heritage". However, since there is limited understanding of 'sustainable tourism', the GATD puts a lot of energy into engaging key stakeholders, especially community representatives, to promote the principles of sustainable tourism. It will support those communities that choose tourism as a development strategy, but critically, it will also respect those that choose to resist tourism. When introducing foreign investors, it will encourage them to promote local employment, and to use local food and building materials, again adding value to the product and helping to satisfy consumer demand for the 'authentic' local product.

Natour Communications has run a series of short online campaigns to change the negative perception of Venezuela as a tourist destination, using a database of over 8,000 e-mail addresses of travel agents, operators, media interested in the natural world and tourism. The campaign consisted of between 8 and 10 issues over three months depending on the specific messages, to promote the country's natural attractions and activities, and generating interest for a familiarisation trip for 24 international media and operators.

Familiarisation visits ('fam trips') bring invited press and selected operators to destinations to sample the product. These are especially of value to emerging destinations and to showcase new products in more established destinations. Tourist boards tend to sponsor and support these, and in some instances run them. Typically a fam trip takes 8 to 12 weeks to set up because it requires targeting participants, raising awareness, organising logistics and tailoring the trip to their particular needs. Natour Communications run a fam trip to the Caribbean island of Trinidad coinciding with the 3rd annual Shandy Carib Adventure Festival to showcase adventure, nature and cultural opportunities.

Tour Operators

These are organisations that sell holidays and travel products to consumers, taking a commission or margin on the product (or package of products) sold, which they have purchased from suppliers or are selling (as an agent) on behalf of suppliers. Additional income is gained through the sale of other travel-related products, such as travel insurance and foreign currency. In some cases, they will establish a 'partnership' relationship with their suppliers, working collaboratively with them on destination management, product development and direct marketing activities.

The key tool for tour operators is the 'service agreement', the contract between operator and supplier, whether an airline, accommodation or excursion provider or ground handler. It defines the service standards, including quality as well as health and safety requirements. The results of customer satisfaction questionnaires in areas such as food, facilities, staff and overall quality, often determine bonuses being added or compensation being paid if the supplier varies significantly from the required standard.

Some tour operators are starting to introduce environmental standards, but with only limited consumer demand, few are yet willing to link these to contractual obligations and financial penalties. The general approach is one of encouragement, with operators identifying key suppliers that might need to improve their environmental performance and are consequently offered mainly training and advice, and in fewer instances financial incentives. A large proportion of the work done by large tour operators to improve the sustainability of their service providers is by promoting the economic advantages of reducing water, waste and energy costs through being more environmentally friendly.

There are fewer examples of tour operators engaging their suppliers in improving their socioeconomic records, for example by providing better labour relations, support to communities or the use of local produce. For many specialist tour operators, sustainability is part of the product quality sought by tourists. In this case there are few examples for supplier development, but usually because a minimum sustainability requirement was part of the selection criteria.

Most tour operators are not likely to pay a higher price to their suppliers for sustainability. Generally they argue that sustainability is an element of the expected quality, and that it will also bring (in particular in the area of environmental practices in the accommodation sector) major cost savings. Supplier development initiatives are generally voluntary, with few examples of tour operators making them mandatory. Several large tour operators have reported that between 10 and 25% of suppliers have met the voluntary 'sustainability related' standards (for example Kuoni Switzerland, TUI, MyTravel Northern Europe, First Choice, Hotelplan). Tour operators are most successful in convincing long-term suppliers, and those that are owned or managed by the same parent company. Few tour operators highlight those suppliers that are more sustainable in their brochures.

The Reiseanalyse 2002 survey in Germany showed that tourists demand such information, but it is likely that many tour operators will not want to do so until a certain volume of their products have met the necessary standards, and they can send a positive reassuring message to the market.

The large German tour operator LTU Touristik distributed 16,000 environmental management manuals to accommodation suppliers in German, English, French, Italian, Spanish, and Greek. Impacts are rated by time and cost required to make a significant improvement. The manual is the result of long term development involving suppliers and destinations, and LTU Touristik requires feedback from hoteliers on the manual's usefulness and the hotels' performance. Hotels implementing this manual best are those managed by LTU itself and those where LTU brings a high percentage of their business.

Hello Tuscany promotes to young people a positive experience of sustainable tourism: the Summer Camps in Tuscany. Summer camps seem to be a very pleasant experience, since they combine the attraction of natural parks, a real interaction with a beautiful environment, and with local people with their own historical traditions. Kel 12 is a small Italian tour operator specialising in adventure holidays mainly in Africa, even though their presence is now widespread everywhere from the Sahara to China to South America.

It promotes the marketing of sustainable tourism products by working with destination agencies that share the same philosophy, including sustainability as purchasing criteria, running conservation and community projects in the field, and engaging consumers in projects. Examples of projects include protecting part of the Gabon forest, buying the rights on territories instead of the concessions involved in cutting wood, as well as a Sahara project to prevent accumulating big amounts of plastic waste using plastic tanks for water instead of plastic bottles.

The Dutch Tour Operator Association ANVR requires members to appoint and train a responsible tourism coordinator; develop and implement a responsible tourism policy; report annually to ANVR on at least one sustainability measure per each of five areas (accommodation, transport, recreation/excursions, consumers information and internal sustainability); and not offer travel products that are forbidden according to the developed list of irresponsible travel products. Similar requirements are being introduced in the UK through the Federation of Tour Operators.

Guidebooks

Most guidebooks are produced by independent commercial publishers. Although some guides might be openly commissioned as marketing tools by individual travel companies, guidebook publishers are generally independent of the travel industry. They identify products and destinations, giving objective opinions (both good and bad), and are sold to consumers, including conventional tourists and business travellers. These guides rely on the quality and objectivity of their messages to be trusted by travellers. Additional revenue can be earned from advertising and the production of associated online editions, but the most trusted guidebooks keep their information independent from commercial ties.

Freelance travel writers are commissioned to write individual books. In general, the appointed writers receive a very specific brief by the guidebook editing team, which outlines the guide. the structure to follow, including the characteristics of the companies to be included in the guide. The authors also receive (in particular if their task is an 'update') all the information collected on the country and in particular on hotels and tourism services that they will have to personally review. The briefs are developed taking into account the specific target audience. In general however, travel guides are increasingly including sustainability charters, as well as sections on environmental and socioeconomic issues at the destinations.

These writers research hotels, restaurants and attractions following the criteria of the travel guide according to their market positioning and unique selling proposition. Many guidebooks emphasise unique, exciting and interesting products that are aligned to the principles of sustainable tourism, although few will use explicit criteria for the selection of what towns and companies are to be included, and the final decision depends on space and a balance between different destinations and types of product. Sustainability is often referred to as far as it is part of the exciting and unique attributes that the independent tourist is seeking.

The companies publishing traditional guidebooks are evolving to produce customised guidebooks, spin-off guides and unique travel information, licensed use of web engine or travel information, and to selling photographs. Travel information is now not only coming in the typical guidebook form, but also increasingly in electronic form, whether on websites or in phone/PDA formats. All of these provide new niche opportunities for tourism companies and destinations. Highly professional guidebooks are now also being produced by non-governmental organisations and campaign groups, for which the motivation is development assistance, rather than commercial profit. The focus is increasingly shifting to the consumer, since publishers are discovering that these publications meet a market need, giving objective (and entirely noncommercial) advice on obscure community-led tourism products, offering consumers access to 'authentic experiences' with less of the more negative aspects of tourism. By being produced by not-for-profit organisations, consumers treat contents as a strong seal of quality assurance, which helps increase sales of sustainable tourism products, which in turn promotes best practice in tourism and across the industry.

As in the case of travel media, the ability to be included in a guidebook depends on whether the product can be presented as being exciting, quirky and unique. Sustainability is sometimes the reason why a product is interesting, but the message has to be tailored with the tourist experience as the centre of attention. The guidebooks support sustainable tourism products within the limits of having to honestly report about quality of the services provided, and when a company with a sustainable ideology provides sub-standard services, this has to be highlighted.

Over 100,000 Lonely Planet travellers use the electronic Thorn Tree travellers' bulletin boards on a regular basis, where travellers can exchange information on destinations and experiences, and plan their next adventure. This makes Lonelyplanet.com a vibrant heavily trafficked global travel resource. Lonely Planet also sends a monthly email newsletter to thousands of readers.

Lonely Planet's Shoestring guides have a large readership amongst young people travelling for the first time. These guides include extensive information on responsible behaviour in their travels, and the choices of places to visit reinforce this *philosophy. Lonely Planet has however been questioned for publishing a guide that encourages tourism to Burma* (Myanmar (Burma). *8th ed., 2002.), despite their claims that the guide raises awareness and supports the type of firms that will least* support financially the oppressive regime.

Sustainability is at the core of Lonely Planet, although this has so far happened more intuitively than strategically. The company is now examining how they formalise their commitment to sustainability. Their French branch has produced an Ethical Charter, and Lonely Planet Europe would consider explicit sustainability guidelines for both their authors of guides, and for the suppliers of services to be featured. In their own forecast they estimate that in 10 years, 40 to 50% of the products listed in their guides could have verified sustainability credentials.

Tourism Concern, which "campaigns for ethical and fairly traded tourism" is currently planning the third edition of it's the Good Alternative Travel Guide. *Working through its large international network of tourism stakeholders, known as the 'Fair* Trade in Tourism Network', it is able to identify a wide range of sustainable tourism products, including community-based tourism initiatives primarily and responsible tour operators.

With Access to Extensive Language skills, the Organisation is not constrained by having to communicate in English, and is able to research many products in often remote and marginal destinations. Products that pass a preliminary review are sent a questionnaire (in an appropriate language), which is used as the basis of assessment and to determine which products meet sufficient criteria of fair trade and responsibility to be included. There is no fee for inclusion, although there is some income from advertising, and those that are rejected are offered advice and guidance on best practice, since "the objective is to change the industry". Two hundred products were included in the guide's second edition, of which 10,000 copies have been sold, and which is supplemented by promotion at trade fairs and online listings. Tourism Concern's website receives 9,000 unique site visits each month, making this a highly effective medium. Feedback from suppliers has been extremely positive, with over 100 new suppliers contacting.

Tourism Concern in the past twelve months seeking inclusion in the next edition, reflecting the recommendations and value placed on the medium by existing suppliers. According to Tourism Concern, the guide is particularly valued by suppliers, because the organisation "shares information across its network", promoting best practice and contributing to the development of 'fair trade in tourism'. Whilst for consumers, *who are "a bit more socially* *responsible" and "want to take a different kind of holiday", its value is that it is "not just a marketing tool", but is "*effectively *a certification scheme". Some consumers seek product endorsement, whilst suppliers* recognise the benefits of working with an independent organisation with fifteen years of international network experience. Insofar as the guide is a tool for normalising sustainability and promoting best practice, Tourism Concern describes the guide's contents as "tourism that's developed in the context of sustainable development".

Media

Media includes the travel section of mainstream newspapers and consumer magazines, as well as dedicated travel magazines. Most income comes from advertising revenue, whilst the content primarily consists of stories, reviews and features about particular destinations and products. Newspapers also offer commercial opportunities through affiliate marketing initiatives (endorsing and featuring holiday offers in the newspapers for a commission for the newspaper instead of paying a price for the advert). The travel pages of newspapers are the key promotional channel for specialist tour operators other than word of mouth.

But, just as the point of newspapers is to sell news, the point of travel journalism is to promote travel. Therefore, according to *The Independent*, sustainability is "not an issue", because ultimately "people want to go on holiday, even if they want to travel more *thoughtfully*". The newspaper has certain values, which means that it will tend to encourage community-led tourism and promote small guest houses, cycling and public transport, but it also has a commercial need to gain advertising revenue, which cannot be constrained by considerations of sustainability, on which there is no specific policy. The editorial view is that for consumers, the theme of 'sustainable tourism' is "boring... like travel insurance", but that at the same time 'sustainable tourism products' are generally "more interesting", (said the freelance journalists interviewed for this report).

Travel pages of newspapers have a small team of staff editors that commission the work from freelance editors, who have to pitch ideas that are original, new, interesting and also good ideas for holidays. Freelance writers look for ideas that will sell. Funnelling interesting stories from the tourism provider and the travel media is the gap. Training tourism companies on how the media operates, and how to identify the relevant freelance journalists with the right stories is crucial. Original, quirky, interesting stories of exciting and unique places to go and things to do have the greatest potential to be featured in the travel pages. The emphasis sought by freelance journalists and travel editors is on why these are good holidays. Giving money to charities, investing in schools, saving turtles all play a part in the feature, but not in the opening paragraphs. In doing so the media contributes to consumer education in a more subliminal way. A feature on the importance of responsible tourism per se would only be a story once, while this way there is a way to keep communicating the underlying principles.

Tourism firms need to plan the message to be communicated, emphasising first why it is exciting and unique. They require thinking from the point of view of the consumer, and not focusing first on conservation, and they first have to make an interesting travel proposition.

Messages need to be newsworthy, so products are easiest to be featured when they are new. For products that have been on the market for some time, companies need to think of ways to reinvent messages in the public relations tradition to ensure their products have maximum exposure. For example, the UK project promoting bicycle routes 'Sustrans' had already received extensive exposure for their work in the 1990s, and yet they are being featured again for introducing public artwork along their routes to attract more families to cycling. Celebrities visiting a sustainable tourism company and supporting the cause is another way of getting repeated exposure.

Several newspapers run travel awards that highlight good practice and have become great marketing methods for the few companies winning. *The Times* dedicated four pages to the winners of their Responsible Tourism Awards (organized by the online travel agent responsibletravel.com, in association with *The Times*, World Travel Market and *Geographical Magazine*). Many independent tour operators use their winning status to promote themselves, and a number of sustainable tourism products have dramatically increased their bookings and reputation through winning one of these awards.

The Guardian *newspaper in the UK runs a monthly column called The Green Light, featuring responsible holidays, based on market research that identified a gap in the market. "Go diving with octopuses" was the incentive to read about an* Earthwatch project in Costa Rica monitoring octopuses and their habitat. The tour operator Discovery Initiatives was featured in two mainstream UK television travel programmes, The Holiday Programme and Wish You Were Here. In both cases the productions were well received and stimulated a great deal of interest. The Holiday Programme feature was further repeated in at least one revised format suggesting recognition by the producers of the value of this type of holiday.

Certification Schemes

Certification schemes highlight sustainable tourism products. They have a dual function of helping tourism suppliers to raise their sustainability standards, and providing market mechanisms to increase trade gained from having the brand of the ecolabel. There are over 60 initiatives, targeting mostly the accommodation sector, and mainly in Europe. Most of them have started since the mid 1990s, with 20 more in development at present.

These schemes have the dual role of increasing industry performance by providing guidelines on how to be more sustainable, directing applicants towards sources of help and in some cases providing advice directly, and at the same time providing marketing benefits. As the certification programs grow, they are promoting the certified companies to both distribution channels and to consumers.

However, there are too many labels, with few certified products each, to have an impact on the market. Consolidation of current labels for international recognition, and repositioning of the labels as being an extension to traditional product quality (particularly for ecotourism markets) are obvious avenues forward. In only a few instances will sustainability be a unique selling proposition that can be meaningfully branded.

The certified product is not meaningful to the consumer for two reasons: firstly, lack of awareness, and secondly, the perception that it does not have significantly different attributes. Consumers cannot tell from the available information whether a certified product is better than the average product, on the points that matter to the tourist. The small number of certified companies, and the fact that the basic quality attributes are very different (a 5 star hotel and a guest house can have the same environmental label) means that choosing providers based on an ecolabel is not likely. This is partly attributed to the fact that certification programs have no in-house marketing or communications specialists.

VISIT is the acronym for 'Voluntary Initiatives for Sustainability In Tourism', the result of 10 ecolabels uniting forces to raise standards across Europe and to benefit from the economies of scale of joint marketing and lobbying. The EU funded project Tourlink supports tour operators to standardise their sustainability checklists with those of certification programmes. This will create more transparent and cost-effective distribution systems for certified companies, and reduce technical barriers to trade from multiple but similar standards.

Green Travel Market offers tour operators a tool for receiving reliable, up-to-date information on more sustainable tourism products currently available on the market, screened for quality and sustainability. Amongst others it includes over 1000 certified accommodation providers in Europe. The Sustainable Tourism Certification Network of the Americas aims to make sustainable tourism firms more competitive by providing market advantages through certification. The goal is to involve 175 enterprises in certification by 2007.

Technical assistance to suppliers to date includes 21 trainers trained, 507 entrepreneurs trained, and 1686 introduced to best management practices through seminars. This effort is being implemented in four pilot countries by Rainforest Alliance-Costa Rica, Alianza Verde in Guatemala, the Ecuadorian Ecotourism Association (ASEC),and Programme for Belize.

Consumer and Trade Fairs

Travel and tourism suppliers ranging from individual products to national tourist boards use fairs to present their goods and services to travel trade buyers and consumers, including prospective tourists and business organisations. Key sectors of the fairs market include leisure tourism, independent travel and MICE (Meetings, Incentives, Conferences & Exhibitions although in North America and Asia Pacific, the 'C' is usually 'Conventions').

The number of specialised fairs addressing the topic of sustainable, eco and responsible tourism is increasing, while traditional national fairs are developing these themes as well by offering specific events or pavilions and forum of discussions. Individual companies are unlikely to attend many fairs, particularly small providers, for cost reasons. Learning about the market is useful, particularly at the early stages of developing a company. The majority of firms will not be able to justify the cost, even when they are selling under the umbrella of the national tourist board's stand.

Business travel, as evidenced by the MICE sector, has traditionally not been considered particularly relevant to sustainable tourism, but this is changing. With the growing importance of 'corporate governance' in business and the associated shareholder exposure to corporate risk, buyers are increasingly seeking out suppliers that have strong sustainability credentials, and are asking to see companies' environmental policies and evidence of 'corporate social responsibility'.

The Centre for the Promotion of Imports for Developing Countries, an agency of the Netherlands' Ministry of Foreign Affairs, sponsors community based tourism and NGO's under certain conditions and provides marketing assistance prior, during and after the Vakantiebeurs' Fair in Utrecht, Netherlands, such as brochure and website design and negotiation skills, as well as organising meetings with relevant tour operators.

Reisepavillon is the alternative travel fair running annually in Hanover, Germany, attracting 250 stands from 50 countries in 2004 (the 13th year of operations, up 10% from 2003). There is a high exhibitor turnover, with 39% of new exhibitors, and 20% of non returns. Networking of experts provides the edge to this fair, with parallel meetings and project briefings by associations and institutions such as Ecotrans, Bund für Umwelt-und Naturschutz, Viabono, WWF, Naturfreunde and GTZ, the German Agency for Environmental Co-Operation. GTZ supports the fair by organising the industry networking and training event, Tourismus Forum International (TFI), and also bringing 20% of the stands by showcasing developing ecotourism projects from developing countries.

Consumer fairs such as Chicago and New York have rebranded from specialist adventure shows to more mainstream to attract a broader public and companies. In doing so they have attracted first time buyers for specific product types such as adventure and eco tourism because the fairs showcase products not usually found in travel agencies, with actual sales made on the show. These fairs are days out, with 22,000 people paying USD 15,00 each to enter the New York Adventure and Travel Expo. The activity holidays and shortbreak tour operator Inntravel organises a day long travel fairs where suppliers from all over Europe are invited to the UK to meet directly with customers. The fairs are held every three years in different parts of the country, with the most recent in December 2004 in North Yorkshire. About 120 suppliers (including hotel owners, restauranteurs and service providers such as ski-hire companies) presented their products and services to 1000 customers and potential customers. Attendance is by ticket only because of the high demand, although tickets are free. Inntravel staff – including directors, product managers and sales staff are on hand to answer enquiries and take bookings.

IMEX is the leading MICE fair held each year in Frankfurt, with three schemes to showcase best practice and to promote corporate social responsibility in its sector. These are gaining in prestige and each year attract a growing number of applications. The Programmes of Purpose Award for Social Responsibility "recognises meeting organisers who have put together meetings or incentives benefiting the local community – undertaking charitable acts can be inspirational to participants as well as lastingly beneficial to the community concerned".

The Environmentally Responsible Meetings Award (in association with IHEI and Oceans Blue Foundation) "recognises environmental awareness amongst meeting organisers, highlighting the opportunities that now exist to stage business tourism events in 'green-minded' venues, whilst also planning an agenda in which sustainability issues have been taken fully into account". The Free Wild Card Places is one of the most innovative awards, enabling emerging destinations with MICE potential to participate and access new markets.

Internet Retailers

These are on-line retailers, in some cases complementing conventional operators and agents, but usually they are a global distribution system for mainstream products. This category also includes holiday auction sites and over-branded in-house websites used to sell distressed stock. There are very few sites that are selective and control their product according to strict quality criteria, and sometimes they act as 'matchmakers' between suppliers and operators. Retailers act as sales agents and sell products direct to consumers, and also via travel agents. Income is mainly from commission, and also advertising revenue and registration fees. The distinction between 'matchmakers' and 'sales agents' is both practical and legal. Whilst both might gain a commission from the transaction, a 'matchmaker' introduces potential clients to suppliers (and sometimes vice versa), whilst an 'agent' sells the tourism services of a supplier directly to customers, although consumers might be under the impression that they are dealing directly with the supplier.

Internet retailers can also be divided into two categories: high volume-low margin and low volume-high margin. The large internet retailers compete on price and supply a commodity market, whilst the many small ones focus on specialist products, particular niche markets or are dedicated to a small number of suppliers, sometimes in a single destination. The smaller retailers therefore gain tremendous expertise, but at the expense of a balanced portfolio, which would reduce their exposure to the risk of an unexpected fall in their chosen field.

The websites of vertically integrated tour operators, such as TUI, Thomas Cook and MyTravel, and those of other large tourism service providers, such as international hotel groups, airlines and car hire firms, are not considered here. This is because such websites are an extension of conventional retailing, rather than representing a specialist distribution channel.

However, unlike holidays booked through tour operators (whether online, by telephone or through a travel agent), consumers will often not have the same protection provided them by the Council Directive on package travel, package holidays and package tours (90/314/EEC of 13 June 1990). Thus, whilst the larger internet retailers have developed fairly comprehensive contractual and regulatory frameworks that offer a measure of protection to consumers, the smaller ones have adopted a more precautionary approach, to protect both their customers and their own businesses. Many have therefore adopted more of a 'matchmaking' role, so that their legal agency (and liability) is limited, but their ability to freely make a much wider range of specific recommendations is enhanced. Consumer confidence in the smaller retailers thus becomes a function of commercial independence and transparency.

One of the fastest growing internet retailers is the UK-based responsibletravel.com, which has grown by 250% each year since its launch in April 2001. It acts as an 'introducer' for suppliers, matching suppliers to customers and also bringing together suppliers and operators. Its 260 suppliers in 140 countries are known as 'partners' or 'members' and between them offer 2,000 individual products; its customers are primarily in English-speaking markets, with 80% in the UK, but this is changing.

Every supplier is carefully screened and each product must fulfil specific criteria that include environmental, social and economic policy. This process typically takes 7-10 days. All partners must have the capacity to respond to email enquiries in English within 48 hours. Each partner pays an annual fee, which ranges from nothing for community-led enterprises to more than £5,000 for the largest tour operator, plus commission per converted enquiry, which is never more than 10%. The company insists that it is "not a middle man, because the supplier knows best". Thus, it generates booking enquiries for its partners, who are then responsible for converting these into sales.

With a strapline inviting visitors to "Find 1000's of holidays to 100's of places not ravaged by mass tourism", the company distinguishes itself from the larger internet retailers, like lastminute.com and Expedia, both of which have huge brand recognition but which lack the capacity to deal so individually with customers. Its objective is to "market responsible tourism as a different and better product than less responsible tourism". Many of responsibletravel.com's "best sellers are wildlife trips, walking holidays... [and] more adventurous family holidays". Given that such products are nowadays in fact very mainstream, this indicates that the online marketing of sustainable tourism is no longer a niche activity. A leading UK tour operator has reported that it achieves more sales through responsibletravel.com than through any other internet retailer.

Consumers of such products however inevitably require a lot of information which only the supplier can furnish. A customer identifies a product through the company's website (with every page individually subjected to highly sophisticated search engine optimization) or through one of its increasingly numerous newspaper supplements, sends an enquiry (via the website) to the supplier, who responds with full information and booking details. Such a service could not be offered by large retailers, if only because enabling such communication would put their commission at risk, but it is part of the unique proposition of responsible travel.com. This process is, of course, subject to audit which is possible for a relatively small operation.

Known primarily as a B2C agent, responsibletravel.com is particularly proud of some of its B2B activities: enabling tiny community tourism businesses to engage with leading international tour operators, helping numerous journalists to identify some excellent sustainable tourism products, generating significant PR opportunities and additional business for its members. It has rarely lost a member, because it offers good value for money and has created a community of suppliers and customers that value authenticity and the direct approach. Apart from offering all the usual add-on products, such as flights, travel clothes and insurance, the company also offers 'Tips for responsible travellers'.

Consumer Organizations

Consumer organisations promote the rights and interests of their members, through product testing, policy lobbying and conducting information campaigns. Consumer organisations whose mandate is to protect consumer rights are increasingly showing interest in the sustainability of products as part of their overall quality, and as such are reporting quality and sustainability standards to their members.

These communicate and distribute a range of information to their members that influences purchasing behaviour, and in many cases they also provide holiday accommodation and booking services. Consumer organisations' recommendations to their members are powerful marketing tools because of high member loyalty and because their assessments are perceived as independent.

In addition to general consumer organisations, there are 'membership' associations such as automobile and caravanning associations. The Alliance Internationale de Tourisme (AIT) and the Federation Internationale del' Automobile (FIA) have more than 42 million members in Europe, and 100 million plus members globally. They are champions of the 'mobile consumer', with the focus of their public policy agenda being sustainable mobility, road safety, consumer protection and testing, environment and tourism. Their work has focused on increasing the quality and safety of driving, and within this, driving holidays. These clubs promote cleaner emissions, reducing road congestion and increasing safety.

Promoting sustainable tourism has to be seen within the remits of both organisations. For automobile clubs this means they are information providers within the mandate of consumer protection. They have enormous media resources and reach with strong brands and reputations. The ADAC association in Germany is considered more credible by young people than the Church and Green Peace, while in the Netherlands three out five households have ANWB membership. The services these consumer organisations provide to their members include hotel guides, camping and caravanning guides, maps, holiday guide books and route planners amongst others based on the clubs' own inspections, evaluations and assessments which take some sustainable practices into account.

Camping and caravanning associations, in particular, have engaged with a range of environmental actions for their own sites, and setting criteria for other sites. In the UK the Caravan Club has an alliance with the Royal Society for the Protection of Birds as 11% of CC members are members of RSBP. AIT & FIA conduct environmental audits for camping and caravan sites, support for the new European tourist accommodation Eco-label, and the monitoring of European Bathing Water Quality.

The Consumers Union (USA) is considering sustainability certification as the criteria for including tourism suppliers in their travel directory. This is within their organisational remit of providing unbiased product testing and consumer information to protect the interests of consumers. Their publications have 6 million subscribers in the United States alone, and are part of the Consumers International global network of 250 organisations in 110 countries. The Alliance Internationale de Tourisme & Federation Internationale del'Automobile would consider a policy to increase the coverage of sustainable tourism issues in the magazines of their national member associations within Europe. *The Camping and Caravanning Club (UK) operates over 100 club sites, and is starting to operate franchised sites. With over 400,000 loyal members, the club provides one of the strongest camp site brands. One of their most recent acquisitions in the Lake District has been renovated to the gold standard in the Cumbria for Excellence 2004 awards in the Caravan Holiday Park category, and was quoted by* The Guardian *newspaper as possibly the greenest camp site in the UK.*

Analysis

Traditionally governments, inter-governmental organisations and non-governmental organisations have encouraged sustainable tourism by focusing mainly on the supply side of the tourism industry, or on promoting responsible citizenship through consumer education, with the aim of increasing demand. Matching supply and demand is the missing link. Specific policies should then be designed to support the linkage between sustainable consumers and sustainable tourism products by strengthening the opportunities offered by the various distribution tools.

The four issues used to assess each of the eight distribution channels under consideration are designed to indicate the relative value of each tool. It is generally recommended that policies should be based on the ability to promote change of tourism suppliers that is equitable, with potential for market penetration, a positive cost-benefit analysis, and normalization or mainstreaming potential.

Supplier equity: High/Low-'High' indicating that this tool/ channel is extremely accessible on fair terms to a wide range of suppliers Market penetration potential: Strong/Weak-'Strong' indicating that this tool/channel has significant reach (B2B or B2C) Cost benefit analysis (supplier perspective): Positive/Negative-'Positive' indicating that the receipts and other business benefits produced by this tool/channel can reasonably be expected to outweigh any costs associated with participation Normalisation potential: Strong/Weak-'Strong' indicating that this tool/channel has the potential to be used to promote and encourage a more sustainable development and environmental management of travel and tourism products

Supplier Equity

Equity, understood as the ability of companies to have the same opportunities to access knowledge, loans, distribution channels, and to promote their products, is the first attribute used to analyse these tools. Public sector intervention in the marketplace has usually been justified on the basis of promoting equal access. Policy makers should promote equitable tools, and contribute to the equity of the different tools, because otherwise the danger is that only a few privileged companies will be able to market themselves as sustainable, through no fault of the remaining companies.

Destination management companies, tourist boards and guidebooks have the highest level of equity in as far as all companies can have the same access to use these channels. Communicating and distributing through tour operators and internet retailers have varied equity because it depends on the ability to set commercial relations with them, and to accept the commissions they charge. Media, travel fairs and certification schemes have low equity, because they require capital investment usually with little guarantee of return, only few companies can be featured, or there are no schemes available.

Training at an early stage is crucial to support product and destination planning. Marketing training will help to set realistic targets, and to create more level playing fields that will make all instruments more equitable. Policies should support companies and destination management organisations to learn about their markets, particularly about expectations and purchasing patterns, and how this affects the marketing and service delivery. Development plans should be realistic and market the marketable, as part of a plan for sustained and balanced growth.

Market Penetration Potential

Some distribution channels have the potential to make a considerable contribution towards changing the behaviour of the market they target. For all these markets, the greatest potential is to change behaviour in the adventure, ecotourism, nature tourism markets where sustainability is part of the quality of the product both experienced and expected, as the potential market is already sympathetic to the philosophies of sustainable tourism.

DMOs and tourist boards rarely reach the actual markets, although increasingly internet marketing portals are achieving where print publications failed. These are custodians of the destination brand and as such can create interest in a certain destination. Providing an internet sales portal that allows efficient bookings increases the potential for market penetration.

Suppliers can achieve considerable market penetration through tour operators, with many examples in the past of over relying on few operators, that subsequently meant suppliers losing entrepreneurial skills and self-control. Travel guides are important marketing tools because they reach a large number of people within one given target market, and the readership of these travel guides use the information to make purchasing choices. However, individual suppliers need to consider working with travel guides as a mid-term investment, as there is no guarantee that they will be featured, and there is a considerable lead time between preparing information and the publication date. The media can generate short-term interest in specific destinations and provide a boost to companies starting with creative, unique concepts. But media has a short self life and cannot be relied on.

Certification has limited potential for market penetration at present because the marketing know-how as well as resources of certification programs are insufficient to reach consumers. The focus should therefore be on business to business marketing and lobbying tour operators that certified products can guarantee sustainability. While progress is being made in this respect, it is too early to say what the potential actually is. Travel fairs have very limited potential for market penetration, particularly business to consumer. They are better tools to reaffirm current working relationships with distribution channels, and to learn about market trends. Internet retailers also have a high potential for market penetration, although this depends on the type of product and market targeted, and there is often a high commission to pay for internet retailers. "Dynamic packaging" that allows consumers to pick and choose different components of a holiday from the same travel site to form a personalized package. Finally, direct marketing has good potential for niche marketing, and to encourage repeat purchases.

Companies should think about promoting to the domestic market, and the extension of current products, before trying to attract new "hard-to-reach" international tourists. Donor-funded projects in particular should be realistic about the ability to generate markets from small interventions. Many funded projects cannot be self-financed in the long run through poor understanding of market needs, simply incorporating tourism as a form of income generation for conservation projects without developing the necessary skills, or market-led product planning which sets unachievable expectations.

Cost-benefit Analysis

Cost-effectiveness is the third key issue reviewed here to consider the suitability of different tools. These are considered both from the point of view of government intervention as well as the investment for tourism companies. DMOs and tourist boards are cost-effective ways for small firms to market themselves, membership costs are usually low for the service received as these organisations receive central funding to contribute to their fixed costs. Most governments undertake economic impact assessments that suggest that public sector investment in marketing functions generates a return on investment into the economy through tourism revenues in the region of 8 to 1. Policy makers are also increasingly being asked to contribute to the running of certification programs, as an extension of their duties in quality assurance.

The challenge here is that all these programs require substantial subsidies, and despite individual examples of good practice, the impact on the market is not sufficient to justify the investment. These certification programs need to move towards being self-financing. In the same way, many travel fairs require subsidies and growth is hindered by the potential benefits they can deliver, and by how many fairs one company can attend.

Distribution tools that do not require public financial support include tour operators, guidebooks, and internet retailers. Marketing to tour operators is also a cost-effective method to reach markets. There are directories of outbound operators for most key markets, and the national tourist boards of the destination country should provide the necessary market intelligence to support targeted campaigns. In the same way, marketing to internet retailers is cost-effective if the company can survive with the commissions charged, and if reasonable yield management arrangements are made. Guidebooks are a cost-effective method for unique products with a high chance of being included. However, as there is no control of how the product is featured, the supplier might not agree with how they are portrayed. Getting a good review in the media can make a significant difference to the launch of a product. But spending too long on a media campaign could be cost ineffective if the product does not have uniqueness. Finally, direct marketing can be cost-effective for specific markets and to capitalize on consumer loyalty.

5

Cooperation in Tourism

More on Co-Operation in Tourism

Statistical support is one of the major tools needed for a better understanding of the tourism sector. The finalisation of a new Statistical Regulation in the field of tourism is in an advanced state and it is expected to enter in force in 2010. At the same time, the Commission, together with Member States and in collaboration with OECD and the World Tourism Organisation, is promoting the introduction of TSA (Tourism Satellite Account) in Member States. TSA is a statistical accounting framework in the field of tourism to measure the goods and services according to international standards of concepts, classifications and definitions, which allow valid comparisons from country to country in a consistent manner. A complete TSA contains detailed production accounts of the tourism industry and their linkages to other industries, employment, capital formation and additional nonmonetary information on tourism.

Enhancing the visibility of European tourism is another of our main goals. To draw attention to the value, diversity and shared characteristics of European tourist destinations, and to promote destinations where the economic growth objective is pursued in such a way as to ensure the social, cultural and environmental sustainability of tourism, the European Commission is running the European Destinations of Excellence (EDEN) preparatory action. Some of the main aims of such a preparatory action are enhancing visibility of the emerging European tourist destinations of excellence, especially the lesser known, and creating awareness of Europe's tourist diversity and quality.

The Commission also intends highlighting the richness and diversity of European tourism through its Calypso programme, which seeks to facilitate tourism exchanges in Europe.

Finally, again in the direction of cooperation with other actors of the tourism sector, and with the aim of strengthening European tourism, the Commission proposed an operational framework through the organisation of a number of events. Such events are deemed important in order to improve the interface between European tourism stakeholders. One of the measures provided are an annual European Tourism Forum, which normally brings together more than 300 leading representatives from the tourism industry, civil society, European Institutions, national and regional authorities dealing with tourism, and international organisations to discuss the challenges of the sector. Every year the Forum focuses on specific themes of interest.

E-Collaboration: A Universal Key to Solve Fierce Competition in Tourism Industry?

The development of Internet technology and the dramatic spread of its use throughout the world in the past decade brought business into a new stage, a stage known 'e-time'.

Before 'e' time, tourism industry players mainly maintained workable vertical relationships with its suppliers and their sales force (Appleman & Go 2002). The walls of each company's office were not just physical bricks; they were also the spiritual boundaries isolating the company from its horizontal neighbours who do similar business. While drivers in the business environment such as globalization, regionalization, information technology and e-commerce decreased barrier effect of brick walls (Timothy 2003). Consumers are becoming more experienced. Competition between organisations by throwing bricks to each other can no longer lead to success (Stern & Hicks 2000).

This article starts with relevant definitions of e-collaboration and the description of the change in the business environment and then analyses these motivations, advantages and the problems of e-collaboration in the tourism industry. Multinatinational enterprise (MNE) and small business/tourism organisations are tending to adapt e-collaborative strategies. Gartner (2001) predicts that 70% of firms will have a coherent e-business strategy within a year. However, this is not a universal key if being used improperly. Addressing the theories of collaboration and e-business in other industries and trying to find a way of applying them to today's tourism industry players to create and guide thriving e-collaboration strategies is the main aim of this article.

E-collaboration bridges national borders and continents. E-collaboration and collaborative systems bring geographically dispersed teams together, supporting communication, coordination and cooperation. Indeed, it has become a cornerstone of global competition (Doz & Hamel 1998; Timothy 2003). It is a logical and timely response to the quick change in the economic and IT world and split organizations into two competition divisions: one for the global market, one for the future development.

Relevant Definitions

E-Business

This field of activity is relatively young and evolving rapidly, and as such no single definition of the term has become accepted as the universal norm (Clegg *et al* 2001). E-business was initially limited to the financial transactions online. It was coined with a meaning of conducting business on the Internet by IBM back in 1997 as part of an advertising campaign. For the purposes of this essay, both business-to-business (B2B) and business-to-consumer (B2C) transactions and relationships are considered. Thus, e-business here is defined as the transaction of commercial activities on global open networks between an ever-increasing number of corporate and individual participants (Richmond *et al.* 1998).

Collaboration

According to Cambridge Advanced Learner's Dictionary (2003), collaboration means working jointly with others or together for some purpose or achieve the same thing. Words like strategic alliance, collaborative partnership, collaborative form, collaboration, partnership, and coalition are interchangeable utilized (Fyall & Spyriadis 2003).

E-collaboration is an extension from the old collaboration type in e-age. It is Internet-based cooperation/collaboration with exchange of information, materials, or cash among entities (Brown & Sappenfield 2003).

The Changing of the Business Environment

Information is the "lifeblood" of tourism. Since the tourism products can not be pre-tested, the access to accurate, timely and relevant information is therefore essential to consumers. Before the spread of Internet, telephone, fax, letter and face-to-face meeting were the main communication channels between suppliers and buyers. The generation, gathering, processing, application and communication of information was time consuming (O'Connor *et al* 2002).

Consumers almost completely relied on representation and description to make an appropriate choice (Go and Pine 1995). Intermediaries played a very important role between disciplines and end-customers. Collaborations between horizontal tourism players were very rare.

While technology can act as a 'creator, enhancer, focal point and/or destroyer of the tourism experience' as O'Connor (2002 p332) indicated, the development of IT brought the business world a revolution of electronic. Business-related "dotcom" Web sites emerged all over the virtual world. A matching between buyer and seller was set up. Andy Grove, the chairman of Intel, predicted in 1999 that, within five years, all companies will be Internet companies or they will not exist.

As web-based technologies expanded, core back-office processes, including order management, procurement, logistics, financial management, and supply chain planning was incorporated (Gould 2004). The barriers and distance competitors were reduced. Information flows among the client, intermediaries and each of the suppliers involved in serving the client's needs. New relationships with customers, new relationships between competitors and suppliers and buyers, new business process, new information and communications technologies came into being and empowered employees are required.

Motivations for Collaboration

Globalization and regionalisation are emerging worldwide. This macro environment stimulates the development of IT; and the development of IT enhances the integration inversely. Hastings (1993) states that the need for 'quality, as well as the high costs and complexity of servicing global markets' is forcing organisations into collaborating with their clients, their suppliers and with their competitors in many new ways.

The power of IT allows information to be managed more effectively, and transported worldwide almost instantly (Frew and Pringle 1995). The physical boundaries between brick walls or territories can't block the information flow. Smaller countries, organisations, in particular, can benefit by gaining access to a much larger market than that in their own territories; large economic regions become available to them for sale of their goods and services (Timothy 2003).

From horizontal view, market is limited, the more ratio one company occupies, the less other companies occupies. But competitors in well-matched strength always exist. It's time for antagonists to begin to use the bricks to build something useful instead of throwing bricks at one another (Stern & Hicks 2000). Collaboration offers a way to pursue business development, revenue increase, cost reductions in promotions and marketing and enhance market image and reputation (Fyall & Spyriadis 2003). A partnership of collaboration is a tailored business relationship based on mutual trust, openness, shared risk and shared rewards that yields a competitive advantage, resulting in business performance greater than would be achieved by the firms individually.

In an executive report, META pointed that by 2001/02, high-performing enterprises will recognize the value of business collaboration to achieve flexibility, speed, and agility. By 2004, more than 30% of G2000 companies will have developed a collaborative competency and will use collaborative tools to extract superior value from their collaborative efforts (Passori 2000).

Types of Collaboration

There are three types of collaboration: vertical relationships, horizontal relationships and diagonal relationships. (Fyall & Spyriadis 2003) This is a classifying according to the different structure of collaboration and could suit *International Business Research* October 2008

Vertical Relationship

Vertical relationship is the collaboration between suppliers and buyers e.g. travel operator and travel agency, travel agency and hotel. There is growing emphasis in modern supply chain literature on the importance of forming collaborative strategic partnerships with select trading partners (Kolluru & Meredith 2001). The official site of Scotland's tourism board is one example. The links to travel agencies which sales its products can be found in this website. It offers you the service of journey booking while not owning a travel agency itself.

Horizontal Relationship

Horizontal relationship is the collaboration between competing companies selling similar products or services, e.g. hotel and hotel (Bernal *et al* 2002). In tourism industry, horizontal collaboration happens more often than other two types with the spread of IT. This collaboration can be either inter-organisational which refers to licensing, franchising, sub-contracting and etc under one brand or alliance between different brands. Whichever horizontal collaboration the tourism industry players join, they are separated organisations by law. Orbitz.com, for instance, was initially started by five airlines-American, Continental, Delta, Northwest and United to serve customers better and only sell flight tickets of these five owners. To gain more "click", it encourages other airlines to sell their tickets through its website. At the same time, other airlines are seeking for multi-distribution channels to explore market. Now Orbitz's inventory has hundreds of choices of airlines for customers.

Marriott International has just signed a deal with Hotels.com. As part of the agreement, Marriott will have a direct link to the websites from its own central reservation systems. It will make its inventory of hotel rooms available to the sites.

Diagonal Relationship

Diagonal relationship is the relation where companies in different industries and sectors are working jointly. It's a dynamic structure and is growing follow closely to the other two types of e-collaboration (Brenner 2004).

Grandheritage.com can illustrate this type of collaboration. Grandheritage.com is an online hotel booking website, but it has collaboration with Currency Converter, BBC Weather, Multi Map, British Tourist Authority (a site for events & general information), British Airports Authority, London Transport, UK Genealogy (a site for tracing UK ancestry), Festivals.com (festivals and events in Europe), BITOA (The British Incoming Tour Operators Association), (suppliers of water to hotels), and (low cost car hire). The collaboration is not just limited to the vertical supplier and buyer's relationship and horizontal relationship with competitors, but extends to other industries.

The Influence of E-Collaboration

Advantages

Wider market and better competitive position. Collaborative partners share common reservation system and customer databases. In this way tourism destinations, hotels, travel agencies and etc. can access to worldwide markets despite of the territory boundaries (Fyall & Spyriadis 2003). The collaborated members can market as a whole sometimes (Teye 2000). Hospitality industry is witnessing the growth of technology-based collaboration best. An example of this is the Hilton International (UK based unit of Ladbroke Plc.) and Hilton Hotel Corporation (US based) alliance.

These companies have entered into a relationship that involves sharing customer databases throughout the world. According to Hilton, the objective of this collaboration is to grow the brand to be able to compete on a global basis. Hotels.com is another good example for global market. It is one of the fastest growing hotel booking sites on the Internet. It offers savings of up to 70% off regular hotel rates in some of the world's most popular and expensive cities.

What's more, the collaboration of the hotels guarantees traveller a room when cities are sold out. As Bruce Wolff, Marriott's senior vice president of sales and e-commerce strategy, said on Marriott's collaboration with expedia and hotel.com:' We want to ensure the travelers have access to Marriott properties no matter how they prefer to plan and book travel.'

This advantage is especially helpful to small and medium size tourism industry players. Collaboration through Internet enables them to source components and raw materials so as to widen their market and reputation (Gani 2001).

E-collaboration offers the opportunity for companies to increase the numbers of potential suppliers, and for smaller companies to reach a larger trans-national client base (Leadbetter 1999) 'Through a close collaboration between hotels, restaurants, tourism and commerce, we can cater for anyone who wants to arrange their meeting or conference in Kristianstad or the surrounding area,' says Gunnel Ahlbeck of Turism Kristianstad (2003). When cross-border collaboration and cooperation in tourism promotion are formed, the global competitive advantage is likely to increase (Timothy 2003).

Value Creation

Collaboration between competing firms may create favourable conditions for "inter-partner" learning (Dussage *et al.* 1999), allowing one firm to acquire capabilities that they lack from a partner, particularly when partners from different geographic region. Each partner will bring its product markets, technology, and experience to the collaborated group. A high-speed search and accurate results can be offered to customers with the sharing resources contributed by collaborators (O'Connor *et al* 2002). This caters for the increasing business-to-business or business-to-consumer demands for products and services with a wider resource of combination of each partner's limited resource.

What's more, value creation and its role in business network relationships is becoming an area of increasing interest (Blankenburg-Holm *et al.* 1998 in Bernal 2002) and enables firms to focus on combining internal and external resources in innovative ways.

Inventories Reduction

The closer, long-term, collaborative buyer-supplier relationships, i.e. partnerships, are enabled through seamless integration and transfer of information up and down the chain (Kolluru & Meredith 2001). Strategic SCM can lower inventory risks and costs, improve customer service and satisfaction, increase customer retention and more effective marketing. (Horvath 2000) As distributors enter the same web, data on sales and inventories are received; forecasts are much easier to be made. With the forecasting and planning ability's improvement, collaborators will get benefit to know what to do next clearly. For example, Depkon's Hilton properties use a software application called Birch Street that manages the procurement and inventory at the property level. It allows the properties real-time access to suppliers' inventory. The sound e-collaboration makes the hotel managers focus on the day-to-day issues more and saves the hotel 8 percent to 15 percent (Higley 2004).

Better Communication

E-collaboration enhances inter-organizational relationships. Though reduction in face-to-face contact and an increase in the opportunities for dispersed or paperless offices and people-less factories that have proved to be largely unfounded

(Clegg et al 2001), e-collaboration does allow managers/staff to share information dynamically and far more quickly than previously. It enhances the gain from face to face meetings and other types of communication.

Fewer Cultural Conflicts

As more collaborations are made, defining company culture is critical, especially when companies come from different countries. The social cultural environment will impact the company. While e-collaboration is based online, whether to customers or managers, it is more virtual than physical. Communicating while not working and meeting face to face day to day. Emotion and behavior interference will be less (Stern & Hicks 2000).

Key Problems

Collaboration offers a way out of the fierce competition but it is not a universal key. Without good understanding and preparation, e-collaboration can also damage business. Not all collaboration or alliances or cooperation are successful.

America's Tribune newspaper (2003) has reported a trend of hotel operators breaking away from their franchises and going it alone without big brand backing. The following are several key problems exist in e-collaborative relationship.

Unequal Resource Commitments

Perhaps the most critical thing in collaboration is the degree to which the partners' contributions are committed and complementary (Stern & Hicks2000).

Timothy (2000) pointed that the commitment on the part of individual nations to giving up absolute control in some areas is lack, because national interests nearly always outweigh cross-national interests when he talked out the collaboration between countries. It is a common problem throughout the world where collaboration is being undertaken no matter it is a horizontal collaboration, vertical collaboration or diagonal one.

Unbalanced Management and Power

Unbalanced management and power results from unequal commitment. But no party wants to be at a disadvantage in cooperation. The unbalanced situation sometimes leads to inefficient if dealt wrong.

Different Maintenance of Quality Standards between Partners

Every tourism industry player has different internal needs for different technological and organizational systems and external needs for connectivity and shareability of messages, data, applications and processes (Stern & Hicks 2000). But once collaborated, the reputation and services of each collaborator are bounded together. One comparatively worse website or service will lead to the poor impression of the whole group to customer. And also because of the collaboration of huge database, the difficulty of maintenance is increasing (Bernel *et al* 2002).

Losing the Opportunity for a Creative Solution

Problems are sometimes unavoidable no matter what product and what life stage. When an enterprise meets conflicts or problems entering a market, it might find its own way to solve itself. E-collaboration may need certain managers to negotiate with those who have been in the market and link their websites and database to bridge the markets.

Suggestions and Conclusions

E-collaboration is a very vital strategy for tourism industry players in today's business world. Vertical and horizontal e-collaboration is more often to see in tourism industry than diagonal collaboration. But this type of e-collaboration will be a trend when vertical and horizontal collaboration have developed well. Cooperation between different industries will enhance each other and help each industry's development.

Smartly using this strategy can avoid the fierce competition between hotels, travel agencies and travel operators. As discussed above, e-collaboration can help to widen market, enhance competitive position, add value, reduce cost, bridge communication and lessen cultural conflicts. It is a great strategy more SME to compete with stronger competitors. But Zaid Ismail (2003), senior director of the National Chamber of Commerce and Industry of Malaysia (NCCIM), said though many small and medium size companies have their own websites, not all of them are aware of the benefits of e-business and fully utilize this tool.

Either to small business/tourism organisations or multinational enterprise, to take successful e-collaboration strategy to compete in the global market, the following suggestions should be considered:

- Choose your partner carefully. Every enterprise should know clearly its own strengths and weaknesses before collaborating, and then smartly look for partners that can fit its wants.
- Necessary information technology. The information that an organization communicates with its supply chain partners is among the most critical of its assets. Powerful, integrated collaborative technology is the backbone of an e-collaboration (Vlachopoulou and Manthou 2003). Protection must be provided against external threats and from internal abuse (Kolluru & Meredith 2001). The data that is shared between the partners and customers engaged in these different types of relationships varies widely in its criticality, thus requiring different levels of security.
- Managing the balance of power and dependence. Normally a partner who brings differentiating contributions of a more sustainable nature — such as a leading brand— will enjoy a more sustained influence. And the smaller partner is comparably more dependent. The dependence comes from commitments. As the commitments are irreversible, more specific commitments should be done so that every partner is very clear about its role and contribution, for example, the service standard, price, credit policy, service level performance, response time, image and etc. The trust between partners should be well set up as the basis of enduring collaborative relationships.
- Monitoring the quality. Quality is the life core in any industry. Service, price, credit policy, response time, and legal issue warranties and so on detailed things should also be considered carefully. Online service and face-to-face service should be both monitored. Keeping a sustainable good quality can enhance customer's loyalty and then raise the company's reputation.
- Hiring intelligent and empowered employees. Managing e-collaboration will be more difficult than traditional management activities, as the systems become potentially more complex, more tightly coupled, and increasingly involve complex interrelations between people, organizations and technology (Timothy 2003). Companies need more than just good technology to make the most of the Internet (Cairncross 2000).

Evaluation can also not be forgotten while using e-collaboration strategy. Individually, jointly and publicly evaluation all are important to keep the process on its way to success.

This paper addresses the relevant theories on e-business and internet to the specific tourism industry. But as time and resources are limited, no particular case study is offered to support the researcher's ideas. E-trading is the industry witnesses the technology information development first and reacts first. The theories and practice in this industry can be studied more to contribute to tourism. A further research of comparing and analysing the similarities and differences between these two industries, especially the e-market place and online travel agencies can be carried out. What's more, the research of the trend of diagonal e-collaboration in tourism industry is also worth researching.

Interorganisational Collaboration in Tourism

Collaboration between organisations involved in the tourism industry is a widely established practice. Many of the benefits of such participation have been widely reported. For example, organisations have been known to co-ordinate their activities to cope with the turbulence and complexity of their environments, to solve environmentally-related problems, and to enhance sustainable development. Forming such relations, however, is not a simple process.

Frequently, difficulties are confronted. These difficulties derive from the complexity of the 'industry' for it actually involves a collection of businesses, from different sectors, all marketing travel-related services (Leiper, 1990). These tourism organisations, while diverse, are interdependent. This means that any developments or changes in one industry or firm will, in turn, affect another to a greater or lesser degree.

To clearly understand the characteristics of this industry, Leiper (1979) suggested that we should view it as a system. This conceptualisation is laudable as it captures the highly interdependent nature of organisational relationships in tourism. Implicit in this systems explanation is the need for close organisational coordination if tourism activities are to succeed. Leiper (1979: 404) explains:

The behavioural element, (1) tourists, are represented leaving

(2) generating regions, travelling to and staying in (3) destinations, and returning home. The tourist industry element is represented within all three (4) geographic elements. Also symbolic is the representation of part of the tourist element outside the (5) industrial element, signifying the partially industrialised characteristics of the process.

Propositions about Collaboration Environmental Forces

Growth in Tourism

Collaborative marketing was developed to take advantage of growth opportunities and in an attempt to gain sufficient return on investment for stakeholders in tourism development.

Demand Uncertainty

Any problem domain, such as demand uncertainty, of concern to all stakeholders that cannot be satisfactorily managed by a single organisation, will lead to the formation of collaborative marketing.

Growth of Tourism Organisations

The growth of any tourism organisations or associations will facilitate the development and/or initiation of larger-scale collaborations in tourism destination marketing.

Motives

Perceived Benefits : Collaboration will not occur unless two conditions are satisfied: (a) stakeholders share at least one common interest in relation to the proposed collaboration and (b) they recognise the individual and mutual benefits of being involved in collaboration.

Perceived Interdependence

Collaboration in tourism destination marketing requires a recognition of the high degree of interdependence. The formation of any collaboration is enhanced by an initiator or convenor who emphasises the shared responsibility of all stakeholders as well as the potential negative effects of a lack of collaboration in marketing destinations.

Extendedness of a Relationship

Stakeholders will be motivated to collaborate by their expectation of extendedness in a future relationship.

Commitment

Collaboration will require a certain degree of commitment between a firm and its partners.

Legitimacy

An organisation's motives to gain future recognition from other stakeholders is positively related to their decision to participate in collaborative marketing activities.

Trust

Collaboration will be enhanced when stakeholders have trust and/or confidence of the tourism association's ability to market the destination as a whole.

Conditions

Organisational Factors

Organisations with a small budget will collaborate where their budget allows them room to manoeuvre.

Problem Domain

Domain focus and domain consensus facilitate the formation of collaboration. The degree to which this occurs is related to the degree of acceptance of other's claims to specific goals and functions.

The Referent Organisation

A convenor and/or bridging organisation are required to initiate and facilitate collaboration in tourism destination marketing. The role of the convenor is to identify and bring all legitimate stakeholders to the table.

Any effort to involve all stakeholders in the development of collaborative marketing in tourism is likely be thwarted by divergent stakeholder views.

e-Tourism

e-Tourism is a subset of Travel technology with a particular focus on the tourism industry. In June 2003, the United Nations Conference on Trade and Development, UNCTAD, established a Task Force on Sustainable Tourism for Development that proposes the use of the concept of e-tourism as part of a strategy to build sustainable and locally rooted tourism industries. The e-Tourism Initiative aims to promote ICT-driven growth through a participative strategy that includes networking and competitive collaboration for the tourism sector of developing countries.

e-tourism: An Innovative Approach for the small and Medium-Sized Tourism Enterprises (Smtes) in Korea

The definitions of tourism innovation (*e.g.* product, service and technological innovations) remains unclear, with the exception maybe of the Internet. New technologies can produce an essential contribution to tourism development.

For tourism businesses, the Internet offers the potential to make information and booking facilities available to large numbers of tourists at relatively low costs. It also provides a tool for communication between tourism suppliers, intermediaries, as well as end-consumers. OECD (2000) revealed that the advent of Internet-based electronic commerce offers considerable opportunities for firms to expand their customer base, enter new product markets and rationalise their business. WTO (2001) also indicated that electronic business offers SMEs the opportunity to undertake their business in new and more cost-effective ways.

According to WTO, the Internet is revolutionising the distribution of tourism information and sales. An increasing proportion of Internet users are buying on–line and tourism will gain a larger and larger share of the online commerce market. Obviously, the Internet is having a major impact as a source of information for tourism. However, the SMTEs are facing more stringent impediments to the adoption of new information technology, in particular, e-business. Part of the problem relates to the scale and affordability of information technology, as well as the facility of implementation within rapidly growing and changing organisations. In addition, new solutions configured for large, stable, and internationally-oriented firms do not fit well for small, dynamic, and locally-based tourism firms.

Despite these challenges, SMTEs with well-developed and innovative Web sites can now have "equal Internet access" to international tourism markets. This implies equal access to telecom infrastructure, as well as to marketing management and education. According to a UN report (2001), "it is not the cost of being there, on the on-line market place, which must be reckoned with, but the cost of not being there." It is certain that embracing digital communication and information technology is no longer an option, but a necessity. Thus, one of the most important characteristics of electronic commerce is the opportunity and promise it holds for SMTEs to extend their capabilities and grow.

Recent Research on e-Commerce in Tourism Industry

The study of e-commerce in the tourism industry has emerged as a 'frontier area' for information technology. The literature on e-commerce in the tourism industry was critically reviewed with a view to developing a framework suitable for this study. E-commerce is defined as the process of buying and selling or exchanging products, services and information via computer networks including the Internet. However, adoption of Information and Communication Technologies (ICT) is only part of the story. In particular, network access costs, dissemination of information on electronic commerce, training, skill development and human resources provide big challenges for smaller companies.

The difficulty in addressing issues of trust and confidence also makes SMTEs more vulnerable than large firms to problems linked to authentication/certification, data security and confidentiality and the settling of commercial disputes.

However, a SME Electronic Commerce Study done by APEC reported that "Small and medium enterprises are significant players in business-to-business electronic commerce, which constitutes more than 80 percent of all e-commerce activities. SMEs that can demonstrate their capabilities to use e-commerce will have a competitive advantage in the e-commerce marketplace."

Most research suggested that government plays an important role in facilitating the use of electronic commerce for the tourism industry and in increasing their ability to reap the benefits, (*e.g.* via awareness building and training programmes). Governments in partnership with the private sector should establish a more comprehensive and consistent policy approach to the tourism industry and electronic commerce, and apply evaluation mechanisms to assess what works and does not work (UN 2001, OECD, 2000, Korea Information Society Development Institute 2000, APEC-TEL 1999).

Key Factors for Successful e-Commerce for SMTEs

Research was performed to collect the secondary data regarding e-commerce for the tourism industry. Based on those data, a questionnaire was developed to get information on the challenges and opportunities faced by the tourism industry. The survey covered e-commerce activities, benefits, barriers and key success factors. It covered essentially the Korean SMTEs. SMTEs are defined as businesses that have 300 or fewer employees or sales from USD 2 million to 20 million, depending on the characteristics of business.

Benefits of e-Commerce for SMTEs

Respondents considered that the main benefits of e-commerce for tourism enterprises are 'providing easy access to information on tourism services,' 'providing better information on tourism services,' and 'providing convenience for customers'. This result implies that respondents are less aware of many other benefits of e-commerce, such as 'creating new markets,' 'improving customer services,' 'establishing interactive relationships with customers', 'reducing operating cost', 'interacting with other business partners', and 'founding new business partners'.

Barriers of e-Commerce for SMTEs

There are a number of barriers for SMTEs in adopting e-commerce in Korea. These barriers include 'limited knowledge of available technology,' 'lack of awareness,' 'cost of initial investment,' 'lack of confidence in the benefits of e-commerce,' and 'cost of system maintenance.' These barriers also include 'shortage of skilled human resources,' and 'resistance to adoption of e-commerce.' In terms of market situation, one might also mention 'insufficient e-commerce infrastructure,' and 'small e-commerce market size'.

Factors for Successful SMTEs E-Commerce Practices

The two main factors for conducting successful e-commerce are 'security of the e-commerce system' and 'user-friendly Web interface', thus recognising that building customer trust and convenience for customers are essential to succeed. 'Top management support,' 'IT infrastructure,' and 'customer acceptance' were also considered as important factors. On the other hand, most SMTEs do not recognise the importance of 'sharing knowledge and information between SMTEs' and 'business partnerships' as e-commerce successful strategies.

Importance and Performance of SMTEs' e-Commerce

The study used Importance and Performance (IP) analysis to examine e-commerce strategies. For 'Importance' respondents indicated the importance of each of the 16 proposed factors for a successful implementation of e-commerce by SMTEs. For 'Performance,' respondents indicated how well their member economy performs regarding e-commerce, in relation to their response to 'Importance.'

Four IP categories emerge from this analysis. The 'Keep up the good work' category means that both 'Importance' and 'Performance' are high. The category 'concentrated efforts' refers to 'high importance' and 'low performance' responses. The 'low priority' category refers to 'low importance' and 'low performance' responses. The 'Possible overkill' includes 'high performance' with low importance".

Keep up the Good Work

Respondents considered the following factors as important; 'Security of e-commerce,' 'User-friendly Web interface,' 'IT (Information Technology) infrastructure,' 'Level of trust between customer and company,' 'Customer acceptance.' All factors are strongly related to consumer issues such as security and user convenience. These factors were also considered as relatively well-performed.

Concentrated Efforts

The factors in this category include 'Top management support' and 'Skilled human resources'. These factors are considered as very important for implementing e-commerce but are considered as performed insufficiently. Thus, more efforts need to focus on these factors.

Low Priority

'Government support,' 'Sharing knowledge and information between SMTEs,' 'Integration with the existing corporation,' and 'Relationship with other business partners.' received low marks in importance and performance. These factors, however, are actually critical to successful e-commerce of SMTEs. This implies that managers have limited information and knowledge on e-commerce. More information should be delivered to entrepreneurs about the importance of those factors.

Possible Overkill

'Market situation' falls in the 'Possible overkill' category. According to the survey results, managers of SMTEs utilise the Internet for market analysis (may include competitor analysis) but do not consider this factor as important. Researchers believe that this result has some discrepancy with previous reports that SMEs (Small and Medium-Sized Enterprises) usually do not use the Internet for market research.

Remainder

Three factors including 'Specific tourism products or services for e-commerce,' 'Corporation knowledge, culture, and acceptance,' and 'Internal communication' fall somewhere between 'Low Priority' and 'Possible overkill.' One factor, 'Cost of establishing and maintaining e-commerce system' is between the 'Concentrated efforts' and 'Keep up the good work' categories. These factors were assessed relatively similarly as 'low importance' and 'middle performance.'

E-Commerce Strategies for Innovation of the SMTEs

For Rayport and Jaworski (2002), e-commerce strategy should be implemented with the four critical forces: technology, capital, media, and public policy infrastructures. An infrastructure is defined as the foundation of a system. E-commerce strategies refer to these four infrastructures:

- The technology infrastructure means the technological foundation of the Internet, which enables the running of e-commerce enterprises, including the hardware of computers, servers, routers, cables, network technologies, software, and communications. Understanding technology infrastructure – and thus understanding what is and is not achievable – is essential to formulating travel and tourism's vision and strategy.
- The capital infrastructure relates to how to secure funding for an e-business and subsequently value that business.
- The media infrastructure is an important issue for all e-commerce managers because the Internet is a mass communication platform. Managers who run on line enterprises must learn to manage a staff responsible for design interface, stylistic choices, and editorial policies, and content choices associated with the new communication venue. Therefore, the e-commerce manager is now a publisher of digital content on the Web. He/she should make choices about the types of media employed (*e.g.* print, audio, video), the nature of the media,

and editorial policy, including style, content, and look-and-feel.

- Finally, all of the decisions related to technology, capital, media, and strategy are influenced by laws and regulation, that is, public policy decisions. The public policy infrastructure affects not only the specific business but also direct and indirect competitors. E-commerce managers should understand both the current laws and how the laws may affect their businesses and those around them. This paper suggests different strategies according to the e-commerce infrastructure of the business and stage of e-business development:
- Internet start-up SMTEs should adopt a business model appropriate for their own e-business objectives and environments. External service providers have great potential for them. Marketing should be done selectively. Earning a good reputation in the local market should be the top-priority. Internet start-up SMTEs can develop a strategy to access international markets directly to sell their tourism products and services.
- Established SMTEs should focus on two key strategies: 1) expanding the range of services and products and 2) upgrading their quality. They should redesign their Web sites to focus more on 'customer retention' than 'customer acquisition' to ensure quality of service. The Internet is a useful tool to reach international markets. E-partnerships between SMTEs or large firms are important. They should utilise their resource to build an e-community.

Their e-business strategies should be formulated according to their business environments. Linkage to a site of destination management organization (DMO) is critical to success. Development of an online booking system is the most important technological aspect. Various measures to overcome lack of trust and confidence of consumers should be taken, such as utilization of 'about us,' 'frequently asked questions (FAQs),' and 'call center' services.

Established SMTEs should consider e-strategy issues, including; 1) target market segments, 2) building trust and confidence of e-consumers, and 3) expanding e-commerce activities.

Implications for Tourism Policy

The role of government is very important. The key principle is that the private sector leads the market. The government should avoid creating undue obstacles to e-commerce and its aims should be to support and enforce a predictable, minimal, consistent and simple legal environment if governmental involvement is needed. Active government support to foster an entrepreneurial culture is important. Key policy agendas include; 1) improving the legal and regulatory framework, 2) moving government procurement on line, and 3) facilitating e-transformation in industry sectors.

Legal and regulatory issues should consider consumer protection, legal resource mechanisms in disputes (*e.g.* e-commerce mediation committee), intellectual property protection, and validity and enforcement of contracts. The policies cover issues such as what taxes should apply to Internet transactions, the identification and residence of users, and the problem of tax avoidance. The guidelines of international organisations such as APEC and OECD can be a basis for e-commerce laws and regulations. To support consumer trust and confidence, a programme of e-trust certification could be effective. Online government procurement and government participation in e-transformation of industry sectors should be planned and implemented in the medium-and long-term. Government support can be provided in tax reductions, monetary support, and sharing of knowledge and information between industries and research organisations.

In Korea, a pilot project aims to construct a B2B network in all key industries. The government has also implemented a 'System to Certify Venture Tourism Business,' which indirectly supports the industry. In 2001, 11 companies were selected as venture tourism businesses and can receive support and benefits. Applications for the status of venture tourism are evaluated twice a year. Most domestic software companies in Korea do not have distribution channels of their own.

Therefore, they pay a commission of almost 40% to distributors of their products. This is a major disadvantage in the competitive market. To solve this problem the government established a software cybermall. The Internet shopping mall, which opened in 1998, provides product demonstrations and the ability to purchase products electronically. The mall is linked to the sites of many vendors.

Finally, government could help the growth of e-commerce in various ways through, planning, creating the legal and regulatory framework, building capacity in information technology infrastructure, skill formation and manpower planning, and also undertaking promotional and incentive measures. The government should function as a facilitator, promoter, educator, and 'anchor tenant' for testing and pilot deployment of new applications. It is expected that OECD member countries facilitate international strategic alliances at government-to-government (G2G) and industry-to-industry (I2I) levels and help local firms to grow, regionalise and also globalise. Government can also help create markets in emerging areas at the initial stage and help remove regulatory obstacles that may impede the growth of markets and businesses. Again, the ultimate objective of the government remains the promotion of private sector initiatives in e-commerce development (Kahn, 2002).

Conclusions: Recommendations for e-Tourism Innovations

In conclusion, this paper suggests some recommendations for decision makers, entrepreneurs and practitioners in the tourism industry field, particularly for SMTEs. These recommendations are made to the Korean e-tourism market, however, they can probably apply to the tourism industries in other countries.

The government should develop a national vision, a strategic plan and policy guidelines for SMTEs e-commerce activities. The development of e-commerce strategies should involve all tourism stakeholders. The policy makers are also responsible for establishing the appropriate laws, regulations and service standards that will enable to build trust and consumer confidence.

Entrepreneurs need to adopt business models which are tailor-made for their own e-business objectives and the SMTEs environment. SMTEs can combine various e-business models. External service providers have great potential to assist SMTEs.

Stakeholders should also find ways to integrate SMTEs into industry-wide associations. This will encourage SMTEs to stop competing at the destination level, and to develop networks for mutual benefit. In line with this co-operation, they need to formulate and implement networking or strategic alliances through partnerships with other SMTEs or large firms, especially in the area of brand management, customer relationship management, and human resources management.

As regards marketing, association with e-shopping will allow SMTEs to conduct Internet-based e-commerce without bearing all the start-up costs, improvements cost, advertising and technical difficulties, which could be shared by all the merchants in the mall instead. Associations of e-shopping will provide SMTEs with the opportunity to take advantage of e-commerce systems *e.g.* interactivity, mass customisation, real time and a database of customers.

In the established stage, SMTEs may need to redesign their website to focus more on 'customer retention' than 'customer acquisition'. They should also try to develop and manage their own digital brand. Brand power is more important on line than off line because the main stage of e-business is the virtual world where consumers are more dependent on recognised brands.

Finally, both the policy makers and the entrepreneurs should work together to raise awareness of e-commerce through training and education for stakeholders, employees and consumers. E-commerce cannot be implemented without empowering and enabling tourism stakeholders to take advantage of new Internet and e-commerce technologies.

Helping Developing Countries to become Autonomous

Tourism is one of the main exports of the 50 least developed countries (LDCs). But at the same time, leakages (repatriation of profits) in this sector total up to 85 percent in some African LDCs, more than 80 percent in the Caribbean, 70 percent in Thailand and 40 percent in India.

In order to minimize leakages and to promote sustainable growth and poverty alleviation, it is now essential for tourism destinations and local small and medium-sized enterprises (SMEs) to increase their autonomy, and to include all tourism stakeholders. To deal with this issue, UNCTAD has developed the e-Tourism Initiative, with the aim of helping developing countries, and particularly the LDCs, to make the most of their tourism potential.

Launched at the eleventh UNCTAD quadrennial ministerial conference in Sao Paulo, Brazil, in June 2004, the E-Tourism Initiative is part of UNCTAD's task force on sustainable tourism for development. The Initiative is part of the UNCTAD XI Information and Communication Technologies for Development

Partnership. This partnership encompasses activities in the areas of free and open-source software, e-tourism, ICT policies, e-measurement, ICT indicators and e-finance.

Linking sustainable tourism and ICTs for development, the demand-driven E-Tourism Initiative will strengthen developing country capacities to promote their tourism product and dynamically match it to worldwide demand.

The Initiative focuses on the development and implementation of ICT-based tools that will help communities tap the international market by strengthening and including local institutional and human capacities in the global market and promoting local involvement and ownership.

Purpose of the Initiative

For many developing countries, and particularly the LDCs, the small economies and the island developing States, tourism provides a significant potential for poverty reduction, economic growth and development. It is often their primary source of hard currency and is also one of the largest sources of employment.

ICTs can make developing countries more autonomous and self-sufficient in constructing their own brand images and promoting their own tourist attractions. In maximizing their comparative advantage in this sector, developing countries can adjust their tourism services to suit their own development strategies and become better integrated in the world economy.

The target population for this project is composed of ministries of tourism, national tourism boards, destination management organizations, local tourism stakeholders and other relevant partners.

The immediate objective is to design, create and establish a steady e-commerce market place by identifying, promoting and integrating the providers of national goods and services with regard to international business. Other objectives are to enable destination countries to organize their tourism services, to develop new tourism products, to improve the quality of their services and foster public-private partnerships to improve the competitiveness of the sector.

A Package

The E-Tourism Initiative is structured around a tool, a method and a partnership-building approach.

The tool is a country platform aimed at helping developing countries identify, standardize, coordinate and propose tourism services in response to varying world demand.

The Initiative also provides a method for collecting the relevant information, standardizing it and disseminating it on the Internet. The aim of the method is to encourage active cooperation among partners, and learning and capacities enhancement, in order to promote sustainable development.

Partnerships will enable all concerned stakeholders to coordinate their resources and objectives. They may be formed in the private sector (private-private), in the public sector (public-public) or between the private and public sectors.

A Tool

Technically, the tool is a *web-site generator*, which is reproducible and adaptable, and which builds around a group of databases and multi-criterion search engines. This genuine decision-making, management and promotional tool will offer visibility to the destination countries in the global market place.

Designed to be inclusive, decentralized and commercial, this tool contributes to the organization of national markets by encouraging organizational and functional links between private and public entities in the sector, and allows tourism services to be promoted in accordance with countries' development objectives.

The electronic platform acts as a virtual travel agent and offers personalized information. This tool aims at increasing the online consumer rate.

It has the potential to give a real boost to national growth, notably among SMEs, by shaping a national identity for destination countries. Developing countries will be able to promote their products and services and diversify their economies.

A Method

As well as providing an Internet platform, the Initiative provides a method and relevant mechanisms for collating the relevant information, standardizing it and disseminating it on the Internet.

As the approach is business oriented, it includes a corresponding generic business model, educational material, various guides and related road maps for building user skills, with the aim of strengthening national capacity in this field. The business model is adapted to conditions in the country to ensure the platform's sustainability.

A guide that gives full directions for using the portal, and special records for the various entities, operating in the sector will be produced and distributed. Each participant is responsible for its own part and is given a road map and blueprints for measuring and evaluating results. At the end of the project this informal arrangement should be firmed up and kept in operation in accordance with the associated business plan.

The success of such an initiative depends on the involvement of local entities, from the start, in taking ownership of the project and jointly defining its framework. Their responsibilities towards each other should be clearly understood, accepted and followed up. This is, in the long run, the purpose of the awareness-raising seminar planned for the start of the project.

Partnership-Building

The E-Tourism Initiative is based on a collaborative public and private approach. Some partnerships will be pursued when planning begins, others at the development stage to support the project, and others when the product is actually introduced in the target countries, all in close cooperation with international partners, such as the World Tourism Organization (WTO), sub regional, national and local partners, NGOs, local communities and local traders. Finally, further partnerships will be developed to build skills at the local level.

6

Operation in Hotel Management

Tourism and hospitality is the fastest growing industry in the world with over 72.4 million jobs within the industry. Through the growth of e-commerce and globalization, a wide variety of career opportunities have emerged in the meeting and convention, attractions, event planning, travel, gaming, transportations, airline, recreation and food and beverage fields.

Many modern words readily associated with hospitality are evolved from the same hypothetical Proto-Indo-European root *ghosti (1) meaning: stranger, guest, host: properly 'someone with whom one has reciprocal duties of hospitality' (American Heritage Dictionary, 2001). The word guest came from the Middle English gest, evolved from Old Norse gestr, and from Old High German gast, both come from Germanic *gastiz. *Ghosti also evolved to the Latin root hostis, meaning enemy, army, and where host (multitude) and hostile find their origin; and the Latin root hostia, meaning sacrifice, host (Eucharistic). The combination of *ghosti and another Proto-Indo-European root *poti powerful, gave the compound root *ghos-pot-, *ghos-pon (d)-, which evolved to the Latin hospes and eventually into hospice, hospitable, hospital, hospitality, host (giver of hospitality), hostage and hostel. The Greek languages also evolved from the same Proto-Indo-European base; *ghosti gave the Greek xenos which has the interchangeable meaning guest, host or stranger. Hospitality, then, 'represents a kind of guarantee of reciprocity—one protects the stranger in order to be protected from him'.

Grecian Hospitality Mythology

In Ancient Greece, it was not known if the stranger knocking at the door was going to be hostile or hospitable, whether they were a god disguised, or watching from above and passing judgment. This was not considered important for 'it is hard for mortals to see divinity'. Hospitality was a way of honouring the gods, which was so essential, so fundamental to civilized life, that its patron was the god of gods.

In true hospitality, it doesn't matter who the guest is, nor their apparent status in life. Generous hospitality freely given to a stranger was the same as that given to a god. Reese (1993) in his analysis of the writings attributed to Homer identifies 18 'hospitality' scenes. It is clear from these scenes in the Homeric writings that hospitality brought expectations. As the traveller would not usually be wandering without cause from their home into the dangers of the world.

Hospitality management is the academic study of the hospitality industry. A degree in Hospitality management is often conferred from either a university college dedicated to the studies of hospitality management or a business school with a department in hospitality management studies. Hospitality management is the academic study of the hospitality industry. A degree in Hospitality management is often conferred from either a university college dedicated to the studies of hospitality management or a business school with a department in hospitality management studies.

Hospitality and Tourism Management

In America, Hospitality and Tourism Management (HTM) can be a business major in either a Bachelors of Science, Bachelors of Commerce or a Bachelors of Arts.

Graduate students graduate with a Masters of Business Administration, a Masters or Science, or a Doctorate of Philosophy in Hospitality and Tourism Management.

It is a focus that is studied by individuals that are intending to work in the Hospitality Industry, examples of which are; Hotels, Resorts, Casinos, Restaurants, and Events.

Within the HTM concentration there is generally:

- Food Management and Operations (Examples: Food Science, Food Selection and Preparation, Food and Beverage Operations)
- Lodging Operations (Examples: Hotel Operations, Resort Management, Lodging Management, Financial

Management and Cost Control for Hospitality Organizations)

- Global Tourism (Examples: Travel and Tourism Management, Tourism Analysis, Hospitality and Research Methods)
- Sustainable Tourism (Examples: Natural Destination Management, Responsible Tourism, Green Tourism and Eco-Tourism, Alternative and more Environmentally friendly ways of working within the whole Tourism industry)
- Tourist Attractions Management (Examples: Heritage Attractions, Arts and Cultural Attractions, Industrial Attractions, City Based Attractions, Retail Attractions, Natural Attractions)
- Entertainment Management (Examples: Theme Park Management, Theatre Management, Cinema Management, Museology, Live Music and Music Festival Management).
- Event Management (Examples: Hospitality Sales, Catering Management, Hospitality Marketing Management).

Several large corporations such as Marriott, IHG, Hyatt, Starwood, Wyndham and Hilton Hotels have summer internships in training programs for students majoring in Hospitality and Tourism Management, to help students get valuable work experience.

Hospitality and Tourism Management

In America, Hospitality and Tourism Management (HTM) can be a business major in either a Bachelors of Science, Bachelors of Commerce or a Bachelors of Arts.

Graduate students graduate with a Masters of Business Administration, a Masters or Science, or a Doctorate of Philosophy in Hospitality and Tourism Management.

It is a focus that is studied by individuals that are intending to work in the Hospitality Industry, examples of which are; Hotels, Resorts, Casinos, Restaurants, and Events.

Within the HTM concentration there is generally:

- Food Management and Operations (Examples: Food Science, Food Selection and Preparation, Food and Beverage Operations)

- Lodging Operations (Examples: Hotel Operations, Resort Management, Lodging Management, Financial Management and Cost Control for Hospitality Organizations)
- Global Tourism (Examples: Travel and Tourism Management, Tourism Analysis, Hospitality and Research Methods)
- Sustainable Tourism (Examples: Natural Destination Management, Responsible Tourism, Green Tourism and Eco-Tourism, Alternative and more Environmentally friendly ways of working within the whole Tourism industry)
- Tourist Attractions Management (Examples: Heritage Attractions, Arts and Cultural Attractions, Industrial Attractions, City Based Attractions, Retail Attractions, Natural Attractions)
- Entertainment Management (Examples: Theme Park Management, Theatre Management, Cinema Management, Museology, Live Music and Music Festival Management).
- Event Management (Examples: Hospitality Sales, Catering Management, Hospitality Marketing Management).

Several large corporations such as Marriott, IHG, Hyatt, Starwood, Wyndham and Hilton Hotels have summer internships in training programs for students majoring in Hospitality and Tourism Management, to help students get valuable work experience.

Hospitality Industry

The hospitality industry consists of broad category of fields within the service industry that includes lodging, restaurants, event planning, theme parks, transportation, cruise line, and additional fields within the tourism industry.

The hospitality industry is a several billion dollar industry that mostly depends on the availability of leisure time and disposable income. A hospitality unit such as a restaurant, hotel, or even an amusement park consists of multiple groups such as facility maintenance, direct operations (servers, housekeepers, porters, kitchen workers, bartenders, etc.), management, marketing, and human resources. Usage rate is an important variable for the hospitality industry. Just as a factory owner would wish to have his or her productive asset in use as much as possible (as opposed to having to pay fixed costs while the factory isn't producing), so do restaurants, hotels, and theme parks seek to maximize the number of customers they "process".

In viewing various industries, "barriers to entry" by newcomers and competitive advantages between current players are very important. Among other things, hospitality industry players find advantage in old classics (location), initial and ongoing investment support (reflected in the material upkeep of facilities and the luxuries located therein), and particular themes adopted by the marketing arm of the organization in question (such as a restaurant called the 51st fighter group that has a WW2 theme in music and other environmental aspects). Very important is also the characteristics of the personnel working in direct contact with the customers. The authenticity, professionalism, and actual concern for the happiness and well-being of the customers that is communicated by successful organizations is a clear competitive advantage.

Hotel Company Practices

Hotel

A hotel is an establishment that provides paid lodging on a short-term basis. The provision of basic accommodation, in times past, consisting only of a room with a bed, a cupboard, a small table and a washstand has largely been replaced by rooms with modern facilities, including en-suite bathrooms and air conditioning or climate control. Additional common features found in hotel rooms are a telephone, an alarm clock, a television, and Internet connectivity; snack foods and drinks may be supplied in a mini-bar, and facilities for making hot drinks. Larger hotels may provide a number of additional guest facilities such as a restaurant, a swimming pool or childcare, and have conference and social function services. Hotels rooms are usually numbered to allow guests identify their room.

Some hotels offer meals as part of a room and board arrangement. In the United Kingdom, a hotel is required by law to serve food and drinks to all guests within certain stated hours; to avoid this requirement it is not uncommon to come across *private hotels* which are not subject to this requirement. In Japan, capsule hotels provide a minimized amount of room space and shared facilities. In the United Kingdom, Australia, Canada and Ireland (and rarely in some parts of the United States), the word may also refer to a pub or bar and might not offer accommodation. In India and Bangladesh, the word may also refer to a restaurant.

Etymology

The word *hotel* is derived from the French *hotel* (coming from *hotel* meaning *host*), which referred to a French version of a townhouse or any other building seeing frequent visitors, rather than a place offering accommodation. In contemporary French usage, *hôtel* now has the same meaning as the English term, and *hôtel particulier* is used for the old meaning. The French spelling, with the circumflex, was also used in English, but is now rare. The circumflex replaces the 's' found in the earlier *hostel* spelling, which over time took on a new, but closely related meaning. Grammatically, hotels usually take the definite article-hence "The Astoria Hotel" or simply "The Astoria".

Classification

The cost and quality of hotels are usually indicative of the range and type of services available. Due to the enormous increase in tourism worldwide during the last decades of the 20th century, standards, especially those of smaller establishments, have improved considerably. For the sake of greater comparability, rating systems have been introduced, with the one to five stars classification being most common and with higher star ratings indicating more luxury. Hotels are independently assessed in traditional systems and these rely heavily on the facilities provided. Some consider this disadvantageous to smaller hotels whose quality of accommodation could fall into one class but the lack of an item such as an elevator would prevent it from reaching a higher categorization. In some countries, there is an official body with standard criteria for classifying hotels, but in many others there is none. There have been attempts at unifying the classification system so that it becomes an internationally recognized and reliable standard but large differences exist in the quality of the accommodation and the food within one category of hotel, sometimes even in the same country. The American Automobile Association (AAA) and their affiliated bodies use diamonds instead of stars to express hotel and restaurant ratings levels.

Hotels are also classified by service type ranging for all-inclusive full-service resorts that cater to vacationers to small limited service hotels that cater to transient business travelers. The main categories of hotels are as follows;

- Full Service Upscale
  - o *Examples include Conrad Hotels, Ritz Carlton, Four Seasons Hotels, and JW Marriott*
- Full Service
  - o *Examples include Hilton, Marriott, Doubletree, and Hyatt*
- Select Service
  - o *Examples include Courtyard by Marriott and Hilton Garden Inn*
- Limited Service
  - o *Examples include Hampton Inn, Fairfield Inn, Days Inn, and La Quinta Inn*
- Extended Stay
  - o *Examples include Homewood Suites by Hilton, Residence Inn by Marriott, and Extended Stay Hotels*
- Timeshare
  - o *Examples include Marriott Vacation Club, Westgate Resorts, and Disney Vacation Club*
- Destination Club.

Historic Hotels

Some hotels have gained their renown through tradition, by hosting significant events or persons, such as Schloss Cecilienhof in Potsdam, Germany, which derives its fame from the Potsdam Conference of the World War II allies Winston Churchill, Harry Truman and Joseph Stalin in 1945. The Taj Mahal Palace & Tower in Mumbai is one of India's most famous and historic hotels because of its association with the Indian independence movement. Some establishments have given name to a particular meal or beverage, as is the case with the Waldorf Astoria in New York City, United States where the Waldorf Salad was first created or the Hotel Sacher in Vienna, Austria, home of the Sachertorte. Others have achieved fame by association with dishes or cocktails created on their premises, such as the Hotel de Paris where the crepe Suzette was invented or the Raffles Hotel in Singapore, where the Singapore Sling cocktail was devised.

A number of hotels have entered the public consciousness through popular culture, such as the Ritz Hotel in London, United

Kingdom, through its association with Irving Berlin's song, 'Puttin' on the Ritz'. The Algonquin Hotel in New York City is famed as the meeting place of the literary group, the Algonquin Round Table, and Hotel Chelsea, also in New York City, has been the subject of a number of songs and the scene of the stabbing of Nancy Spungen (allegedly by her boyfriend Sid Vicious). The Waldorf Astoria and Statler hotels in New York City are also immortalized in the names of Muppets Statler and Waldorf. The luxurious Grand Hotel Europe in Saint Petersburg, Russia achieved fame with its inclusion in the James Bond film Golden Eye.

Unusual Hotels

Many hotels can be considered destinations in themselves, by dint of unusual features of the lodging or its immediate environment:

Treehouse Hotels

Some hotels are built with living trees as structural elements, for example the Costa Rica Tree House in the Gandoca-Manzanillo Wildlife Refuge, Costa Rica; the Treetops Hotel in Aberdare National Park, Kenya; the Ariau Towers near Manaus, Brazil, on the Rio Negro in the Amazon; and Bayram's Tree Houses in Olympos, Turkey.

Bunker Hotels

The Null Stern Hotel in Teufen, Appenzellerland, Switzerland and the Concrete Mushrooms in Albania are former nuclear bunkers transformed into hotels.

Cave Hotels

Desert Cave Hotel in Coober Pedy, South Australia and the Cuevas Pedro Antonio de Alarcon (named after the author) in Guadix, Spain, as well as several hotels in Cappadocia, Turkey, are notable for being built into natural cave formations, some with rooms underground.

Capsule Hotels

Capsule hotels are a type of economical hotel that are found in Japan, where people sleep in stacks of rectangular containers.

Ice and Snow Hotels

The Ice Hotel in Jukkasjarvi, Sweden, and the Hotel de Glace in Duschenay, Canada, melt every spring and are rebuilt each winter; the Mammut Snow Hotel in Finland is located within the walls of the Kemi snow castle; and the Lainio Snow Hotel is part of a snow village near Yllas, Finland.

Garden Hotels

Garden hotels, famous for their gardens before they became hotels, include Gravetye Manor, the home of garden designer William Robinson, and Cliveden, designed by Charles Barry with a rose garden by Geoffrey Jellicoe.

Underwater Hotels

Some hotels have accommodation underwater, such as Utter Inn in Lake Malaren, Sweden. Hydropolis, project cancelled 2004 in Dubai, would have had suites on the bottom of the Persian Gulf, and Jules Undersea Lodge in Key Largo, Florida requires scuba diving to access its rooms.

Other Unusual Hotels

- The Library Hotel in New York City, is unique in that each of its ten floors is assigned one category from the Dewey Decimal System.
- The Burj al-Arab hotel in Dubai, United Arab Emirates, built on an artificial island, is structured in the shape of a boat's sail.
- The Jailhotel Löwengraben in Lucerne, Switzerland is a converted prison now used as a hotel.
- The Luxor, a hotel and casino on the Las Vegas Strip in Paradise, Nevada, United States due to its pyramidal structure.
- The Liberty Hotel in Boston, used to be the Charles Street Jail.
- Built in Scotland and completed in 1936, The former ocean liner RMS *Queen Mary* in Long Beach, California, United States uses its first-class staterooms as a hotel, after retiring in 1967 from Transatlantic service.

Resort Hotels

Some hotels are built specifically to create a captive trade, example at casinos and holiday resorts. Though of course hotels have always been built in popular desinations, the defining characteristic of a resort hotel is that it exists purely to serve another attraction, the two having the same owners.

In Las Vegas there is a tradition of one-upmanship with luxurious and extravagant hotels in a concentrated area known as the Las Vegas Strip. This trend now has extended to other resorts worldwide, but the concentration in Las Vegas is still the world's highest: nineteen of the world's twenty-five largest hotels by room count are on the Strip, with a total of over 67,000 rooms.

In Europe Center Parcs might be considered a chain of resort hotels, since the sites are largely man-made (though set in natural surroundings such as country parks) with captive trade, whereas holiday camps such as Butlins and Pontin's are probably not considered as resort hotels, since they are set at traditional holiday destinations which existed before the camps.

Railway Hotels

Frequently, expanding railway companies built grand hotels at their termini, such as the Midland Hotel, Manchester next to the former Manchester Central Station and in London the ones above St Pancras railway station and Charing Cross railway station also in London is the Chiltern Court Hotel above Baker Street tube station and Canada's grand railway hotels. They are or were mostly, but not exclusively, used by those travelling by rail.

Motels

A motel (Motor Hotel) is a hotel which is for a short stay, usually for a night, for motorists on long journeys. It has direct access from the room to the vehicle (for example a central parking lot around which the buildings are set), and is built conveniently close to major roads and intersections.

World Record Setting Hotels

Largest

In 2006, Guinness World Records listed the First World Hotel in Genting Highlands, Malaysia as the world's largest hotel with a total of 6,118 rooms.

Oldest

According to the Guinness Book of World Records, the oldest hotel still in operation is the Hoshi Ryokan, in the Awazu Onsen area of Komatsu, Japan which opened in 718.

Tallest

Burj Al Arab in United Arab Emirates is the tallest building used exclusively as a hotel. However, the Rose Tower, also in Dubai, which has already topped Burj Al Arab's height at 333 m (1,093 ft.), will take away this title upon its opening.

Hotel Rooms as an Investment

Some hotels sell individual rooms to investors. The buyer is allowed to stay in the room without charge or at a reduced rate for a given number of days each year. The investor is paid a share of the takings for the room. Rooms can be sold on a leasehold basis, sometimes on a 999 year lease. Room owners are free to sell at any time.

Living in Hotels

A number of public figures have notably chosen to take up semi-permanent or permanent residence in hotels. Actor Richard Harris lived at the Savoy Hotel while in London. Hotel archivist Susan Scott recounts an anecdote that when he was being taken out of the building on a stretcher shortly before his death he raised his hand and told the diners "it was the food".

Fictitious Hotels

Hotels have been used as the settings for television programmes such as the British situation comedies Fawlty Towers and I'm Alan Partridge, the British soap opera Crossroads, and in films such as the Bates Motel in Hitchcock's 1960 film Psycho.

Hospitality Service

The concept of Hospitality Exchange, also known as "accommodation sharing", "hospitality services" (short "hospex"), and "home stay networks", refers to centrally organized social networks of individuals, generally travelers, who offer or seek accommcdation without monetary exchange. Generally, these services connect users via the internet.

History

In 1949, Bob Luitweiler founded the first hospitality service called Servas Open Doors as a cross national, non-profit, volunteer run organization advocating interracial and international peace. In 1965, John Wilcock set up the Traveller's Directory as a listing of his friends willing to host each other when travelling. In 1988, Joy Lily rescued the organization from imminent shutdown, forming Hospitality Exchange. In 2000, Veit Kuhne founded Hospitality Club, the first Internet-based service. In 2004, Casey

Fenton started CouchSurfing, now the largest hospitality exchange organization.

How they Work

Generally, after registering, members have the option of providing very detailed information and pictures of themselves and of the sleeping accommodation being offered, if any. The more information provided by a member improves the chances that someone will find the member trustworthy enough to be their host or guest. Names and addresses may be verified by volunteers. Members looking for accommodation can search for hosts using several parameters such as age, location, sex, and activity level. Home stays are entirely consensual between the host and guest, and the duration, nature, and terms of the guest's stay are generally worked out in advance to the convenience of both parties. No monetary exchange takes place except under certain circumstances (e.g. the guest may compensate the host for food). After using the service, members can leave a noticeable reference about their host or guest.

Instead of or in addition to accommodation, members also offer to provide guide services or travel-related advice. The websites of the networks also provide editable travel guides and forums where members may seek travel partners or advice. Many such organizations are also focused on "social networking" and members organize activities such as camping trips, bar crawls, meetings, and sporting events.

Some networks cater to specific niche markets such as students, activists, religious pilgrims, and even occupational groups like police officers.

Monetary Savings

As these networks provide accommodation at no charge, monetary savings can be significant.

Local Contact

Hospitality exchange gives travelers the chance to experience what life is like for people living in other places. In addition, making interpersonal connections and fostering understanding of different cultures may in the long run also be important to international relations. During hospitality exchanges, hosts may show off their local knowledge and exciting places "off the tourist map". Not only may travelers get a distinct experience, but they will also get a feel for the everyday lives of local residents.

Reciprocity

These systems foster richer and more convenient travel experiences not so much on the premise of altruism, but on the basis of social exchange theory. Implicit in the agreement to host travelers is the ability to ask to be hosted by them in the future. If one enjoys having interesting guests in their home, this works out well for both parties. It works comparatively better if you are visited by travelers from a locale you find particularly attractive. Thus, hosting someone from New York City in Gainesville, Florida seems to be an unbelievable opportunity. Moreover, if you are a Westerner visiting someone in a developing country, your stay might be the only way that this individual or family could afford a trip to a rich nation. This may mean more than just a relaxing vacation for such disadvantaged parties.

Drawbacks

Lack of Guarantee

There is no contractual agreement between users in these systems. Reservations are made, but if they are for some reason broken, there is no higher authority to which one could plead for a refund or other compensation. The only repercussion will be the poor rating you give that user and your only consolation will be that your warning will deter others from visiting or hosting them. For those who feel insecure unless their travel arrangements are written in stone before departure, this system will not be comforting.

Potential Interpersonal Conflict or Awkwardness

There is a chance that guest and host will not get along. Perhaps there will be scheduling or ideological conflicts. Maybe you will find that hosts or visitors have misrepresented themselves. Perhaps the experience will not live up to your expectations. Intense interpersonal communications in advance and a flexibility once you have arrived is your best bet. These experiences require additional planning and courtesy towards the demands of your host. Thus, your living conditions, length of stay, and overall experience will be circumscribed by the living conditions you enter into.

Digital Divide and Demographic Segregation

As use of these services generally requires access to the internet and knowledge of the English language, the sample population found in searches of these databases is really much less diverse than a geographical representation of worldwide users might suggest.

Security

Staying in someone's house, or inviting people into your house leaves open the possibility of being taken advantage of.

Example Networks

There are countless websites that serve the idea of hospitality service, with new ones appearing as this phenomenon becomes more popular. While this page is not intended to be a directory listing, here is a small sample of the well-established and long-standing networks:

- CouchSurfing-A very active network with over 1.3 million members in more than 200 countries
- Hospitality Club-A very active network with over 550,000 members in more than 200 countries
- Servas International-human rights and global peace oriented since 1949. A relatively small network now with over 15,000 members(?) with a very long history.
- Be Welcome.

Hilton Hotels Corporation Announces Global Sustainability Goals

Hilton Hotels Corporation recently announced short and long term goals and objectives towards building sustainability into the core fabric of its businesses worldwide. Christopher J. Nassetta, President & CEO, outlined directional targets for improvement in the company's sustainability performance throughout the next five years within systemwide hotels globally. By 2014, goals for the Hilton Family of Hotels are to:

- Reduce energy consumption from direct operations by 20%
- Reduce Co2 emissions by 20%
- Reduce output of waste by 20% and
- Reduce water consumption by 10%.

"Upon becoming a truly global company with the acquisition of Hilton International and following the acquisition of our company by Blackstone late last year, we are in an ideal position to lay down a framework for sustainability within our global hotels and corporate offices," said Nassetta.

As a global business serving more than a quarter billion guests a year in more than 3000 hotels across 74 countries, the Hilton family of Hotels, including Hilton, Conrad Hotels & Resorts, Doubletree, Embassy Suites Hotels, Hampton Inn and Suites, Hilton Garden Inn, Hilton Grand Vacations, Homewood Suites by Hilton and The Waldorf=Astoria Collection, are well-positioned to make a difference environmentally, socially, culturally and economically.

"Population growth and global industrialization are accelerating the depletion of our natural resources. Around the world, demand for energy continues to grow and fresh water scarcity is becoming a global reality. How we respond to these challenges will determine the sustainability of our future lifestyles, the sustainability of our communities as we know them, and ultimately the sustainability of our planet.

"To meet the growing demand of increased travel around the world, we must be able to do so in a sustainable fashion while still delivering unsurpassed levels of hospitality, including a better night's sleep, an enhanced dining experience and a more productive meeting," Nassetta continued. "We must operate our business in ways that provide for our current needs while allowing future generations to meet their own needs. This is the essence of sustainability and the path we must follow. Not only is it the right thing to do as responsible global citizens, it's the right thing to do for our business."

Long-Term, High-Impact Goals

In addition to the stated measurable short-term targets, the company also has committed to focus on several high-impact areas that offer significant long-term benefits. Sustainable buildings and operations, including the advancement of sustainable design and construction, operations, chemical management and purchasing will be one key area. The company is also committed to the advancement of renewable energy as a source of power for its operations, not only to reduce its carbon footprint but to develop a viable commercial infrastructure for powering hotels and corporate offices.

External Assessment by Leading Consulting Group

In the past year, Hilton Hotels Corporation conducted a thorough assessment of its global operations with the goal of identifying current impacts, and creating a strategy to define, galvanize and build sustainability into the business. To lead this effort, HHC brought in Blu Skye Sustainability Consulting, led by company founder and CEO Jib Ellison.

Blu Skye visited a cross-section of Hilton Family hotels, interviewed various business units and analyzed the company's operating procedures. As a result of these efforts, corporate and brand management teams, together with Blu Skye, were able to identify specific areas of focus to build the company's sustainability framework focusing on short and long term value creation. "Hilton is building on its strong history of environmental stewardship by launching these ambitious goals," said Ellison. "Their comprehensive sustainability strategy has put them on a path to leadership in the hospitality industry."

Support Strategy

Under the direction of a newly appointed vice president – global sustainability Christopher Corpuel, HHC will build out a team to develop and implement its sustainability strategy. This team will support all of HHC's core businesses and work closely with hotel ownership and management groups to achieve its stated goals.

In addition, Hilton Hotels Corporation is supporting its portfolio of commitments in a number of ways, by:

- Building out educational and engagement programs for all brands and team members, including online learning, centralized web content, and various training modules.
- Measuring and reporting on our progress. The internal environmental management tool used within company-managed hotels will be extended to all properties, allowing us to track and report on our commitments and design processes and programs that identify areas of opportunity to drive innovation and efficiencies.
- Revising brand operational, and design and construction standards for 2009 to ensure both internal and external best practices are shared, adopted and transparent around the globe.

- Evaluating all current and future purchasing policies and practices across the brands to ensure that the range of products placed in hotels not only enhance the guest experience but drive value for owners while supporting the company's overall sustainability efforts.

Current Practices

Hilton Hotels Corporation has demonstrated its commitment to sustainability with several projects that currently are underway. In the European region, energy and water consumption already have been reduced by 10% during the last two years. In the U.K. and Ireland, the introduction of carbon-free electricity has reduced CO_2 emissions in participating Hilton hotels by more than 64,000 tons, or 56% of our carbon footprint. In the United States, Hilton was the first in the industry to complete the installation of a commercial fuel cell power system, atop the Hilton New York, delivering one of the cleanest power generating technologies available today.

Galvanizing the spirit demonstrated by its recent and past successes together with its current commitments, Hilton Hotels Corporation has created a Mission Statement that will carry forward throughout its business practices.

Mission Statement

The Hilton Family of Hotels will manage our business through a lens of sustainability to benefit this generation and those that follow. Through action and innovation, we will lead our industry in products and programs that:

- Enhance the guest experience
- Engage our employees
- Improve operational efficiency
- Advance building design
- Strengthen our partnerships
- Serve our communities
- Protect our global environment
- Enrich our Family of Brands.

Summary

"If we can use the lens of sustainability and find ways to enhance our leadership position in the industry, I am confident we will not only drive business value in the short and long term, but innovate our products and offerings in ways we never imagined," said Nassetta. "We can create better experiences for our guests, better business opportunities for our partners and investors, better work facilities for our colleagues, and better serve our communities, giving back in ways that actually restore resources instead of removing them, and improving the well-being of all involved. The platform for change we create now is one that will serve us for many years to come and support our goal of being the world's pre-eminent hospitality company."

About the Hilton Hotels Corporation

Hilton Hotels Corporation is the leading global hospitality company, with more than 3,000 hotels and 500,000 rooms in 74 countries, with more than 135,000 team members worldwide. The company owns, manages or franchises some of the best known and highly regarded hotel brands including Hilton®, Conrad® Hotels & Resorts, Doubletree®, Embassy Suites Hotels®, Hampton Inn®, Hampton Inn & Suites®, Hilton Garden Inn®, Hilton Grand Vacations™, Homewood Suites by Hilton® and The Waldorf=Astoria Collection™.

Hilton Hotels Corporation is an Official Sponsor of the U.S. Olympic Team, which will extend through the 2010 Olympic and Paralympic Winter Games in Vancouver, the 2012 Olympic and Paralympic Games in London, the 2010/2012 U.S. Paralympic Team and the 2011 U.S. Pan American Team.

The Hilton Family of Hotels adheres to founder Conrad Hilton's philosophy that, "It has been, and continues to be, our responsibility to fill the earth with the light and warmth of hospitality." The company put a name to its unique brand of service that has made it the best known and most highly regarded hotel company: be hospitable®. The philosophy is shared by all brands in the Hilton Family of Hotels, and is the inspiration for its overarching message of kindness and generosity.

Selecting and Attracting the Right Customers

The following case is completely against the above statement made by Ratan Tata. One day in the month of December Mr.X and his friend Mr.Y went to deposit cash in one of the leading Multi National commercial Bank, They entered the bank premises found one of their executives attending only selective customers which they felt that it is unfair treatment but still they approached him, enquired for pay-in-slip they got it and filled it, later joined the queue with other customers towards the teller counter to deposit the cash which took more than five minutes, employee at the teller counter said "please collect the token for depositing the cash", They left the queue and went to the token machine and opted for non customer with deposit of Rupees less than 50000 and they got the token with (NW72) number and they were waiting for their turn to come and also observing the pattern of calling the customers, customers who came after them were provided priority services, in first 10-12 minutes they came to a conclusion that first preference was given to the customers of the bank itself, They immediately went to the token machine and opted for an another token as customer of the bank with deposit of Rupees less than 50000 and got the token with (CD81) number, their turn came just after fourth customer.

They deposited the money and went to see the manager and put forth their complaint to him that the treatment what a non customer is getting is unreasonable and it is unfair on the part of the bank, the bank manager says that "this is a system where in non customers have been provided a separate counter and as an when their turn comes they will get the service and he was arguing with them and goes on explaining the system, procedure etc., But Mr. X & Y were not at all impressed with his justification and his indifferent comments on the problem made them felt awful, They thanked the Bank Manager and left his cabin.

This is nothing but over automation where in there is no personal touch or humane touch in their approach. This conversation have created an permanent negative image of the bank in their minds that they would never ever be a customer of such Bank or its sister concern and will never suggest any of their friends, relatives and even strangers to be a customer of that bank. Does any customer wants to hear "what are the company's systems and procedures, rules & regulations etc., As a direct or indirect customer one would never want to hear all those justifications, they just want quick service. And there is every possibility that automation of customer service will be abandoned in the frontline and induction of specialists in customer services in front office will be a future trend now which can be observed in Aviation industry. As of now few financial institutions are serving their customers in depositing money, withdrawals, financial planning and tax planning etc., at customer's premises.

The following example explains how indirectly a customer can be a valuable asset for an organization.

Eg: An individual who spends merely an average dollar amount per month with a wireless phone provider might be considered even more valuable if the wireless company knew the customer's spouse was responsible for selecting the wireless service plan for 5,000 workers at a large company.

In general there is misconception in the peoples mind that Public sector undertakings are poor at customer service, to some extent this comment may be right, but not completely true. Here are two public sector banks 'C' Bank (CB) and 'O' Bank (OB). Whose services are far better than that of Indian Multi National Bank. In the month of December Mr. X have been to CB to collect a Demand Draft, it took him more than half an hour when he asked about the time delay in issuing Demand Draft the Assistant Manager was courteous enough to say that "Sir, please wait for few minutes it will be done" and he did it in next ten minutes. Though Mr. X felt bad about the delay in issuing the draft but Mr. X was pleased by the response of the Assistant Manger. This episode haven't made him much disappointed and have not provoked him to erase completely CB from his mind; He still wanted to open an account because it is convenient for him to transact and staff's aptitude to handle customer services are better. And Mr. X still felt CB is bankable and there are better chances that he would suggest his friends to bank at CB.

Unfortunately on the same day itself a situation came, where in he was forced to take one more Demand Draft, he visited OB and enquired about DD form at the counter, the employee just shown the place where they were, with a pathetic face, he took the form and his first question to the bank employee was "How much time does it take to issue a Demand Draft" there was no response from that bank employee who was sitting at the counter, suddenly there was a unexpected response which he heard from an unusual person, a middle aged woman, who is just a Peon " Sir it will just take five minutes" He was convinced with her approach of attending him, he simply paid the amount at the teller and stood near the counter, rest she took over the Job. During this time, she was doing her job simultaneously interacting with him by posing soft questions like "Are you in a hurry Sir?" Where do you come from? And other few similar questions. By the time he answered her questions, the Demand Draft was ready. It took only seven minutes as compared to official time to make a DD is twenty minutes, though it was delayed by two minutes as promised, he was extremely satisfied with that Lady's service. He felt like it would have been better if she would have placed in front office as an executive instead of Peon. Mr. X was extremely impressed by that lady's ability to engage customer at POP, One would definitely feel that the big companies and their big projects of Customer Relationship Management are of no use when there are no people to implement it all the levels.

"According to a research by Reichheld and Sasser in the Harvard Business Review, 5% increase in customer retention can increase profitability by 35% in banking business, 50% in insurance and brokerage, and 125% in the consumer credit card market. Therefore, banks are now stressing on retaining customers and increasing market share".

The above situations like these are definitely creating an impression in the mind of customers that the corporate are denying legitimate right, needs and requirements.

Right from the days of customer centric market, this has been a regular activity that there are problems in customer care. In today's business environment there is no such industry, where customer care problems does not exist, even in the field of hospitality industry and service industry where in these industry's core business is custom care and the gap between the customers and their expectations and the service providers are increasing day by day. Today in the Heighten world lot many new innovative products and services are being invented, but at the same time does any company thought that the product/service they offer are really needed by the customers or it is just because the products are being produced and are dumped into the market.

As people are very much aware that there are whole variety of products and services available in the market. But how many of them do really buy them even though they are of top quality, with marvellous features and at affordable prices.

Managers at middle level and supervisory levels of Indian corporate are not ready to treat customers equally. Unless the attitude of the managers changes towards customers problems pertaining to service will always exist.

How companies are responding to the bad experiences of using the product or service, what are the measures taken to avoid such experiences by the customers. Companies must ensure that customers get a new experience in purchasing and using their products and the impact of such purchase must be for a long time and which can be encased into new opportunities in the long run. And differentiating from competitors, there by extending the change in purchasing experience.

One would definitely agree that, it is not always possible to give such a kind of experience and personal attention to each and every customer, but a company must make sure that customers should not leave the premises without satisfaction, and it is the right of the customer to expect highest degree of respect, let it be in the case of, hospitality, product availability, price, features or any other service (E.g.: Fiat is known for its best designed and engineered cars in the world, but in India it could not capture the market as expected because, after sales service levels were not up to the expectations of the customer, In order to boost sales in India, Tata Motors and Fiat came together and announced a strategic relationship in passenger car segment for sales and marketing of Fiat cars through Tata dealerships. Through these dealerships display a wide selection of Fiat cars along with service and spares will be provided across Tata dealerships in India. Dealers will display the Fiat models along with Tata cars)

And most importantly the consumer complaining behavior process is unique; it has to deal with at most importance. And it distinguishes between negative word-of-mouth that occurs prior to seeking redress (or in lieu of seeking redress) and negative word-of-mouth that occurs after seeking redress.

There is an argument from the company's point of view i.e. how can any company spend time and manpower to attend a default and fraudulent customer and how treat them in the same manner as genuine and productive customer.

Certainly they must be treated in a cordial way but one should not forget that they too deserve some importance in one way or the other.

There is every possibility that companies make mistakes but they must be such that they should be forgivable by the customer, meaning even though companies make mistakes and try to rectify at the earliest and inform customers that the mistake which has been committed is been rectified and at most precautions have been taken, not to repeat the mistake.

Eg: What Cadbury has done by giving advertisements in the media, that it has rectified its mistakes and promised the customer that it won't repeat the same mistake again.

If a person is a regular customer of friendly neighborhood grocery shop or any other shop or bank, one will definitely know the painless punch of corporate businesses. They might misguide, mislead with the bashing effect, display, intense publicity, promotion and enchasing on personal intimacy. One should be aware that in one way or the other the suppliers are the customers and consumers of their own produce. The individuals who supply the produce at certain rate cannot afford to purchase the same product just because it is been packed and placed in fully decorated place. In this kind of situation, are you (customer) the beneficiary, just ask yourself. Who do you think is the real beneficiary; if your answer is, neither the supplier nor the consumer, then one will get to know there is nothing, which is called as "Service".

Most Indians are habituated to have every thing fresh and never had tradition of packing food, let it be cooked or uncooked food, they prefer to have them in a natural way. e.g: Fresh vegetables and fruits, do they really need packing, is there any need for branding products which are grown naturally or cultivated, does anyone feel it is absolutely necessary?

The ever changing customer expectations are forcing the corporate to provide excellent service which is not possible to each an every company, organizations which provides service beyond customer expectations will survive the future rest will be out of business. Organizations who wanted to survive are exploring, proliferating them selves by establishing new businesses in big way, there by depending on higher volumes. Some of them are collaboratively sharing their customer data there by offering vide variety of products to the same customer and leveraging customer base. These strategies adopted by the companies constantly put the pressure on the customer by offering vide range of product and there is fare chance that one might ignore such product offerings which are marketed by different departments, which are in a race generate revenue of their own. There is always a risk that customer may encounter different service levels of the different department of the same company.

For many years, Indian economy has been guarded from invasion of foreign companies in the form of Joint venture or fully owned or capitalistic form of economy. Only some state owned companies which were in key areas like Defense, Telecom, Oil and other essential commodities. A set of few private owned companies who were into consumer items, engineering and manufacturing prospered during that period. Right from the days of closely guarded economy and till the days of economic liberalization in late 1990, the private owned companies in the seller's market were very successful. But the whole scenario chanced after post liberalization.

Ever since the golden days (customer centric market) i.e. Since last thirty years to till date, marketers have been saying "Customer is the King" but, is the customer really a king? This is the main question which comes to everybody's mind and other questions such as how customers are treated? What quality of products do marketers offer? Are the products are user friendly? Etc., if these questions are answered completely with good outlook, a company can build up a brand which will be unique in any or combination of all the following attributes Price, Design, Quality, Usability, Service and shopping experience there by creating own and distinguished Brand. As an human being every individual expects to be treated with courtesy, similarly it is prime duty of marketers to treat customer with at most respect which he/she deserves. Here is a situation where CRM come in to picture, the essence of CRM should be understood as any activity which is completely customer centric and which enhances customer's expectations and satisfaction levels by giving him/her a wow effect with a human touch, at the same time maximize revenues from such services.

"CRM would help organizations to serve the customers on an individual basis, to enjoy a long-term relationship and to get rid of barriers and distortions created by non-value adding intermediaries. He also says that CRM would also help organizations to reduce marketing costs, target specific customers by focusing on their needs and to track the effectiveness of a given marketing action" by Dr. Thapan K. Panda, IIM Indore.

"CRM has power to help bankers quickly and directly improve customer satisfaction. CRM is an added dimension to ensure that what the customer expects is consistent with what the bank is prepared to deliver. One expert in bank CRM initiatives recently said that CRM is an approach that is less focused on providing the right services to the customer than attracting customers who are the right fit for what the bank has to offer. Further, the primary value of CRM is its potential as a customer retention tool. People are starting to measure CRM in terms of increased customer satisfaction rather than ROI" by Rob Keene, Director, Banking Practice.

In the vide spectrum of business, in after adopting and practicing latest technologies like CRM, people soft and other similar technologies. How do people interpret and understand the meaning of Customer Relationship Management, many experts expressed their view in different forms but there are few seminaries which revolve round the "Customer's needs, expectations and satisfaction"

In the field of consumer service management, many unexpected problem do arise and they pose challenges to be solved, a doubt may arise in the minds of individuals that adopting all these CRM technologies are of waste of money and time. May be not, as per the latest studies, customer service problems are marginalized to some extent but could not overcome them completely. We cannot imagine big businesses without such customer service technologies. Company's internal environment (employees) and external environment (Customer traffic, Business expansion etc.,) do influence on implementation of such technologies, Employees must be trained continuously to implement it and also change their mind set to adapt to such changing environment (customer centric). Unless people from top to bottom level in all departments focus and act on, what they actually wanted achieve in customer relationship management, interactive Customer Relationship Management software solutions will never deliver expected results.

It can be concluded that if any company intends to survive in today's competitive market it is essential that they must to treat customer as a king irrespective of using any technology. And giving at most importance to the direct or an indirect customer. Who knows a non productive customer of yours, may be a highly productive customer of your competitor.

International Trade Theory, Practice and Policy

International trade is exchange of capital, goods, and services across international borders or territories. It refers to exports of goods and services by a firm to a foreign-based buyer (importer) In most countries, it represents a significant share of gross domestic product (GDP). While international trade has been present throughout much of history, its economic, social, and political importance has been on the rise in recent centuries.

Industrialization, advanced transportation, globalization, multinational corporations, and outsourcing are all having a major impact on the international trade system. Increasing international trade is crucial to the continuance of globalization. International trade is a major source of economic revenue for any nation that is considered a world power. Without international trade, nations would be limited to the goods and services produced within their own borders.

International trade is in principle not different from domestic trade as the motivation and the behavior of parties involved in a trade do not change fundamentally regardless of whether trade is across a border or not. The main difference is that international trade is typically more costly than domestic trade. The reason is that a border typically imposes additional costs such as tariffs, time costs due to border delays and costs associated with country differences such as language, the legal system or culture.

Another difference between domestic and international trade is that factors of production such as capital and labour are typically more mobile within a country than across countries. Thus international trade is mostly restricted to trade in goods and services, and only to a lesser extent to trade in capital, labour or other factors of production. Then trade in goods and services can serve as a substitute for trade in factors of production. Instead of importing a factor of production, a country can import goods that make intensive use of the factor of production and are thus embodying the respective factor. An example is the import of labour-intensive goods by the United States from China. Instead of importing Chinese labour the United States is importing goods from China that were produced with Chinese labour.

International trade uses a variety of currencies, the most important of which are held as foreign reserves by governments and central banks. Here the percentage of global cummulative reserves held for each currency between 1995 and 2005 are shown: the US dollar is the most sought-after currency, with the Euro in strong demand as well.

Models

Several different models have been proposed to predict patterns of trade and to analyse the effects of trade policies such as tariffs.

Ricardian Model

The Ricardian model focuses on comparative advantage and is perhaps the most important concept in international trade theory. In a Ricardian model, countries specialize in producing what they produce best. Unlike other models, the Ricardian framework predicts that countries will fully specialize instead of producing a broad array of goods.

Also, the Ricardian model does not directly consider factor endowments, such as the relative amounts of labour and capital within a country. The main merit of Ricardin model is that it assumes technology differences between countries. Technology gap is easily included in the Ricardian and Ricardo-Sraffa model.

The Ricardian model makes the following assumptions:

1. Labour is the only primary input to production (labour is considered to be the ultimate source of value).
2. Constant Marginal Product of Labour (MPL) (Labour productivity is constant, constant returns to scale, and simple technology.)
3. Limited amount of labour in the economy
4. Labour is perfectly mobile among sectors but not internationally.
5. Perfect competition (price-takers).

The Ricardian model measures in the short-run, therefore technology differs internationally. This supports the fact that countries follow their comparative advantage and allows for specialization.

Modern Development of the Ricardian Model

The Ricardian trade model was studied by Graham, Jones, McKenzie and others. All the theories excluded intermediate goods, or traded input goods such as materials and capital goods. McKenzie(1954), Jones(1961) and Samuelson(2001) emphasized that considerable gains from trade would be lost once intermediate goods were excluded from trade. In a famous comment McKenzie (1954,) pointed that "A moment's consideration will convince one that Lancashire would be unlikely to produce cotton cloth if the cotton had to be grown in England." Recently, the theory was extended to the case that includes traded intermediates. Thus the "labour only" assumption was removed from the theory. Thus the new Ricardian theory, or the Ricardo-Sraffa model, as it is sometimes named, theoretically includes capital goods such as machines and materials, which are traded across countries. In the time of global trade, this assumption is much more realistic than the Heckscher-Ohlin model, which assumes that capital is fixed inside the country and does not move internationally.

Heckscher-Ohlin Model

In the early 1900s an international trade theory called factor proportions theory emerged by two Swedish economists, Eli Heckscher and Bertil Ohlin. This theory is also called the Heckscher-Ohlin theory. The Heckscher-Ohlin theory stresses that countries should produce and export goods that require resources (factors) that are abundant and import goods that require resources in short supply. This theory differs from the theories of comparative advantage and absolute advantage since these theory focuses on the productivity of the production process for a particular good. On the contrary, the Heckscher-Ohlin theory states that a country should specialise production and export using the factors that are most abundant, and thus the cheapest. Not to produce, as earlier theories stated, the goods it produces most efficiently.

The Heckscher-Ohlin model was produced as an alternative to the Ricardian model of basic comparative advantage. Despite its greater complexity it did not prove much more accurate in its predictions. However from a theoretical point of view it did provide an elegant solution by incorporating the neoclassical price mechanism into international trade theory.

The theory argues that the pattern of international trade is determined by differences in factor endowments. It predicts that countries will export those goods that make intensive use of locally abundant factors and will import goods that make intensive use of factors that are locally scarce. Empirical problems with the H-O model, known as the Leontief paradox, were exposed in empirical tests by Wassily Leontief who found that the United States tended to export labour intensive goods despite having a capital abundance.

The H-O model makes the following core assumptions:

1. Labour and capital flow freely between sectors

2. The production of shoes is labour intensive and computers is capital intensive
3. The amount of labour and capital in two countries differ (difference in endowments)
4. free trade
5. technology is the same across countries (long-term)
6. Tastes are the same.

The problem with the H-O theory is that it excludes the trade of capital goods (including materials and fuels). In the H-O theory, labour and capital are fixed entities endowed to each country. In a modern economy, capital goods are traded internationally. Gains from trade of intermediate goods are considerable, as it was emphasized by Samuelson (2001).

Reality and Applicability of the Heckscher-Ohlin Model

The Heckscher-Ohlin theory is preferred to the Ricardo theory by many economists, because it makes fewer simplifying assumptions. In 1953, Wassily Leontief published a study, where he tested the validity of the Heckscher-Ohlin theory. The study showed that the U.S was more abundant in capital compared to other countries, therefore the U.S would export capital-intensive goods and import labour-intensive goods. Leontief found out that the U.S's export was less capital intensive than import.

After the appearance of Leontief's paradox, many researchers tried to save the Heckscher-Ohlin theory, either by new methods of measurement, or either by new interpretations. Leamer emphasized that Leontief did not interpret HO theory properly and claimed that with a right interpretation paradox did not occur. Brecher and Choudri found that, if Leamer was right, the American workers consumption per head should be lower than the workers world average consumption.

Many other trials followed but most of them failed. Many of famous textbook writers, including Krugman and Obstfeld and Bowen, Hollander and Viane, are negative about the validity of H-O model. After examining the long history of empirical research, Bowen, Hollander and Viane concluded: "Recent tests of the factor abundance theory [H-O theory and its developed form into many-commodity and many-factor case] that directly examine the H-O-V equations also indicate the rejection of the theory." Heckscher-Ohlin theory is not well adapted to the analyse South-North trade problems. The assumptions of HO are less realistic with respect to N-S than N-N (or S-S) trade. Income differences between North and South is the one that third world cares most. The factor price equalization [a consequence of HO theory] has not shown much sign of realization. HO model assumes identical production functions between countries. This is highly unrealistic. Technological gap between developed and developing countries is the main concern of the poor countries.

Specific Factors Model

Global Competitiveness Index (2008-2009): competitiveness is an important determinant for the well-being of states in an international trade environment.

In this model, labour mobility between industries is possible while capital is immobile between industries in the short-run. Thus, this model can be interpreted as a 'short run' version of the Heckscher-Ohlin model. The specific factors name refers to the given that in the short-run, specific factors of production such as physical capital are not easily transferable between industries. The theory suggests that if there is an increase in the price of a good, the owners of the factor of production specific to that good will profit in real terms.

Additionally, owners of opposing specific factors of production (i.e. labour and capital) are likely to have opposing agendas when lobbying for controls over immigration of labour. Conversely, both owners of capital and labour profit in real terms from an increase in the capital endowment. This model is ideal for particular industries. This model is ideal for understanding income distribution but awkward for discussing the pattern of trade.

New Trade Theory

Main Article: New Trade Theory

New Trade theory tries to explain several facts about trade, which the two main models above have difficulty with. These include the fact that most trade is between countries with similar factor endowment and productivity levels, and the large amount of multinational production(i.e.foreign direct investment) which exists. In one example of this framework, the economy exhibits monopolistic competition and increasing returns to scale. There are three basic theories that global marketer has to comprehend:

1. Comparative Advantage Theory 2. Trade or product trade cycle theory 3. Business orientation theory

Gravity Model

The Gravity model of trade presents a more empirical analysis of trading patterns rather than the more theoretical models discussed above. The gravity model, in its basic form, predicts trade based on the distance between countries and the interaction of the countries' economic sizes. The model mimics the Newtonian law of gravity which also considers distance and physical size between two objects. The model has been proven to be empirically strong through econometric analysis. Other factors such as income level, diplomatic relationships between countries, and trade policies are also included in expanded versions of the model.

Regulation of International Trade

Traditionally trade was regulated through bilateral treaties between two nations. For centuries under the belief in mercantilism most nations had high tariffs and many restrictions on international trade. In the 19th century, especially in the United Kingdom, a belief in free trade became paramount. This belief became the dominant thinking among western nations since then. In the years since the Second World War, controversial multilateral treaties like the General Agreement on Tariffs and Trade (GATT) and World Trade Organization have attempted to promote free trade while creating a globally regulated trade structure. These trade agreements have often resulted in discontent and protest with claims of unfair trade that is not beneficial to developing countries.

Free trade is usually most strongly supported by the most economically powerful nations, though they often engage in selective protectionism for those industries which are strategically important such as the protective tariffs applied to agriculture by the United States and Europe. The Netherlands and the United Kingdom were both strong advocates of free trade when they were economically dominant, today the United States, the United Kingdom, Australia and Japan are its greatest proponents. However, many other countries (such as India, China and Russia) are increasingly becoming advocates of free trade as they become more economically powerful themselves. As tariff levels fall there is also an increasing willingness to negotiate non tariff measures, including foreign direct investment, procurement and trade facilitation. The latter looks at the transaction cost associated with meeting trade and customs procedures.

Traditionally agricultural interests are usually in favour of free trade while manufacturing sectors often support protectionism. This has changed somewhat in recent years, however. In fact, agricultural lobbies, particularly in the United States, Europe and Japan, are chiefly responsible for particular rules in the major international trade treaties which allow for more protectionist measures in agriculture than for most other goods and services.

During recessions there is often strong domestic pressure to increase tariffs to protect domestic industries. This occurred around the world during the Great Depression. Many economists have attempted to portray tariffs as the underlining reason behind the collapse in world trade that many believe seriously deepened the depression.

The regulation of international trade is done through the World Trade Organization at the global level, and through several other regional arrangements such as MERCOSUR in South America, the North American Free Trade Agreement (NAFTA) between the United States, Canada and Mexico, and the European Union between 27 independent states. The 2005 Buenos Aires talks on the planned establishment of the Free Trade Area of the Americas (FTAA) failed largely because of opposition from the populations of Latin American nations. Similar agreements such as the Multilateral Agreement on Investment (MAI) have also failed in recent years.

Risk in International Trade

Companies doing business across international borders face many of the same risks as would normally be evident in strictly domestic transactions. For example,

- Buyer insolvency (purchaser cannot pay);
- Non-acceptance (buyer rejects goods as different from the agreed upon specifications);
- Credit risk (allowing the buyer to take possession of goods prior to payment);
- Regulatory risk (e.g., a change in rules that prevents the transaction);
- Intervention (governmental action to prevent a transaction being completed);

- Political risk (change in leadership interfering with transactions or prices); and
- War and other uncontrollable events.

In addition, international trade also faces the risk of unfavourable exchange rate movements (and, the potential benefit of favourable movements).

The Measurement of Efficiency and Productivity

Market orientation efficiency is conceptualized as the speed by which a company gathers information about customers and competitors, disseminates the information throughout the organization, arrives at a shared meaning, and implements a response. A reliable scale with demonstrated content and convergent validity is developed and the impact of market orientation efficiency on business performance is assessed based on multiple informant data drawn from two industries. From a managerial perspective, the scale can be used to evaluate a given firm's level of market orientation efficiency as a baseline measure and again as a measure of success once strategies designed to improve market orientation efficiency are set into motion.

Ultimate Goal of Operations Research

The term Operations Research (OR) describes the discipline that is focused on the application of information technology for informed decision-making. In other words, OR represents the study of optimal resource allocation. The goal of OR is to provide rational bases for decision making by seeking to understand and structure complex situations, and to utilize this understanding to predict system behavior and improve system performance. Much of the actual work is conducted by using analytical and numerical techniques to develop and manipulate mathematical models of organizational systems that are composed of people, machines, and procedures. This article introduces some of the methods and application that are affiliated with OR, and elaborates on some of the benefits that may be gained by incorporating OR into the actual business framework.

OR Activities

OR's role in both, the public and the private sectors is increasing rapidly. In general, OR addresses a wide variety of issues in transportation, inventory planning, production planning, communication operations, computer operations, financial assets, risk management, revenue management, and many other fields where improving business productivity is paramount. In the public sector, OR studies may focus on energy policy, defense, health care, water resource planning, design and operation of urban emergency systems, or criminal justice. To reiterate, OR reflects an analytical method of problem solving and decision-making that is useful in the management of organizations. In OR, problems are (1) decomposed into basic components and (2) solved via mathematical analysis. Some of the analytical methods used in OR include mathematical logic, simulation, network analysis, queuing theory, and game theory. The actual

OR process can in general be described via three steps. (1) A set of potential solutions to a problem is identified and developed (the set may be rather large). (2) The alternatives derived in the first step are analyzed, and reduced to a smaller set of solutions (the solutions have to be feasible and workable). (3) The alternatives derived in the second step are subjected to simulated implementation and, if feasible, exposed

to an actual analysis in a real-world environment. It has to be pointed out that in the final step, psychology and management sciences often play a rather important role. Generally speaking, OR improves the effectiveness and the efficiency of an institution, hence some of the benefits offered by OR include:

- Decrease Cost or Investment
- Increase Revenue or Return on Investment
- Increase Market Share
- Manage and Reduce Risk
- Improve Quality
- Increase Throughput while Decreasing Delays
- Achieve Improved Utilization form Limited Resources
- Demonstrate Feasibility and Workability.

OR Functions and Methods

OR may assist decision-makers in almost any management function. To illustrate, OR supports the key decision making process, allows to solve urgent problems, can be utilized to design improved multistep operations (processes), setup policies, supports the planning and forecasting steps, and measures actual results.

OR can be applied at the non-manager levels as well, as engineers or consumers alike can benefit from the improved and streamlined decision-making process.

When first encountered, the methods commonly utilized in OR may seem obscure. Technical labels such as multi-criteria decision analysis, linear and non-linear programming, discrete-event Dominique A. Heger, Fortuitous Technology, Austin, TX, 2006 simulation, queuing and stochastic process modeling, conjoint analysis, or neural networking further foster this general impression. Despite the wealth of labels available in the filed of OR, most projects apply one of three broad groups of methods, which may be described as:

- *Simulation methods,* where the goal is to develop simulators that provide the decision-maker with the ability to conduct sensitivity studies to (1) search for improvements, and (2) to test and benchmark the improvement ideas that are being made.
- *Optimization methods,* where the goal is to enable the decision maker to search among possible choices in an efficient and effective manner, in environments where thousands or millions of choices may actually be feasible, or where some of the comparing choices are rather complex. The ultimate goal is to identify and locate the very best choice based on certain criteria's.
- *Data-analysis methods,* where the goal is to aid the decision-maker in detecting actual patterns and inter-connections in the data set. This method is rather useful in numerous applications including forecasting and data mining based business environments.

Within each of the three basic groups, many probabilistic methods provide the ability to assess risk and uncertainty factors.

OR in Manufacturing

As OR has made (over the years) significant contributions in virtually all industries, in almost all managerial and decision-making functions, and at most organizational levels, the list of OR applications is prodigious. Hence, this article focuses in the next few paragraphs on the manufacturing industry, and introduces some of the application where OR is being used. The term operations in OR may suggests that the manufacturing application category represents the original home of OR. That is not quite accurate, as the name originated from military operations, not business operations. Nevertheless, it is a true statement that OR's successes in contemporary business pervade manufacturing and service operations, logistics, distribution, transportation, and telecommunication. The myriad applications include scheduling, routing, workflow improvements, elimination of bottlenecks, inventory control, business process re-engineering, site selection, or facility and

general operational planning. Revenue and supply chain management reflect two growing applications that are distinguished by their use of several OR methods to cover several functions. Revenue management entails first to accurately forecasting the demand, and secondly to adjust the price structure over time to more profitably allocate fixed capacity. Supply chain decisions describe the who, what, when, and where abstractions from purchasing and transporting raw materials and parts, through manufacturing actual

products and goods, and finally distributing and delivering the items to the customers. The prime management goal here may be to reduce overall cost while processing customer orders more efficiently than before.

The power of utilizing OR methods allows examining this rather complex and convoluted chain in a comprehensive manner, and to search among a vast number of combinations for the resource optimization and allocation strategy that seem most effective, and hence beneficial to the operation.

Production Systems

Businesses and organizations frequently face challenging operational problems whose successful solution requires certain expertise in applied statistics, optimization, stochastic modeling, or a combination of these areas. To illustrate, a company may need to design a sampling plan in order to meet specific quality control objectives. In a manufacturing environment, operations that compete for the same resources must be scheduled in a way that deadlines are not violated. The manager of a supermarket must determine

how many checkout lines to keep open at various times during the day and evening so that shoppers are not unnecessarily delayed.

Or as a final example, the size of the areas reserved for storing work in process at a Dominique A. Heger, Fortuitous Technology, Austin, TX, 2006 number of bottleneck stations has to be determined so that a smooth flow of work results, even at the busiest (peak) production times.

The area of operations research that concentrates on real-world operational problems is called production systems. Production systems problems may arise in settings that include, but are not limited to, manufacturing, telecommunications, health-care delivery, facility location and layout, and staffing. The area of production systems presents special challenges for operations researchers. Production problems are operations research problems, hence solving them requires a solid foundation in operations research

fundamentals. Additionally, the solution of production systems problems frequently draws on expertise in more than one of the primary areas of operations research, implying that the successful production researcher can not be one-dimensional. Furthermore, production systems problems can not be solved without an in-depth understanding of the real problem, since invoking assumptions that simplify the mathematical structure of the problem may lead to an elegant solution for the wrong problem. Common sense and practical insight are common attributes of successful production planners.

At the current time, the filed of OR is extremely dynamic and ever evolving.

To name a few of the contemporary (primary) research projects, current work in OR seeks to develop software for material flow analysis and design of flexible manufacturing facilities using pattern recognition and graph theory algorithms. Further, approaches for the design of re-configurable manufacturing systems and progressive automation of discrete manufacturing systems are under development. Additional OR projects focus on the industrial deployment of computer-based methods for assembly line balancing, business process reengineering, capacity planning, pull scheduling, and setup reduction, primarily through the integration of the philosophies of the Theory of Constraints and Lean Manufacturing. Please see Appendix A for a short introduction to the objectives and key principles of the Lean Manufacturing principles).

Identifying Sources of Operational Risk

An operational risk is a risk arising from execution of a company's business functions. As such, it is a very broad concept including e.g. fraud risks, legal risks, physical or environmental risks, etc. The term operational risk is most commonly found in risk management programs of financial institutions that must organize their risk management program according to Basel II. In Basel II, risk management is divided into credit, market, liquidity and operational risk management. In many cases, credit and market risks are handled through a company's financial department, whereas operational risk management is perhaps coordinated centrally but most commonly implemented in different operational units (e.g. the IT department takes care of information risks, the HR department takes care of personnel risks, etc.)

More specifically, Basel II defines operational risk as the risk of loss resulting from inadequate or failed internal processes, people and systems, or from external events. Although the risks apply to any organization in business, this particular way of framing risk management is of particular relevance to the banking regime where regulators are responsible for establishing safeguards to protect against systemic failure of the banking system and the economy.

Background

Since the mid-1990s, the topics of market risk and credit risk have been the subject of much debate and research, with the result that financial institutions have made significant progress in the identification, measurement and management of both these forms of risk. However, it is worth mentioning that the near collapse of the U.S. financial system in September 2008 is a clear indication that our ability to measure market and credit risk is far from perfect.

Globalization and deregulation in financial markets, combined with increased sophistication in financial technology, have introduced more complexities into the activities of banks and therefore their risk profiles. These reasons underscore banks' and supervisors' growing focus upon the identification and measurement of operational risk.

Events such as the September 11 terrorist attacks, rogue trading losses at Societe Generale, Barings, AIB and National Australia

Bank serve to highlight the fact that the scope of risk management extends beyond merely market and credit risk.

The list of risks (and, more importantly, the scale of these risks) faced by banks today includes fraud, system failures, terrorism and employee compensation claims. These types of risk are generally classified under the term 'operational risk'.

The identification and measurement of operational risk is a real and live issue for modern-day banks, particularly since the decision by the Basel Committee on Banking Supervision (BCBS) to introduce a capital charge for this risk as part of the new capital adequacy framework (Basel II).

Definition

The Basel Committee defines operational risk as: "The risk of loss resulting from inadequate or failed internal processes, people and systems or from external events." However, the Basel Committee recognizes that operational risk is a term that has a variety of meanings and therefore, for internal purposes, banks are permitted to adopt their own definitions of operational risk, provided the minimum elements in the Committee's definition are included.

Scope Exclusions

The Basel II definition of operational risk excludes, for example, strategic risk-the risk of a loss arising from a poor strategic business decision. Other risk terms are seen as potential consequences of operational risk events. For example, reputational risk (damage to an organization through loss of its reputation or standing) can arise as a consequence (or impact) of operational failures-as well as from other events.

Basel II Event Type Categories

The following lists the official Basel II defined event types with some examples for each category:

1. Internal Fraud-misappropriation of assets, tax evasion, intentional mismarking of positions, bribery
2. External Fraud-theft of information, hacking damage, third-party theft and forgery
3. Employment Practices and Workplace Safety-discrimination, workers compensation, employee health and safety

4. Clients, Products, & Business Practice-market manipulation, antitrust, improper trade, product defects, fiduciary breaches, account churning
5. Damage to Physical Assets-natural disasters, terrorism, vandalism
6. Business Disruption & Systems Failures-utility disruptions, software failures, hardware failures
7. Execution, Delivery, & Process Management-data entry errors, accounting errors, failed mandatory reporting, negligent loss of client assets.

Difficulties

It is relatively straightforward for an organization to set and observe specific, measurable levels of market risk and credit risk. By contrast it is relatively difficult to identify or assess levels of operational risk and its many sources. Historically organizations have accepted operational risk as an unavoidable cost of doing business.

Methods of Operational Risk Management

Basel II and various Supervisory bodies of the countries have prescribed various soundness standards for Operational Risk Management for Banks and similar Financial Institutions. To complement these standards, Basel II has given guidance to 3 broad methods of Capital calculation for Operational Risk

- Basic Indicator Approach-based on annual revenue of the Financial Institution
- Standardized Approach-based on annual revenue of each of the broad business lines of the Financial Institution
- Advanced Measurement Approaches-based on the internally developed risk measurement framework of the bank adhering to the standards prescribed (methods include IMA, LDA, Scenario-based, Scorecard etc.)

The Operational Risk Management framework should include identification, measurement, monitoring, reporting, control and mitigation frameworks for Operational Risk.

Operational disasters in financial institutions have grabbed any number of headlines in newspapers around the world in the last few years-as the case studies on our Wheel of Misfortune demonstrate.

For managers, these tales of incompetence, corruption and simple bad luck are both entertaining and disconcerting.

Disconcerting because, as the tally has risen, it's become clear that gross operational error and failure is much less isolated from the problem of day-to-day management than the financial industry had imagined.

Researchers now reckon that catastrophic events are the visible part of a wider spectrum of cover-ups, "near misses", and costly but undramatic events that plague most firms-and signal a failure in risk management practice and technology.

Operational risk has also turned out to be more costly in terms of capital than most institutions realised-recent estimates put it at 25% or more of risk capital. And that's rising, as operational risk emerges from beneath New Economy business models such as Internet banking, electronic trading and the outsourcing of core bank functions.

Meanwhile, as our scroll-over timeline explains, the regulators of international banking are about to ask major banks to set aside specific amounts of capital for operational risk. It's part of their long-term project to tie capital charges more directly to risk-taking.

Bank regulators are not alone in demanding a new approach. Corporate governance experts and stockmarket analysts have begun to address disingenuous questions to all sorts of financial institutions. Shouldn't top executives be able to name any "sudden death" risks that their firm is exposed to? Or at least have some idea of the scale of potential operational losses in their industry?

Top executives are themselves wondering whether decisions based on risk-adjusted return on capital (RAROC) might be flawed if operational risk is not taken into account. Might they simply exchange business lines with transparent market or credit risks for those with hidden risks?

All this explains why controlling operational risks at business-line level-simply "getting it right"-is no longer enough for many professionals. But, so far, financial institutions lack a framework of methodologies and tools to push operational risks through a coherent risk management cycle.

Some of the new ideas have grown out of established risk management disciplines in financial institutions such as Audit and Market Risk, while others are drawn from activities as diverse as healthcare and the space industry. As we go along, we'll explain the new concepts that are driving operational risk management, hear from some Expert Witnesses, and offer links to key information points on the web.

Saying what You Mean-The Definitional Problem

Defining operational risk sounds easy-it's the risk of something going unexpectedly wrong! Bankers add the caveat "outside of market and credit risk" because they already have specialist risk managers for these areas. But general definitions are less useful when a manager or regulator tries to do something about enterprise-wide operational risk-such as improve operational risk controls across the board, or reserve capital against operational risk.

Counting something, or controlling it, means putting a line around it. Soon, regulators and RAROC analysts will need to decide whether to include, say, strategic business risks or reputational risk in their allocation of regulatory and enterprise-wide capital.

And managers will need to know whether their assessment of operational risk in a business line should include, say, the risk of a trader misunderstanding a sophisticated financial model. Some experts are sure model risk should be included, while others are sure it forms a more natural component of market risk-the button below maps out some other tricky boundary clashes.

Luckily, busy practitioners can sidestep this industry debate by selecting a suitable definition from those below. For the moment, there's really no "right" general definition save one that's boldly drawn and fits the purpose.

Definitions developed by industry bodies and regulators have some practical advantages, so let's take a closer look at the components of operational risk as defined by the London-based British Bankers Association-a body that has been active in developing standard approaches to operational risk.

For the BBA, "Operational risk is the risk of direct or indirect loss resulting from inadequate or failed internal processes, people, and systems or from external events."

Patching up Processes

Historically, most financial institutions have built expert "ways of doing things" to achieve their objectives-whether that's administering a checking account in the retail business, or confirming the details of a million-dollar swap transaction in the money markets.

Processes of a more or less formal kind surround many of the risky activities of a bank. Some are routines performed by humans while others are part of the core infrastructure of the institution. The button below lists some key processes surrounding a capital markets trader.

Key Processes-From Hire to Fire

Connecting a discrete set of actions into a procedure, and than a formal process, offers huge benefits to financial institutions-as it does to manufacturing industries-in terms of scaling, risk control and standardisation.

Processes also help to defuse risk by institutionalising skills that would otherwise reside in a single individual. But processes can make a firm vulnerable in other ways.

Few employees understand a complex bank process as a whole, so the implications of sloppiness or breakdowns in the process chain are often unclear. And devious individuals find a process easier to exploit than a savvy manager because there's no immediate "sense check" of their actions.

Meanwhile, because turning a procedure into a process is usually associated with an increase in business line volumes and notional amounts at the expense of profit margins, processes tend to concentrate and leverage any existing operational risks. If something goes wrong, it goes wrong big time.

This cycle continues as processes speed up and are automated using the institution's computer systems-automation tends to improve consistency but it does not guarantee that the underlying process is structurally safe.

In financial institutions, most processes are designed with audited fail-safes and checking procedures. These might be built into the process itself or take the form of independent monitoring by risk control groups such as Compliance.

But because processes interact with other risky variables-the external environment, business strategy, people-it's difficult to sound the all clear. For example, are the fail-safes and "checks and balances" of the process appropriate now that the firm has opened offices in a new jurisdiction?

Given the new products a firm has introduced, could the firm suffer a massive loss if a step in the procedure is compromised? Does the process efficiently manage transactions that are exceptions to the norm, or are staff barely coping? Is risk information flowing from the process to decision-makers speedily enough to match market developments?

These questions help to show why the problem of risk managing processes has become more urgent over the over the last ten years as the rate of change in the financial industry has accelerated.

Institutions have automated processes, re-engineered them after mergers and acquisitions, and adapted them to improvements in industry-wide infrastructure and communications capabilities. Increasingly, banks have been rewarded with high margins for entering immature markets where, by definition, safe processes are not yet established.

They have also extended their activities overseas-beyond the easy reach of their established process infrastructure and monitoring capabilities.

And they have introduced new processes to monitor underlying processes-New Product Approval Process and formal Technology Audits being only two examples.

The Problem with People

It's said that the greatest asset of a services business goes up and down in the office lift every day. But like any other asset, people are a source of risk as well as reward.

Until recently, the risk associated with the staff of financial institutions was largely thought of in terms of simple fraud. The figures here remain eye-opening-FBI statistics for 1998 show that some 32% of convictions for crimes against US financial institutions involved bank employees. The internet age has also opened up a new frontier for fraudsters.

But people also cause damage to institutions through incompetence, error, bad decision-making and rule breaking. And institutions can become dangerously dependent on key individuals, or on teams that are suffering a high staff turnover rate. As we explain below, some firms are starting to identify this kind of key dependency and to monitor business lines for the key people risk indicators.

Even in the case of fraud, greed in its simplest form is not always the most important factor. Traders who exceed their trading limits-rogue traders-often seem to incur the most damaging losses as they try to gamble themselves back into a break-even position.

The original rule-breaking might be motivated by an attempt to improve a bonus, but it's the fear of discovery and its consequences that encourages traders to go for double-or-quits.

That's why, as our next Expert Witness explains, there's increasing interest in the psychology of risk and decision taking.

Modern electronic trading and information systems can help by physically preventing certain actions as well as by automatically reporting infringements to risk managers and escalating key information through the management hierarchy. These increasingly intelligent process control tools help to turn reliance on people into reliance on properly designed systems.

But even where a business line or market has the electronic infrastructure to make this kind of monitoring practical-many derivatives markets, for example, continue to rely on phone and fax trading-people risk is reduced, not removed.

Systems that are used by people are always vulnerable to compromise by them. And a real-time risk report delivered by a state-of-the-art system is of little use if managers do not react to it appropriately.

It's also difficult to enforce control through automatic systems when businesses are immature or when volumes have grown suddenly. Other kinds of financial business-such as advisory services or those dependent on third-party agency sales-are structurally reliant on people for expertise or distribution in a way that is difficult to engineer away.

That's why financial institutions have started to look at individual and group behaviour as a way of understanding risk. Researchers believe the reason why individuals break rules-more crucially, why their colleagues let them get away with it-is sometimes rooted in the corporate culture of an institution.

Does the institution reward success without looking closely at how it is achieved? Do senior managers favour dominant personalities and connive with the bullying of subordinates?

Making sure that reporting systems are independent of business lines, risk sensitive, automatic, consistent and secure is an important aspect of the control of operational risk. But in many cases on our Wheel of Misfortune, losses spiralled out of control because a compromised executive was high enough in the hierarchy to disguise the losses.

Often, the problem is a fatal reliance upon an individual by senior managers and committees, compounded by the reluctance of staff further down the reporting line to break rank and voice concern.

Increasingly, corporate governance rules around the globe are encouraging firms to establish formal mechanisms for individuals to step outside the normal reporting line-to blow the whistle on wrong doing that has either a social cost or a cost to shareholders.

And as our last Expert Witness mentioned, the way that groups of professionals take critical decisions is also coming under scrutiny. Many disastrous losses-often misleadingly recorded as credit and market risk losses-happen because a group of managers or an oversight committee take a decision in a way that, with hindsight, seems to ignore extreme risks in favour of attaining pre-agreed goals.

One palliative is to make sure the person or committee with the power to take action on the risk information understands what they are being told, and its implications. This is, in part, a problem of risk communication. The development of methodologies such as value-at-risk in recent years is, in part, an attempt to get to grips with this problem.

But confused or wrong-headed decisions are also rooted in poor corporate governance and tie in with the problem of enterprise-wide risk management.

All Systems Down

The reliance of most financial institutions on computer systems and technology infrastructure is absolute, as the avalanche of reports produced in advance of the millennium date-change made clear.

From individual business lines to the core support functions of an institution, systems are the principal means for storing and managing vast amounts of transactional, financial and corporate data. They are used to analyse that information, to automate all or part of many critical bank processes, and to communicate with customers.

It's a mistake to think of these systems as an interconnected whole. Instead, most institutions rely on a series of partially interconnected systems of various shape, size and age.

Often, management information systems or data warehouses are used to extract information from underlying systems and present it to managers to help them in making strategic and risky decisions.

Some of the most intractable system risks reside in the relationship between the system and an institution's business plans. Technicians cannot plan for flexibility in capacity, levels of redundancy or absolute levels of security without clear directions from business managers.

As business plans or volumes change, it's important that these decisions are revisited and that the firm as a whole monitors its system dependencies. If a system is left unaltered, a risk decision has been taken-albeit unconsciously.

Systems audits can help to make these tacit decisions more transparent, but they do not necessarily help managers in weighing up the risks and rewards of new system investments.

Some researchers believe that the new science of real options-the application of financial options concepts to the valuation of decisions about physical assets-will help managers in the future.

But at a more practical level, as our Expert Witness explains, the most pressing problem for senior managers is to identify, monitor and manage critical risks in the huge range of systems supporting their institution-including those supporting emerging e-commerce and multi-channel banking initiatives.

Enemy at the Gate-External Risks

External risks take many forms, but they have one defining feature-it's difficult for firms to influence whether the risk event takes place. So the risk management of an external event focuses on mitigating its effect.

The most dramatic external risks are natural and man-made physical catastrophes such as the bombing of Canary Wharf, London's financial district, by terrorists in 1992.

The direct physical impact of these risks is insurable. But payouts cannot compensate for an interrupted relationship with a customer, or for the effect on future business plans or staff.

The problem of ensuring that a business can continue despite a physical catastrophe-business continuity-has evolved into a small industry.

Major banks now spend millions of dollars each year to ensure that, if disaster strikes, they can relocate within hours to a functional version of their main or trading offices-complete with IT systems that are constantly primed with back-up data from the bank.

But this cannot remove the vulnerability of institutions to public or financial market infrastructure. A recent and dramatic example of this was the systems failure at the London Stock Exchange in the summer of 2000 which prevented the exchange from opening.

Fundamental social and technological trends can also threaten institutions-from a rise in general fraud to sustained attacks on corporate web sites by external hackers and fraudsters.

In the summer of 2000, the UK's financial services regulator Howard Davies echoed the concerns of regulators around the world when he claimed that banks systems were being "probed for weaknesses hundreds of times a day"-and that there was sometimes insufficient segregation between the internal systems of banks.

But regulators are themselves a source of external risk. An unforeseen shift in the regulatory or political environment can ruin the profitability of an institution, or leave it vulnerable to catastrophic litigation.

The Big Picture

Many of the operational risks described above are already managed by specific risk functions within institutions-line managers, operations managers, market risk, credit risk, technology risk, internal audit, security, legal, compliance, insurance and so on. But most of these functions have responsibility for specific risks, services or business lines. They cannot give a firm a wide-angle view of its operational risks.

The reasons why institutions and experts think this wider view is important tend to vary according to individual priorities. But the most pressing are the efficient monitoring of critical risks across an organisation, the interaction of risks, risk measurement and the efficient use of capital, and corporate support for risk-reducing investments at business-line level.

Some leading financial institutions have established specific operational risk managers at a senior level to give them this wider view-the purist approach, in that the operational risk function can then itself be checked over by the institution's internal audit group.

Other firms have extended the remit of internal audit to include operational risk management, arguing that their audit group has to hand the skills, infrastructure and manpower to take action on operational risk.

Some firms report that giving internal audit a wider remit makes the function more efficient. Rather than simply ensuring that the proper reporting and control procedures are in place in each unit, audit can take a more active view of risk/reward and reduce duplicated checks and controls.

Whatever the framework, taking the wider view means bringing together information about risk in a consistent fashion so that corporate management and the specific owners of the risk can take action. The button opposite offers easy access to some of the new information management tools that are being marketed to help managers do this more efficiently.

One interesting aspect of these tools is that by making approaches to operational risk control and measurement more consistent within and across firms, they also make it easier for firms to benchmark their risk standards and publish this information to external audiences of regulators, investors-and key customers.

Seeing the Wood for the Trees-Critical Dependencies and what-if Scenarios

One approach to identifying operational risk is to look for critical dependencies in people, processes, systems and external structures. Once identified, the dependencies can be managed or engineered away by adding fail-safes and system redundancies.

This approach is commonsensical, and has the great advantage that the risk of an event happening does not have to be measured in any quantitative way. It simply has to be identified as critical to the safety of the firm or process.

Many of the formal ideas that have come into the financial industry for system and process analysis have their roots in engineering-appropriately enough, given the increasing dependence of financial institutions on technology.

For example, some consulting firms now specialise in identifying the critical dependencies in power, communication and security systems-such as the failure of a critical power line, cable or firewall. Click the dependency diagram opposite to read how our next Expert Witness tracks back to a specific critical risk.

Dependencies often arise out of the interplay between business plans, process design and system architecture-which means that senior managers and business line managers must be involved in risk identification as well as risk management solutions.

And because a disaster would affect the whole firm, senior managers need to understand enough about the risks and their relationships to take the right decision.

It's not just a question of identifying physical dependencies. Many firms have begun to bring together groups of experts to discuss all the various risks in their part of a financial business line or process.

These structured discussions are different from most traditional forms of risk audit in financial institutions because they concentrate not on checking control procedures, or on the filling in of periodic reports, but on risk identification, the promotion of risk awareness in business line personnel, and detailed risk scenario building.

Risk scenarios are important because they help managers to work through what might happen if a particular mishap occurred. These "what if" scenarios are often simply descriptive and hypothetical. But some institutions are experimenting with more formal, quantitative techniques that model firms as systems.

The approaches include applying the latest scientific ideas on network topologies and complexity theory.

At the moment, though, it's difficult to apply this kind of sophisticated analysis to whole firms-so it's mainly being used to track down dependencies in specific business lines and processes.

The Data Game-More Questions than Answers

When a risk threatens a whole firm, and can be removed simply and cheaply, decision-making is easy. But some decisions demand hard numbers.

It costs money to install redundant systems-how much should be spent? If the chosen means of managing the risk is to reserve capital, how much capital is required?

If a company decides to insure itself, how does it assess whether a high premium is worth paying?

It's difficult for firms to answer these questions-and move through the risk management decision cycle we identified earlier-without first answering three questions that depend upon data.

How frequent are the events that generate each specific risk?

How costly will any loss event be if it occurs?

How likely is it that risk control efforts will reduce either of these numbers?

These questions are similar to those asked by market and credit risk specialists. But operational risk is a more difficult nut to crack because of the paucity of data, the many different frequencies and severities of loss, the multiple categories of risk that have to be considered, and the difficulty of linking a loss event to a single cause.

As our next Expert Witness explains, some key concepts here are expected, unexpected and catastrophic types of event. These concepts can help managers compare the character oi risk profile associated with different business lines, and they also help explain part of the data problem.

Take the case of a failure to process a transaction of some kind. In institutions that process large volumes of transactions, these failures are relatively frequent. Firms are likely to be able to gather significant data on the more common low-impact costs associated with these breaks-fines, penalties, reimbursement to customers or counterparties, cost of mending the transaction, and so on.

Other kinds of medium-impact risk, such as significant bank fraud, are more difficult for banks to analyse because they do not have enough data on loss and frequency within the institution to support a valid statistical analysis. This is not always because data do not exist-sometimes it's a question of availability and quality.

For example, in the US bank fraud and money laundering data is already gathered systematically by the regulatory authorities. But it was only in October 2000, after pressure from industry associations, that the US Treasury's Financial Crimes Enforcement Network indicated it might publish the data periodically in association with the American Banking Association.

It is not yet clear whether the data will be released with enough contextual detail to make it useful for quantifying the risk of different kinds of fraud in different kinds of institutions. For many kinds of medium-frequency, medium-impact risk, however, there are simply no readily available databases of loss. So one of the most exciting developments in operational risk is the emergence of banking industry initiatives to solve this problem.

In the summer of 2000, the British Bankers Association announced that over 20 financial firms were joining together to collect data on operational risk events. By autumn 2000, some of the firms were actually supplying their internally collected data to the BBA, using the association's standard categorisation of loss and risk types.

The BBA pools the data and removes any identifying tags before republishing the complete dataset to contributing banks.

A similar venture, MORE, has been set up by Connecticut-based risk consultancy NetRisk, with the support of industry associations and various Canadian and US banks.

The most important feature of both these efforts is the attempt to produce a rich but standard set of data that will help banks quantify risk and link it to root causes, while at the same time preserving bank confidentiality.

These initiatives should help the banking industry to put numbers against the operational risks that are frequent and also those that are unexpected. But they will not solve the problem of the most extreme and infrequent events.

Extremely high impact, but low frequency, risks pose a different kind of problem. This kind of loss is difficult to conceal from shareholders, and is often reported in the press, so some data is publicly available. Bringing this data together in a consistent form is a significant task, but a number of consultancies-listed in our Operational Risks Tools button above-offer such public loss databases as packages.

But the real problem is that, even at an industry level, there are not enough extreme events of a particular type to allow the statistical modelling of their frequency or severity. Most firms respond to these extreme risks through attempting to prevent them or by insuring against them, rather than by reserving specific amounts of capital against them.

But they can't be ignored in the numbers game, or institutions will be building a blind spot for the most deadly risks of all. The regulators are also keen that these risks are accounted for in the total levels of capital available to the financial industry.

One of the cutting-edges of operational risk research is therefore the application of a body of theory known as Extreme Value Theory to the scarce data that is available on catastrophic risks. Although highly technical, EVT offers some hope that it will become possible to put meaningful figures against the risk of massive operational failure.

But EVT cannot help solve a more fundamental data problem. Data takes time to collect and it often has to be aggregated across institutions to make the sample large enough for statistical analysis.

Some experts point out that aggregate historical data cannot help banks identify the risks specific to their institution, or the risks that are lie in wait over the horizon of the data sample.

Risk Indicators and Scorecards

Collecting historical loss data at an industry or institutional level is one way to put a number against operational risk-but it's not the only way.

Institutions can also try to identify sets of quantitative "risk indicators" that seem likely to be related to the level of operational risk in a business line. As our next Expert Witness explains, quantitative risk indicators could bring a valuable element of objectivity to traditional operational risk assessment techniques.

For example, in a business line that depends upon the safe handling of transactions, some key quantitative risk indicators might include the ratio of reported transaction "breaks" or failures compared to transaction volumes, the ratio of transaction volume to trained staff, and the ratio of system downtime to uptime.

After all, a back-office operation with high volumes, skeleton staff and poor systems would seem more likely to make operational errors than a similar low-volume operation with longer-serving employees and a robust systems infrastructure.

Quantitative risk indicators can be transformed into weighted components of a more general risk scorecard for a business line or whole firm with the help of expert judgement. But this introduces a subjective element into the measurement.

So some leading banks are starting to apply statistical techniques, such as discriminant analysis and principal components analysis, to explore the relationship between a risk indicator and loss levels, and to weight the indicator's relative importance within a larger set of indicators.

In an ideal world, all operational risk indicators would be quantitative, and their weighting within the overall risk score of a business line would be decided statistically, and backtested.

Operational risk modelling would end up looking something like advanced credit modelling-a series of weighted risk ratios back-tested against the available data.

In the real world, some bankers say it's difficult to avoid assessing operational risk using qualitative factors. That's why the new science of quantitative operational risk management sometimes begins to sound like the rather older art of risk auditing-armed with new information management tools and risk/reward concepts.

Indeed, some practitioners argue that risk managers who try to track operational risk at group level should simply incorporate audit scores for each business line into their enterprise-wide risk assessments.

The tension between quantitative and qualitative assessments of risk is likely to be a continuing theme in operational risk management. The problem is at its greatest in business lines and support functions such as fund management or legal risk that that rely heavily on individual expertise and integrity.

But even techniques for awarding qualitative scores can be improved. For example, qualitative scoring can be linked more closely related to risk levels, rather than control levels. That is, the weighting given to each element of the control environment can be modified to reflect the severity of any loss given a failure of control, and the scoring can be made independent, and benchmarked for consistency.

Moving from Measurement to Capital Allocation

Quantitative measures and improved scorecards can be used to compare the risk levels in different business lines, track risk trends, improve controls and prioritise risk management efforts. But some firms are also starting to use them to allocate portions of economic risk capital to particular business lines.

There are various ways to approach this problem. One is to work out the total capital the bank ought to set aside to cover operational risk by looking at the amounts of capital other banks set aside (the benchmarking methodology) or by a statistical analysis of industry-level operational losses in the relevant business lines.

Internal scorecards can then be used to adjust the portion of the capital charge allocated to each particular business line.

This mixed methodology is not the only approach to calculating or allocating capital for operational risk. In the past, firms that allocated capital to operational risk tended to use non-interest expense as a rule of thumb or, alternatively, examined the revenue/ expense volatility associated with a business.

Into the future, many firms hope they will be able to a purely statistical/actuarial approach that links the analysis of data collected at business-line level to firm-and industry-wide loss and risk data.

But for the moment, scorecards have some practical advantages from the point of view of forward-looking line managers and enterprise-wide risk managers.

For a start, the cause of a high score is transparent because it can easily be traced back to the scores on the card. By contrast, if a business line is deemed "risky" because of historical or industry-wide data, it is often unclear what the manager can do to reduce the risk score.

So scorecards help motivate managers to reduce the amount of economic capital allocated to their business line by ironing out problem areas. Likewise, group managers can quickly establish stronger incentives for line managers to improve controls.

From Risk Insurance to Alternative Risk Transfer

Some operational risks are impossible to engineer away or to risk manage adequately. Others are so difficult to identify and scale that an institution can never be sure that its internal risk management has been effective.

Where the potential losses seem likely to be of medium severity, a financial institution can reserve capital or use self-insurance techniques to mitigate their impact. But in the case of a catastrophic risk, institutions either have to accept the risk as part of doing business, or transfer the risk to external providers of risk capital.

Over the last few years, new kinds of insurance and alternative risk transfer mechanisms have held out hope that this kind of risk transfer will become more practical and cheaper. Insurance has developed in two ways. Firstly insurance policies have developed to cover types of operational risk that are ill-served in traditional bank cover. Our next Expert Witness believes an improved set of insurance products will offer a stiff challenge to some novel ideas that have recently been mooted within the banking industry-such as mutual insurance techniques.

Secondly, insurers have begun to offer coverall policies for extreme levels of risk, arguing that the massive amounts of capital available to insurers gives them a special role in managing catastrophic risk. But critics of the insurance strategies for operational risk claim that the insurance market is an opaque and inefficient way of pricing risk. They say the delay and uncertainty associated with insurance payouts might destroy a wounded institution.

In the case of alternative risk transfer mechanisms, on the other hand, capital would already in the hands of the wounded bank. ART tools-so far only a concept in the financial institutions sector-would take the form of structured instruments sold to the capital markets by the bank itself. For example, some time in the near future a financial institution might sell a special bond to investors that offered an above-market interest rate, with the stipulation that the bank would cease paying any interest on the billion-dollar principal in the event of an operational disaster.

The premium the bank had to pay to the market to accept this embedded option would be, in effect, the market price of its operational risk-and the world would have seen the first operational risk derivative for a financial institution. Some investment bankers say this kind of traded market in operational risk would price major bank risks more efficiently than the traditional insurance market. But the banking industry's own internal insurance specialists are more cautious. They say they are still trying to work out how well their existing insurance polices complement the risks the bank is running. They don't think they'll be in a position to understand the cost reduction and risk management benefits of new-fangled instruments for some time to come.

But it would be a pleasant irony if the derivatives technology that lay behind some of the most famous operational losses in the 1990s eventually helped to tame the most unpredictable piece of the risk jigsaw.

7

Staffing for Housekeeping Operations

Staffing is the third sequential function of management. Up until now the executive housekeeper has been concerned with planning and organizing the housekeeping department for the impending opening and operations.

Now the executive housekeeper must think about hiring employees within sufficient time to ensure that three of the activities of staffing—selection (including interviewing), orientation, and training—may be completed before opening. Staffing will be a major task of the last two weeks before opening.

The development of the Area Responsibility Plan and the House Breakout Plan before opening led to preparation of the Department Staffing Guide, which will be a major tool in determining the need for employees in various categories. The housekeeping manager and laundry manager should now be on board and assisting in the development of various job descriptions. (These are described in Appendix B.) The hotel human resources department would also have been preparing for the hiring event. They would have advertised a mass hiring for all categories of personnel to begin on a certain date about two weeks before opening. Even though this chapter reflects a continuation of the executive housekeeper's planning for opening operations, the techniques described apply to any ongoing operation, except that the magnitude of selection, orientation, and training activities will not be as intense. Also, the fourth activity—development of existing employees—is normally missing in opening operations but is highly visible in ongoing operations.

Job Specifications

Job specifications should be written as job descriptions are prepared. Job specifications are simple statements of what the various incumbents to positions will be expected to do. An example of a job specification for a section housekeeper is as follows:

Job Specification—Example

Section Housekeeper (hotels) [often Guestroom Attendant—GRA] The incumbent will work as a member of a housekeeping team, cleaning and servicing for occupancy of approximately 18 hotel guestrooms each day.

Work will generally include the tasks of bed making, vacuuming, dusting, and bathroom cleaning. Incumbent will also be expected to maintain equipment provided for work and load housekeeper's cart before the end of each day's operation. Section housekeepers must be willing to work their share of weekends and be dependable in coming to work each day scheduled.

[Any special qualifications, such as ability to speak a foreign language, might also be listed.]

Employee Requisition

Once job specifications have been developed for every position, employee requisitions are prepared for first hirings (and for any follow-up needs for the human resources department). Note the designation as to whether the requisition is for a new or a replacement position and the number of employees required for a specific requisition number.

The human resources department will advertise, take applications, and screen to fill each requisition by number until all positions are filled. For example, the first requisition for GRAs may be for 20 Staffing Housekeeping Positions GRAs.

The human resources department will continue to advertise for, take applications, and screen employees for the housekeeping department and will provide candidates for interview by department managers until 20 GRAs are hired. Should any be hired and require replacing, a new employee requisition will be required.

Staffing Housekeeping Positions

There are several activities involved in staffing a housekeeping operation. Executive housekeepers must select and interview employees, participate in an orientation program, train newly hired employees, and develop employees for future growth. Each of these activities will now be discussed.

Sources of Employees

Each area of the has its own demographic situations that affect the availability of suitable employees for involvement in housekeeping or environmental service operations. For example, in one area, an exceptionally high response rate from people seeking food service work may occur and a low response rate from people seeking housekeeping positions may occur. In another area, the reverse may be true, and people interested in housekeeping work may far outnumber those interested in food service.

Surveys among hotels or hospitals in your area will indicate the best source for various classifications of employees. Advertising campaigns that will reach these employees are the best method of locating suitable people. Major classified ads associated with mass hirings will specify the need for food service personnel, front desk clerks, food servers, housekeeping personnel, and maintenance people. Such ads may yield surprising results.

If the volume of response for housekeeping personnel is insufficient to provide a suitable hiring base, the following sources may be investigated:

1. Local employment agencies
2. Flyers posted on community bulletin boards
3. Local church organizations
4. Neighborhood canvass for friends of recently hired employees
5. Direct radio appeals to local homemakers
6. Organizations for underprivileged ethnic minorities, and mentally disabled people (It should be noted that many mentally disabled persons are completely capable of performing simple housekeeping tasks and are dependable and responsible people seeking an opportunity to perform in a productive capacity.)

If these sources do not produce the volume of applicants necessary to develop a staff, it may become necessary to search for employees in distant areas and to provide regular transportation for them to and from work.

Staffing for Housekeeping Operations

If aliens are hired, the department manager must take great care to ensure that they are legal residents of this country and that their green cards are valid. More than one hotel department manager has had an entire staff swept away by the Department of Immigration after hiring people who were illegal aliens. Such unfortunate action has required the immediate assistance of all available employees (including management) to fill in.

Processing Applicants

Whether you are involved in a mass hiring or in the recruiting of a single employee, a systematic and courteous procedure for processing applicants is essential.

For example, in the opening of the Los Angeles Airport Marriott, 11,000 applicants were processed to fill approximately 850 positions in a period of about two weeks. The magnitude of such an operation required a near assembly-line technique, but a personable and positive experience for the applicants still had to be maintained.

The efficient handling of lines of employees, courteous attendance, personal concern for employee desires, and reference to suitable departments for those unfamiliar with what the hotel or hospital has to offer all become earmarks for how the company will treat its employees.

The key to proper handling of applicants is the use of a control system whereby employees are conducted through the steps of application, prescreening, and if qualified, reference to a department for interview.

Note the opportunity for employees to express their desires for a specific type of employment. Even though an employee may desire involvement in one classification of work, he or she may be hired for employment in a different department. Also, employees might not be aware of the possibilities available in a particular department at the time of application or may be unable to locate in desired departments at the time of mass hirings.

Employees who perform well should therefore be given the opportunity to transfer to other departments when the opportunities arise.

According to laws regulated by federal and state Fair Employment Practices Agencies (FEPA), no person may be denied the opportunity to submit application for employment for a position of his or her choosing. Not only is the law strict on this point, but companies in any way benefiting from interstate commerce (such as hotels and hospitals) may not discriminate in the hiring of people based on race, color, national origin, or religious preference. Although specific hours and days of the week may be specified, it is a generally accepted fact that hotels and hospitals must maintain personnel operations that provide the opportunity for people to submit applications without prejudice.

Prescreening Applicants

The prescreening interview is a staff function normally provided to all hotel or hospital departments by the *human resources* section of the organization. Prescreening is a preliminary interview process in which unqualified applicants—those applicants who do not meet the criteria for a job as specified in the job specification–special qualifications—are selected (or screened) out.

For example, an applicant for a secretarial job that requires the incumbent to take shorthand and be able to type 60 words a minute may be screened out if the applicant is not able to pass a relevant typing and shorthand test.The results of prescreening are usually coded for internal use and are indicated on the Applicant Processing Record If a candidate is screened out by the personnel section, he or she should be told the reason immediately and thanked for applying for employment.

Applicants who are not screened out should either be referred to a specific department for interview or, if all immediate positions are filled, have their applications

Staffing Housekeeping Positions : placed in a department pending file for future reference. All applicants should be told that hiring decisions will be made by individual department managers based on the best qualifications from among those interviewed.

A suggested agenda for a prescreening interview is as follows:

1. The initial contact should be cordial and helpful. Many employees are lost at this stage because of inefficient systems established for handling applicants.
2. During the prescreening interview, try to determine what the employee is seeking, whether such a position is available, or, if not, when such a position might become available.

3. Review the work history as stated on the application to determine whether the applicant meets the obvious physical and mental qualifications, as well as important human qualifications such as emotional stability, personality, honesty, integrity, and reliability.
4. Do not waste time if the applicant is obviously not qualified or if no immediate position is available. When potential vacancies or a backlog of applicants exists, inform the candidate. Be efficient in stating this to the applicant. Always make sure that the applicant gives you a phone number in order that he or she may be called at some future date. Because most applicants seeking employment are actively seeking immediate work, applications more than 30 days old are usually worthless.
5. If at all possible, an immediate interview by the department manager should be held after screening. If this is not possible, a definite appointment should be made for the candidate's interview as soon as possible.

The Interview

An interview should be conducted by a manager of the department to which the applicant has been referred. In ongoing operations, it is often wise to also allow the supervisor for whom the new employee will work to visit with the candidate in order that the supervisor may gain a feel for how it would be to work together. The supervisor's view should be considered, since a harmonious relationship at the working level is important. Although the acceptance of an employee remains a prerogative of management, it would be unwise to accept an employee into a position when the supervisor has reservations about the applicant.

Certain personal characteristics should be explored when interviewing an employee. Some of these characteristics are native skills, stability, reliability, experience, attitude toward employment, personality, physical traits, stamina, age, sex, education, previous training, initiative, alertness, appearance, and personal cleanliness. Although employers may not discriminate against race, sex, age, religion, and nationality, overall considerations may involve the capability to lift heavy objects, enter men's or women's restrooms, and so on. In a housekeeping (or environmental services) department, people should be employed who find enjoyment in housework at home. Remember that character and personality cannot be completely judged from a person's appearance. Also, it should be expected that a person's appearance will never be better than when that person is applying for a job. Letters of recommendation and references should be carefully considered. Seldom will a letter of recommendation be adverse, whereas a telephone call might be most revealing.

If it were necessary to select the most important step in the selection process, interviewing would be it. Interviewing is *the* step that separates those who will be employed from those who will not. Poor interviewing techniques can make the process more difficult and may produce a result that can be both frustrating and damaging for both parties. In addition, inadequate interviewing will result in gaining incorrect information, being confused about what has been said, suppression of information, and, in some circumstances, complete withdrawal from the process by the candidate. The following is a well-accepted list of the steps for a successful interview process.

1. *Be prepared.* Have a checklist of significant questions ready to ask the candidate. Such questions may be prepared from the body of the job description. This preparation will allow the interviewer to assume the initiative in the interview.
2. *Find a proper place to conduct the interview. The* applicant should be made to feel comfortable. The interview should be conducted in a quiet, relaxing atmosphere where there is privacy that will bringabout a confidential conversation.
3. *Practice.* People who conduct interviews should practice interviewing skills periodically. Several managers may get together and discuss interviewing techniques that are to be used.
4. *Be tactful and courteous.* Put the applicant at ease, but also control the discussion and lead to important questions.
5. *Be knowledgeable.* Be thoroughly familiar with the position for which the applicant is interviewing in order that all of the applicant's questions may be answered. Also, have a significant background knowledge in order that general information about the company may be given.
6. *Listen.* Encourage the applicant to talk. This may be done by asking questions that are not likely to be answered by a yes or no. If people are comfortable and are asked

questions about themselves, they will usually speak freely and give information that specific questions will not always bring out. Applicants will usually talk if there is a feeling that they are not being misunderstood.

7. *Observe.* Much can be learned about an applicant just by observing reactions to questions, attitudes about work, and, specifically, attitudes about providing service to others. Observation is a vital step in the interviewing process.

Interview Pitfills

Perhaps of equal importance to the interviewing technique are the following pitfalls, which should be avoided while interviewing.

1. Having a feeling that the employee will be just right based on a few outstanding characteristics rather than on the sum of all characteristics noted.
2. Being influenced by neatness, grooming, expensive clothes, and an extroverted personality—none of which has much to do with housekeeping competency.
3. Overgeneralizing, whereby interviewers assume too much from a single remark (for instance, an applicant's assurance that he or she "really wants to work").
4. Hiring the "boomer," that is, the person who always wants to work in a new property; unfortunately, this type of person changes jobs whenever a new property opens.
5. Projecting your own background and social status into the job requirement. Which school the applicant attended or whether the applicant has the "proper look" is beside the point. It is job performance that is going to count.
6. Confusing strengths with weaknesses, and vice versa.

What is construed by one person to be overaggressiveness might be interpreted by another as confidence, ambition, and potential for leadership, the last two traits being in chronic short supply in most housekeeping departments. These are the very characteristics that make it possible for management to promote from within and develop new supervisors and managers.

7. Being impressed by a smooth talker—or the reverse: assuming that silence reflects strength and wisdom. The interviewer should concentrate on what the applicant is

saying rather than on how it is being said, then decide whether his or her personality will fit into the organization.

8. Being tempted by overqualified applicants. People with experience and education that far exceed the job requirements may be unable for some reason to get jobs commensurate with their backgrounds. Even if such applicants are not concealing skeletons in the closet, they still tend to become frustrated and dissatisfied with jobs far below their level of abilities.

The application of the techniques and avoidance of the pitfalls will be valuable tools in the selection of competent personnel for the housekeeping and environmental service departments.

For many years, the approach of many managers was to write a job description and then fill it by attempting to find the perfect person. This approach may overlook many qualified people, such as disadvantaged people or slow learners. Job descriptions may be analyzed in two ways when filling positions: (1) what is actually required to do the work, and (2) what is desirable. Is the ability to read or write really necessary for the job? Is the ability to learn quickly really necessary? A person who does not read or write or who is a slow learner can be trained and can make an excellent employee. True, it may take additional time, but the reward will be a loyal employee as well as less turnover. It has been proven many times that those who are disadvantaged or slightly retarded, once trained, will perform consistently well for longer periods. There are agencies who seek out companies that will try to hire such people.

Results of the Interview

If the results of an interview are negative and rejection is indicated, the candidate should be informed as soon as possible. A pleasant statement, such as "Others interviewed appear to be more qualified," is usually sufficient. This information can be handled in a straightforward and courteous manner and in such a way that the candidate will appreciate the time that has been taken during the interview.

When the results of the interview are positive, a statement indicating a favourably impression is most encouraging. However, no commitment should be made until a *reference check* has been conducted.

Reference Checks

In many cases, reference checks are made only to verify that what has been said in the application and interview is in fact true. Many times applicants are reluctant to explain in detail why previous employment situations have come to an end. It is more important to hear the actual truth about a prior termination from the applicant than it is to hear that they simply have been terminated. Reference checks, in order of desirability, are as follows:

1. Personal meetings with previous employers are the least available but provide the most accurate information when they can be arranged.
2. Telephone discussions are the next best and most often used approach. For all positions, an in-depth conversation by telephone between the potential new manager and the prior manager is most desirable; otherwise a simple verification of data is sufficient to ensure honesty.
3. The least desirable reference is the written recommendation, because managers are extremely reluctant to state a frank and honest opinion that may later be used against them in court.

Applicants who are rated successful at an interview should be told that a check of their references will be conducted, and, pending favourably responses, they will be contacted by the personnel department within two days. Applicants who are currently employed normally ask that their current employer not be contacted for a reference check. This request should be honored at all times. Applicants who are currently working usually want to give proper notice to their current employers. If the applicant chooses not to give notice, chances are no notice will be given at the time he or she leaves your hotel.

In some cases, the applicant gives notice and, upon doing so, is "cut loose" immediately. If such is the case, the applicant should be told to contact the department manager immediately in order that the employee may be put to work as soon as possible.

Staffing for Housekeeping Operations

Interview Skills Versus Turnover

There is no perfect interviewer, interviewee, or resultant hiring or rejection decision in regard to an applicant. We can only hope to improve our interviewing skills in order that the greatest degree of success in employee retention can be obtained. The executive housekeeper should expect that 25 percent of initial hires into a housekeeping department will not be employed for more than three months. (This is primarily because the housekeeping skills are easily learned and the position is paid at or near minimum wage.) Some new housekeeping departments have as much as a 75 percent turnover rate in the first three months of operation. Certainly this figure can be improved upon with adequate attention to the interviewing and selection processes. However, regardless of the outcome of the interview, the processing record should be properly endorsed and returned to the personnel department for processing.

Orientation

A carefully planned, concerned, and informational orientation program is significant to the first impressions that a new employee will have about the hospital or hotel in general and the housekeeping department in particular. Too often, a new employee is told where the work area and restroom are, given a cursory explanation of the job, then put to work.

It is not uncommon to find managers putting employees to work who have not even been processed into the organization, an unfortunate situation that is usually discovered on payday when there is no paycheck for the new employee. Such blatant disregard for the concerns of the employee can only lead to a poor perception of the company.

A planned orientation program will eliminate this type of activity and will bring the employee into the company with personal concern and with a greater possibility for a successful relationship.

A good orientation program is usually made up of four phases: employee acquisition, receipt of an employee's handbook, tour of the facility, and an orientation meeting.

Employee Acquisition

Once a person is accepted for employment, the applicant is told to report for work at a given time and place, and that place should be the personnel department. Preemployment procedures can take as much as one-half day, and department managers eager to start new employees to work should allow time for a proper employee acquisition into the organization.

Employment Checklist similar to those used by most personnel offices to ensure that nothing is overlooked in assimilating a new person into the organization.

At this time it should be ensured that the application is complete and any additional information pertaining to employment history that may be necessary to obtain the necessary work permits and credentials is on hand. Usually the security department records the entry of a new employee into the staff and provides instructions regarding use of employee entrances, removing parcels from the premises, and employee parking areas. Application for work permits, and drug testing, will be scheduled where applicable. All documents required by the hotel's health and welfare insurer should be completed, and instructions should be given about immediately reporting accidents, no matter how slight, to supervisors.

The federal government requires that every employer submit a W-4 (withholding statement) for each employee on the payroll. The employee must complete this document and give it to the company. Mandatory deductions from pay should be explained (federal and state income tax and Social Security FICA), as should other deductions that may be required or desired. At this time, some form of personal action document is usually initiated for the new employee and is placed in the employee's permanent record.

Note the permanent information that will be carried on file. The PAF is serially numbered, is created from data stored on magnetic discs, and is maintained in the employee's personnel file. When a change has to be made, such as job title, marital status, or rate of pay, the PAF is retrieved from the employee's record, changes are made *under* the item to be changed, and the corrected PAF is used to change the data in the computer storage. Once new information is stored, a new PAF is created and placed in the employee's record to await the next need for processing. A long-time employee might have many PAFs stored in the personnel file.

When either regular or special performance appraisals are given, the last (most current) PAF will be used to record the appraisal. A standard form used to record such appraisals, as well as written warnings and matters involving terminations. These forms are usually found on the reverse side of the PAF. Since performance appraisals may signify a raise in pay, the appropriate pay increase information would be indicated on the front side of the PAF. All recordings on PAFs, whether on one side or both, require the submission of data, storage of information, and creation of a new PAF to be stored in the employee's record.

The PAF and performance appraisal system should be thoroughly explained to the new employee, along with assignment of a payroll number. The employer should also explain how and when the staff is paid and when the first paycheck may be expected.

The Employee Handbook

The new employee should be provided with a copy of the hotel or hospital employee's handbook and should be told to read it thoroughly. Since the new housekeeping employee is not working just for the housekeeping department but is to become integrated as a member of the entire staff, reading this handbook is extremely important to ensure that proper instructions in the rules and regulations of the hotel are presented. The handbook should be developed in such a way as to inspire the new employee to become a fully participating member of the organization. As an example, a generic emplcyee's handbook is presented in Appendix C. Note the tone of the welcoming letter and the manner in which the rules and regulations are presented.

Familiarization Tour of the Facilities

Upon completion of the acquisition phase, a facility tour should be conducted for one or all new employees. For new facilities, access to the property should be gained within about one week before opening, and many new employees can be taken on a tour simultaneously. It is possible for employees to work in the hotel housekeeping department for years and never to have visited the showroom, dining rooms, ballrooms, or even the executive office areas. A tour of the complete facility melds employees into the total organization, and a complete informative tour should *never* be neglected.

For ongoing operations, after acquisition, the new employee may be turned over to a department supervisor, who becomes the tour director. An appreciation of the total involvement of each employee is strengthened when a facilities tour is complete and thorough. If necessary, the property tour might be postponed until after the orientation meeting; however, the orientation activity of staffing is not complete until a property tour is conducted.

Orientation Meeting

The meeting should be held in a comfortable setting, with refreshments provided. It is usually conducted by the director of human resources and is attended by as many of the facility managers as possible. Most certainly, the general manager or hospital administration members of the executive committee, the security director, and the new employees' department heads should attend. Each of these managers should have an opportunity to welcome the new employees and give them a chance to associate names with faces. All managers and new employees should wear name tags. In orientation meetings, a brief history of the company and company goals should be presented.

A planned orientation meeting should not be concluded without someone stressing the importance of each position. Every position must have a purpose behind it and is therefore important to the overall functioning of the facility. An excellent statement of this philosophy was once offered by a general manager who said, "The person mopping a floor in the kitchen at 3:00 A.M. is just as valuable to this operation as I am—we just do different things."

The orientation meeting should be scheduled to allow for many questions. And there should be someone in attendance who can answer *all of them.*

Although the new employee will be gaining confidence and security in the position as training ends and work is actually performed, informal orientation may continue for quite some time. The formal orientation, however, ends with the orientation meeting (although the facility tour may be conducted after the meeting). Finally, it should be remembered that good orientation procedures lead to worker satisfaction and help quiet the anxieties and fears that a new employee may have. When a good orientation is neglected, the seeds of dissatisfaction are planted.

Training

General

The efficiency and economy with which any department will operate will depend on the ability of each member of the organization to do his or her job. Such ability will depend in part on past experiences, but more commonly it can be credited to the type and quality of training offered. Employees, regardless of past experiences, always need some degree of training before starting a new job. Small institutions may try to avoid training by hiring people who are already trained in the general functions with which they will be involved. However,most institutions recognize the need for training that is specifically oriented toward the new experience, and will have a documented training program.

Some employers of housekeeping personnel find it easier to train completely unskilled and untrained personnel. In such cases, bad or undesirable practices do not have to be trained out of an employee. Previous experience and education should, however, be analyzed and considered in the training of each new employee in order that efficiencies in training can be recognized. If an understanding of department standards and policies can be demonstrated by a new employee, that portion of training may be shortened or modified. However, skill and ability must be demonstrated before training can be altered. Finally, training is the best method to communicate the company's way of doing things, without which the new employee may do work contrary to company policy.

First Training

First training of a new employee actually starts with a continuation of *department* orientation.When a new employee is turned over to the housekeeping or environmental services department, orientation usually continues by familiarizing the employee with *department rules and regulations.* Many housekeeping departments have their own department employee handbooks. Compare this handbook with that of the generic handbook (Appendix C). Although these handbooks are for completely different types of organizations, the substance of their publications is essentially the same; both are designed to familiarize each new employee with his or her surroundings. Handbooks should be written in such a way as to inspire employees to become team members, committed to company objectives.

A Systematic Approach to Training

Training may be defined as those activities that are designed to help an employee begin performing tasks for which he or she is hired or to help the employee improve performance in a job already assigned. The purpose of training is to enable an employee to begin an assigned job or to improve upon techniques already in use. In hotel or hospital housekeeping operations, there are three basic areas in which training activity should take place: skills, attitudes, and knowledge.

Attitude Guidance

Employees need guidance in their attitudes about the work that must be done. They need to be guided in their thinking about rooms that may present a unique problem in cleaning. Attitudes among section housekeepers need to be such that, occasionally, when rooms require extra effort to be brought back to standard, it is viewed as being a part of rendering service to the guest who paid to enjoy the room. Carol Mondesir, director of housekeeping, Sheraton Centre, Toronto, states that:

- A hotel is meant to be enjoyed and, occasionally, the rooms are left quite messed up.
- However, as long as they're not vandalized, it's part of the territory.
- The whole idea of being in the hospitality business is to make the guest's stay as pleasant as possible.
- Positive relationships with various agencies and people also need to be developed.

The following is a list of areas in which attitude guidance is important:

1. The guest/patient
2. The department manager and immediate supervisor
3. A guestroom that is in a state of great disarray
4. The hotel and company
5. The uniform
6. Appearance
7. Personal hygiene.

Meeting Standards

The most important task of the trainer is to prepare new employees to meet standards. With this aim in mind, sequence of performance in cleaning a guestroom is most important in order that efficiency in accomplishing day-to-day tasks may be developed. In addition, the *best method* of accomplishing a task should be presented to the new trainee. Once the task has been learned, the next thing is to meet standards, which may not necessarily mean doing the job the way the person has been trained.

Knowledge Training

Areas of Knowledge in which the Employee Needs to be Trained are as follows:

1. Thorough knowledge of the hotel layout; employee must be able to give directions and to tell the guest about the hotel, restaurants, and other facilities
2. Knowledge of employee rights and benefits
3. Understanding of grievance procedure
4. Knowing top managers by sight and by name.

Ongoing Training

There is a need to conduct ongoing training for all employees, regardless of how long they have been members of the department. There are two instances when additional training is needed: (1) the purchase of new equipment, and (2) change in or unusual employee behavior while on the job. When new equipment is purchased, employees need to know how the new equipment differs from present equipment, what new skills or knowledge are required to operate the equipment, who will need this knowledge, and when. New equipment may also require new attitudes about work habits.

Employee behavior while on the job that is seen as an indicator for additional training may be divided into two categories: events that the manager witnesses and events that the manager is told about by the employees. Events that the manager witnesses that indicate a need for training are frequent employee absence, considerable spoilage of products, carelessness, a high rate of accidents, and resisting direction by supervisors. Events that the manager might be told about that indicate a need for training are that something doesn't work right (product isn't any good), something is dangerous to work with, something is making work harder. Although training is vital for any organization to function at top efficiency, it is expensive.

The money and man-hours expended must therefore be worth the investment. There must be a balance between the dollars spent training employees and the benefits of productivity and high-efficiency performance. A simple method of determining the need for training is to measure performance of workers: Find out what is going on at present on the job, and match this performance with what should be happening. The difference, if any, describes how much training is needed. In conducting performance analysis, the following question should be asked: Could the employee do the job or task if his or her life depended on the result? If the employee *could not* do the job even if his or her life depended on the outcome, there is a deficiency of knowledge (DK). If the employee could have done the job if his or her life depended on the outcome, but did not, there is a deficiency of execution (DE). Some of the causes of deficiencies of execution include task interference, lack of feedback (employee doesn't know when the job is being performed correctly or incorrectly), and the balance of consequences (some employees like doing certain tasks better than others).

If either deficiency of knowledge or deficiency of execution exists, training must be conducted. The approach or the method of training may differ, however. Deficiencies of knowledge can be corrected by training the employee to do the job, then observing and correcting as necessary until the task is proficiently performed. Deficiency of execution is usually corrected by searching for the underlying cause of lack of performance, not by teaching the actual task.

Training Methods

There are numerous methods or ways to conduct training. Each method has its own advantages and disadvantages, which must be weighed in the light of benefits to be gained. Some methods are more expensive than others but are also more effective in terms of time required for comprehension and proficiency that must be developed. Several useful methods of training housekeeping personnel are listed and discussed.

On-the-job Training. Using on-the-job training (OJT), a technique in which "learning by doing" is the advantage, the instructor demonstrates the procedure and then watches the students perform it. With this technique, one instructor can handle several students. In housekeeping operations, the instructor is usually a GRA who is doing the instructing in the rooms that have been assigned for cleaning that day. The OJT method is not operationally productive until the student is proficient enough in the training tasks to absorb part of the operational load.

Simulation Training. With simulation training, a model room (unrented) is set up and used to train several employees. Whereas OJT requires progress toward daily production of ready rooms, simulation requires that the model room not be rented. In addition, the trainer is not productive in cleaning ready rooms. The advantages of simulation training are that it allows the training process to be stopped, discussed, and repeated if necessary. Simulation is an excellent method, provided the trainer's time is paid for out of training funds, and clean room production is not necessary during the workday.

Coach-Pupil Method. The coach-pupil method is similar to OJT except that each instructor has only one student (a one-to-one relationship). This method is desired, provided that there are enough qualified instructors to have several training units in progress at the same time.

Lectures. The lecture method reaches the largest number of students per instructor. Practically all training programs use this type of instruction for certain segments. Unfortunately, the lecture method can be the dullest training technique, and therefore requires instructors who are gifted in presentation capabilities. In addition, space for lectures may be difficult to obtain and may require special facilities.

Conferences. The conference method of instruction is often referred to as workshop training. This technique involves a group of students who formulate ideas, do problem solving, and report on projects. The conference or workshop technique is excellent for supervisory training.

Demonstrations. When new products or equipment are being introduced, demonstrations are excellent. Many demonstrations may be conducted by vendors and purveyors as a part of the sale of equipment and products. Difficulties may arise when language barriers exist. It is also important that no more information be presented than can be absorbed in a reasonable period of time; otherwise misunderstandings may arise.

Training Aids : Many hotels use training aids in a conference room, or post messages on an employee bulletin board. Aside from the usual training aids such as chalkboards, bulletin boards, charts, graphs, and diagrams, photographs can supply clear and accurate references for how rooms should be set up, maids' carts loaded, and routines accomplished.

Most housekeeping operations have films on guest contact and courtesy that may also be used in training. Motion pictures speak directly to many people who may not understand proper procedures from reading about them. Many training techniques may be combined to develop a well-rounded training plan.

Records and Reports

Whether you are conducting a training or a development program, suitable records of training progress should be maintained both by the training supervisor and the student. Periodic evaluations of the student's progress should be conducted, and successful completion of the program should be recognized. Public recognition of achievement will inspire the newly trained or developed employee to achieve standards of performance and to strive for advancement.

Once an employee is trained or developed and his or her satisfactory performance has been recognized and recorded, the person should perform satisfactorily to standards. Future performance may be based on beginning performance after training. If an employee's performance begins to fall short of standards and expectations, there has to be a reason other than lack of skills.

The reason for unsatisfactory performance must then be sought out and addressed. This type of follow-up is not possible unless suitable records of training and development are maintained and used for comparison.

Index

T

U

W

□□□